MY KINGDOM IS A HORSE

*The Really, Really,
Really
Difficult Way
to Find a Husband*

Emma Crosby Spurling

BRANDEN BOOKS, Boston

Library of Congress Cataloging-in-Publication Data

Spurling, Emma Crosby.
My kingdom is a horse : the really, really, really difficult
way to find a husband / Emma Crosby Spurling. p. cm.
  ISBN 0-8283-2050-0 (alk. paper)
  1. United States—Description and travel.
  2. Spurling, Emma Crosby-journeys-United states.
  3. Travel with horses-United States.
  4. Ponies-United States. I. Title.
IN PROCESS
917.304~dc21   99.33949
CIP

BRANDEN BOOKS
PO Box 812094
Wellesley MA 02482

www.brandenbooks.com

CONTENTS

Prologue   4

Chapter 1-England and elsewhere   6

Chapter 2~Georgia   14

Chapter 3-Alabama   36

Chapter 4~Mississippi   55

Chapter 5-Arkansas   80

Chapter 6-Louisiana   87

Chapter 7~Texas   96

Chapter 8~New Mexico   142

Chapter 9~Arizona   168

Chapter 10-Califoraia   195

Epilogue   217

Equipment   219

PROLOGUE

I couldn't imagine doing something so completely bizarre and possibly dangerous as riding across the United States of America alone, on a pony. I wouldn't even think about packing a couple of canvas bags with enough to live on for eight months and putting them on the back of the first horse I ever owned. I'd never consider spending 202 days in the saddle, freezing in the mountains, sweltering in the summer heat, thirsty, hungry and exhausted for 2,641 very long miles.

You could never convince me to ride that pony from the rough, grey waters of the Atlantic to the sandy beaches of the Pacific. Not now. Not now that I've done it. Even if it was the best thing I ever did. Even if I did love almost every minute of those endless miles and that difficult pony and those nine glorious states. Even if I was to be completely spoiled by a multitude of friendly people from coast to coast.

I would never do it again.

My lovely last night's stop turned into a full-time husband who, fortunately, wouldn't let me! Now we're on an adventure all our own: real life! Better than any fantasy. Those blue canvas saddle bags are hung up for good. Unless someone wants to borrow them...?

Looking back, this trip was made magical by all those wonderful people who helped Smokey and me move on toward that California sunset - helping with food, clean clothes, conversation, hay and water, somewhere to stay, those helpful dollars and a ton of encouragement. It was those generous and friendly people that turned an eight-month-long pony ride into an adventure of a lifetime and showed me that the United States is surely the most beautiful country in the world.

You were wonderful. Thank you. It was my best time.

It started like this:

I was a passenger in a four-hundred dollar station wagon, being driven through the red dust and termite hills of central Australia, dreaming of adventure. There were four others in the bald-tired and rusted car: an eccentric Englishman, taking a year out before beginning his real life as an accountant; a freckled, redheaded, eighteen year old Tom Sawyer; a be-spectacled German hitchhiker who read continuously and hated to pay for anything; and my friend, a Canadian teacher.

We raced from gas station to gas station in the heavily loaded, un-road worthy vehicle, arriving at each one with the wheel rims barely holding on to the slowly deflating tires. We were aiming for Darwin on the northern coast and from there I planned on a couple of lazy weeks on the beach in Bali. I would follow that with a brief stop in England, then on to...? On to...? Well, something very distracting, totally absorbing, extremely time consuming, probably pretty expensive and preferably quite dangerous.

The idea my mind kept jumping back to, the idea that I felt would definitely fulfil all the above criteria, the idea I felt would be just the thing, was to cross the United States of America, East to West. Along and unsupported.

Well, supported only on the back of a horse.

It was perfect. Perfectly ridiculous...but perfect.

Chapter 1

ENGLAND and elsewhere
Turning an old dream into a new reality takes a lot of planning...
and a ton of chocolate biscuits.

I spent two and a half wonderful years with my Canadian. We traveled. After snorkeling off the Australian reef, we canoed in the muddy waters of the Mississippi River; we drank tequila in a Mexican desert, and caught a tan on a Texas beach; we baked bread in our little house on the prairie, and taught our long-eared hound dog to do a high five. Then I disagreed, irredeemably, with his dictatorial father in Montreal. But eventually, I was on a cheap, one way flight back to England, dusting off Plan B.

By the time I was ready to make the return trip to America, sister Harriet and brother-in-law Mick's little family would have expanded by two, and their Emily would be almost in school.

I spent about eight weeks with them in their house, before it was sold. Then we all moved into my newly rented, very cold but friendly little stone cottage, eight miles from the Roman town of Cirencester, in the rolling green hills of Gloucestershire.

Harriet and Emily would be the first to climb down the wooden stairs, and I would wake up to the smell of breakfast cooking and the warmth from a blazing wood fire. We would spend much of the day playing with Emily trying to keep warm, or walking through the rain soaked countryside. Occasionally we'd drive into town to pick up coal, do a bit of shopping; make a trip to the library or to visit our parents. Mostly we stayed, wrapped up, in front of the fire, talking.

For much of that time, we looked back at ourselves as two children living in a tiny four-hundred year old cottage with a teacher-father, two more sisters, my twin brother and our work-at-night, sleep-by-day mother. Money had been very short and the pressure to succeed, academically, very high. While Claire and Kate, the oldest and youngest of the five, were quick learners and devoted to study, my brother Edward, Harriet and I would run off to the woods with bows and arrows. We became Robin Hood and make-believe horses.

From the time our mother came home each morning from her job as a night nurse in a geriatric hospital at 8 or 8:15 until teatime at 6, we'd be out of the house running through the fields and woods, making dens, climbing trees and racing away from capture from imaginary enemies. To be inside was too dangerous. Any noise meant a real pursuit around the apple tree from an angry, tired mother with a wooden spoon in her hand. Even the sound of our Lakeland Terriers barking would bring her stomping downstairs. Quicker than it takes to write, we would be out of the front door, running for the safety of the fields.

With such a common history, we asked each other how we all grew up so differently. Claire and Kate stayed true to their early promise, heading for doctorates at Oxford and St. Andrew's Universities. Edward followed our father's advice to take up civil engineering but ended up as a computer ace, working from home. Harriet was the first to really break away, moving into the shell of a house she'd bought with Mick — a do-er up-er with no front door, or heating or walls.

"I had to get out," she said, referring to life at Gloucester Street with we four girls sleeping in one room. On their tiny salaries — Harriet's as a receptionist at the local paper and Mick's as an apprentice toolmaker. By age 17, they saved the deposit for the three story terraced house. Harriet left the family nest and moved in.

I took the only route really open to me, one that had been plain to see for everyone except my parents. "Never get you anywhere," my Dad said.

At nineteen, after a year's foundation course at Cheltenham, I left home for the Midlands and art college. It was wonderful! I loved it, every minute. The atmosphere, the study, the projects and results, the people and the town of Wolverhampton, and the liberating space!

I had my own piece of air for the first time ever, my own room, grant money, choices and chances. From the rather shy and quiet girl I had been, I developed more confidence and self-respect and the beginning of a way to be. This came from living a real life at college. Be whomever you want to be, whom ever you can be, they said. Draw what you see, where you want to be. Your library is your imagination so open the book. I did .1 left after the three-year degree course, a first class honors in graphic design and illustration in my overall's pocket, my eyes turned to London.

Wild, wild, crazy years! I did use my drawing, had an agent, worked as an illustrator but work became secondary to life; from my first stop in a beautiful Georgian terraced house in Hackney to the one in which I spent a while with fourteen boys in Hampstead; from crazy drunken nights swimming naked on Hampstead Heath to the raucous noisy times we spent sneaking through the back door of the Marquee Club in Wardour Street to listen to heavy metal bands and drink pints of snakebite and black. Then to Camden and my little bed in the coal shed with the damp running down the walls and Christmas lights all year.

It was all directing me somewhere, a real education where the main study was myself. I learned about my personal strengths, my ability to survive on very little money and about my stubborn streak and my soft side. I worked out how far sheer determination will take you and when to give up. Nothing much seemed worth getting too worried over. While Harriet was getting married and progressing with the house and her dream of family, I was still dreaming about being able to fly!

That was about the time I packed up my sleeping bag for the first time, hid a few pounds in the cuffs of my jeans and bought a ticket to Australia.

"You were looking for a bit of space," Harriet said, moving closer to the fire in our tiny cottage.

"I think that's right," I answered, shaking off the memories for the moment. "Just a bit of fresh air and some peace and quiet."

Maybe I was looking for a room of my own. Or, I was still missing a corner piece to my puzzle. Maybe riding across America was it.

One wintry December day, seven weeks later, we were all sitting on packing cases in their new house, drinking instant coffee and eating the compulsory chocolate biscuits. When I returned home later that night, it was to a very quiet and empty little cottage.

The next day, Harriet delivered baby number two, Edward John.

The time for just thinking about it was over; time to be practical now. I took a trip to London, bought a huge map of the United States, a country I loved, where I'd always been happy. I nailed it to my kitchen wall and spent endless hours staring at it, dreaming and planning while alternating between worry and excitement. I didn't tell my parents. I wrote to my American friend, Pat Riley, whom I'd met in Southern Texas, and enlisted his help.

My mind became full of new concerns. What's the best way to tie a horse at night? What to feed it? How often would it need shoes? What was my weight limit? What if it became sick? What would be a good breed and a good saddle? Could I carry a gun?

What about taking a dog? How should I carry money? Where should I start and where would I finish? Am I crazy?

Probably.

I started thinking about equipment and routes. About deserts and mountains, riding in the heat and camping in the cold. And about a horse. I'd never had a horse of my own. I'd never camped overnight with one, or spent more than three or fours hours in the saddle at any time but I had always wanted a horse of my own. My childhood dreams had been full of wild horses, running free, submitting only to the eight, nine, ten year old Emma. All idealistic little girl fantasies from a colorful imagination. I'm a children's book illustrator now, and I make stained glass windows. Everything's tied together. Then, I longed for a horse. Now, I could have one. What would it be like? Could I do it? I thought I could.

I went to night school to learn Spanish, and then took a course in self-defense. I took first-aid and studied Black's Veterinary Dictionary. Any book I could find on America, on travel there, on the countryside and survival, I read avidly, adapting each chapter, each paragraph, each line, to the trip. Every evening I listened to Washington Radio, and each night I dreamt of the adventure ahead. Maps and information started to trickle in from Pat in Texas, and the picture began to develop. I started to make decisions about the route and select equipment. And I saved.

By the end of the first year, the map of the wall was becoming three dimensional. I knew the east would be green and populated. Food for the horse would be easy, and the roads west, plentiful. I could swing north in Mississippi and pick up the historic Oregon Trail in Missouri, or take a more southerly route, joining the old Gila Trail in New Mexico. I would need to start as early as possible in the year to make it across the Rocky Mountains before the first snow. The map described a country that for half its breadth would be pure pleasure riding. The second half would be the test calling on every reserve of endurance, stamina and determination. I was glad the easy miles came first. Once the green grass of eastern Texas faded into the broad, dry, western sweeps, and the barbarous climbs and descents of the mountains, it was going to take more experience and skill than I knew I had. Hopefully, I would have learned enough by the time we reached those Western states.

Early in the second year of my preparations, I found a book in the local library that would turn my imaginary horse into one that was real. It was exactly the book I'd been looking for: long distance travel, on horseback, in difficult country. The book, Saltbush and Sagebrush, described a six hundred mile ride in Southern Australia, followed by an equal distance in south-west Texas, some of the toughest trekking country in the U.S. Inside that book was a description of the type of horse I was looking for: small, stocky, intelligent, strong, -- a survivor. It was the Spanish Mustang, the original horse of the American Indian.

I felt as if I'd discovered gold.

There were two authors of the book. The first, an Australian. The second, a young, professional Texas horsewoman, and an unswayable believer in the Spanish horse. Her address was in the back, and I wrote to her. I was vague in my letter about exactly what I intended to do, but said I was looking for a hardy horse for a distance ride, and would she be kind enough to advise me.

Her name was Vickie Ives Spier, and she wrote back at length, sending photographs of the breed that was her life. Among that small pile, there were two pictures of a little flea-bitten grey pony that one day I would come to know like the scars on my hands, and whom I would learn to depend on and trust, like my closest friend. Her name was Smoking Spear.

As the second year slowly passed by, things started falling into place. I put on paper my ideas for a pair of saddlebags that would hold enough equipment for a year on the road for myself and the horse. At the Cirencester Craftsmen's Market I found a young, talented and creative saddle maker, Emma Baker, and asked her to build them for me. She agreed to do it, tried to wriggle out, then ended up producing a flawless set, that looked as good after the trip, as they did before.

I needed a tent to be my home. After weeks of thought I selected a VauDe two-man lightweight tent. It was green, a good inconspicuous color. It also weighed little over three pounds; was easy and quick to erect, multi-seasonal, and large enough not to give me cabin-fever if I had to spend a day or two inside. There was also the added reassurance of taking a two-man tent, rather than a single, because when the door was closed, nobody could tell if you were alone or sharing it with a 400-pound ill-tempered gorilla..

I already had my sleeping bag. It was my pride and joy, my home on many trips, so valued even my closest friends were never given the chance to use it. Made by North Pole, it was very lightweight and full of the finest down. It was extremely important on a long trip. However difficult my days, the nights would pass in warmth and comfort.

I bought most of my equipment at Cotswold Camping. The selection was good, the quality too. And it was only a few miles away. The helpful staff became used to me studying every item, buying very little, waiting for the May Day Sale. The smallest piece stood trial and had to be judged on ifs value on the road. Did it warrant the space it would take up in the bags? Was the extra weight worth the convenience? Could it be adapted to more than the task it was designed for? Could I live without it? Each decision was carefully weighed using my experience from previous trips and the results of my research. Despite the scrutiny each piece underwent, over three-quarters of my "scientifically" selected equipment lies abandoned across the nine states in America that we crossed.

I divided everything into two piles, summer and winter. And I saved.

I was still receiving letters from Pat in Corpus Christi, but the information I asked him to find was coming back to me frustratingly slowly. I had set him the task, which he said would be an easy one, of finding from among his many friends, the loan of a horse trailer. I needed to be able to transport the horse from Vickie's farm in east Texas to the starting point of the ride, which was likely to be Brunswick, Georgia. I couldn't afford the expense of a professional horse transportation company. Finding this horse trailer gave me more worry than the prospect of being eaten by bears, freezing in the mountains, getting lost in the desert, or being robbed in the cities. I asked him to find maps and weather conditions from around the country, horse organizations, national and state park restrictions, horse boarding facilities and veterinary requirements. All these came back months after I'd asked for them, if at all. But I needed his help.

At the start of the ride, I needed a driver. And to have some support for the first few days on the road would be a comforting thought. Maybe at the end, if my horse and I succeeded, I would need a place to stay before I came home. So I kept writing, kept encouraging and pleading for information. Through it all, I kept being nice. In reality, I was screaming with frustration. However, for what he did do, I will always be grateful.

He was a friend, and I needed one. I knew he had a crush on me. A major crush. Unfortunately, the feeling wasn't mutual. I'd met Pat while traveling with my Canadian in Texas, had worked briefly at his garden center on Padre Island in Texas. He was the creative, sensitive one in a business partnership and we spent interesting hours talking plants and projects. Back in England, I'd written to him, knowing he'd be willing to renew the friendship. He knew I wasn't interested in becoming romantically involved, but he hoped anyway.

Despite all this we began to develop a plan for the first few weeks I'd be in America. First I would fly to Houston, Texas, where Pat would meet me. We'd rest a day or two, picking up the last minute supplies. Pat would then drive me, with the much worried-about horse trailer, to Marshall in the north-eastern corner of the state, to look at Vickie's selection of Spanish Mustangs.

Once the choice of a horse was settled, there would be an intensive few days getting the health certificates, new horse shoes and a saddle together. At the earliest chance, we'd leave for the East coast. It seemed like a good plan.

In January, I bought my ticket to the United States and finally told my parents what I was up to. They surprised me with their calm response and quietly encouraging attitude. I think they thought I'd never really do it. My American sister-in-law, a negative minded woman married to my twin brother, accused me of trying to commit suicide and demanded to know what I was trying to prove. My youngest sister, Kate, the adventurous academic, wanted to come too. My middle sister, Harriet, resigned herself to losing her babysitter and gossipy friend. My older sister, Claire, well, I never found out what she really thought.

As a compensation for all of them, I insured my life for a respectable amount and wrote my will.

My landlord, bless his heart, kindly agreed to rent out my little house, furnished, for as long as I'd be away. Many times in the months that followed, as I sat outside the door to my little tent, I would cheer myself up with the knowledge, that one day, if we made it, I'd be back in my cosy stone cottage, my feet up on the coal stove, burning the backs of my legs, drinking red wine and listening to the radio. When I was tired, I remembered my warm bed. When I was cold, I remembered the warm, friendly kitchen, with the stained glass window, the dresser, the wood drying in the corner and the home-making stove. When I was hungry, I remembered the garden and the vegetables I grew there, the raspberries and strawberries, and the garlic hanging from a nail in the pantry. When I was lonely, well, I never was really lonely.

I had Smokey.

On March 7th, Harriet had baby number three, Thomas Henry.

The last remaining weeks passed by quickly. The flight was booked for the 25th of March. The night before I was due to leave, I lit the fire in the sitting room, ate well, and drank a bottle of cheap red wine. I was nervous. I'd been planning this trip for so long, from those first hours in the Australian desert to the two simmering-away-on-the-back-burner years with my Canadian to the decision to DO IT when the relationship fell apart. It had taken two and a half years of full speed preparation in England to be able to sit in front of the fire that night, drinking a glass of Merlot, saddlebags full, tickets ready. Me? Ready! Well, as ready as I'd ever be anyway. I'd pretty much covered everything, going over all the combinations of possibilities with my neighbor, Pete. There was time for turning around, backing out, but in reality I was already saddled — one horse, one me, riding, comfortable and quiet, along a grand stretch of lonely American highway, Westbound.

But I was nervous. All my personal belongings had been packed into boxes, and were scattered between friends and family. Apart from the basic furniture the house was empty, but the daffodils were blooming in the garden.

For the last time I went over the lists of things to do. It was too late to change much, but I knew I was ready. I had borrowed some money which had been converted into travelers' checks and sewn into the turn-ups of my jeans. (They were "turn ups" then but became "cuffs" after I got to America.) My passport was up to date, my American visa was new, the cheapest possible travel insurance lay on the desk. I'd been to the dentist and the doctor and cut my hair. I had raised twenty pounds from the sale of my rusty old Datsun car.

My will lay signed and sealed next to the insurance. It was time to go.

Chapter 2

GEORGIA
Off to a slow start and slow progress
to something just a bit better. It's not
at all what it was supposed to be.

Pat wasn't there to meet me in Houston. He'd gone to the wrong airport,
which was typical. I waited. To his credit he sent a message, which was
broadcast over the loud speaker, and arrived two and a half hours later. The
next two or three weeks were going to be essential to the success of the
trip. Depending on how they went would be an indication to me whether
we'd see that sparkling Pacific stretched out before us, or a tail-between-the-
legs early ending. After the flight and the long wait I was tired and
exhausted. My mood was grim.

When Pat finally arrived, I smiled, laughed, was glad to see him. It had
been a long flight and I'd slept little, my mind racing with the pieces that
had to fit together over the next week or two. The whole project, much
thought about, discussed, debated, dreamt about and planned suddenly
seemed too big, even though it was of my own making. Some big hunky
hero type should be attempting this, with trailers, and back-up and loads of
money, not one little skinny English girl on a single horse with a small,
inadequate collection of travelers checks stitched into the turn-ups of her
jeans. Sorry. "Cuffs". I'm in America now.

But here I was. In Houston, Texas. A state that before too long would
open its expansive, hospitable arms, and swallow us, that skinny English
thing and her grey pony, whole. Pat hadn't found a horse trailer. I wasn't
surprised, but I was furious, quietly. Hopefully it would resolve itself. Maybe
Vickie Ives Spier in Marshall would lend us one. I tried not to worry, or feel

depressed, but I wanted to go home.

That first days we spent shopping in Houston. I was looking for boots, but bought a sweatshirt, a bit of food, stamps, some gas and a new stove, because the gas wouldn't work in the old one. The next day, we headed up to Marshall. It was a long drive as Marshall is in the top right hand corner of Texas, and Texas is the biggest state, after Alaska, in the Union. Pat was driving his beat-up GMC truck which didn't look capable of making the thousand mile trip to the east coast, especially towing a trailer and thousand pounds of pony. I was also worried about the impression this tatty vehicle was going to make on Vickie. Would she be willing to hand over one of her much loved horses to this low budget outfit?

I was in an irritable mood on that long drive north, made worse by Pat's nasal small talk and his confessions of one sided love. We made it to Marshall, booked into Motel 6. I slumped on the one double bed, trying to build up the courage to phone Vickie to say we'd arrived. I finally did, and her enthusiastic, energetic voice sent welcome, encouragement and direction into the luggage strewn room. My spirits rose. We fixed a time to meet for the following morning.

I slept badly, my face to the wall. Pat ground his teeth, was shocked when I woke him up, asked him to stop it. We woke to the sun streaming under the blinds, promising a good day. It was March 27th. Cool, But sunny.

The road to Karma Farms was bordered by dense banks of wild-flower color. Reds and blues and yellows, trees green with spring leaves. The farm, home to over seventy horses, Vickie, husband Tom, and two daughters, was only seven miles away, and we pulled in a little early. As Pat cut the engine, I looked around to see pens housing long-maned colorful horses and grassy fields dotted with bands of the same breed. They looked happy and healthy, despite the broken boards and bad fencing. Vickie was a small, slightly overweight woman, a long dark plait of hair down her back, with a huge presence. Her confidence, enthusiasm and obvious obsession with each of her horses made even Pat, a non-lover of the animal, fall under their spell. The house was a disaster, cracking a little and short of paint, filled with piles of books, saddles, blankets, papers and five-toed cats. The family energy was directed to the animals outside, and the house was for resting tired muscles and aching bones after a full day in the saddle or in the yards. We were immediately made to feel at home.

I was about to meet the horse that Vicki and I had half selected from photographs Vickie had sent, and the other half on the foolish whim that I liked her name: *Smoking Spear*. She was listed as a Spanish Mustang, fourteen hands high, a flea-bitten grey in color, about twelve years old. She had once run wild in the Stone Cabin area of Nevada. A wild horse. That appealed too. She'd been caught in a Government round up, ten years before, and adopted by the Spiers family. Vickie's teenage daughter, Tori, had won a few rosettes on her, and the family had profited by two handsome foals. She was thought to have no faults or vices, was tough as old boots, and had a sweet and kindly nature.

I was unreasonably nervous on the drive over to view the horse now at the Paul family's home to make a choice between taking her or not,. It was like an arranged wedding. In theory, I was under no obligation to buy this particular animal, despite the trouble the family had gone to - new shoes, inoculations up to your eyeballs, health certificates and those conditioning miles. But I wanted to like her. Wanted to have the horse situation sorted out successfully, so I could cast my worried attention to other things. I also needed to get to the Georgia coast as soon as possible to make the thousands of miles to the west coast before winter. Now every day delayed counted. The horse was the most important item on my worry list. Once that was resolved, things should improve.

She was tied up outside the house, to a tree I think, but I can't remember. She stood there quietly, turning without interest to look at the truck and empty horse trailer pulling into the yard. I thought her ugly. Stocky. Big head and scruffy stub of a tail. She had a thick white coat with dark grey splashes, as if flicked with the end of a paintbrush. I was a little disappointed. Gone were my images of galloping a fire-breathing wild white horse across the western plains.

"What do you think?" they all asked.

"Ooo She's lovely" was the only reply I could think of. Vickie introduced us, pointing out the characteristics that go to make up a good distance horse, and I realized how ignorant a judgment I'd made.

Her head was low set, and quite large, a thick wiry dark grey mane falling to one side, typical of her breed. She had calming big black eyes that followed you with a relaxed and good natured stare. Her legs were short and stocky. Good strong knees and thick bones. I know almost nothing about the anatomical pluses in this type of animal but what I heard was good. Her feet were her best feature. Big and solid and black. Never split and hard as iron. Her back was strong , a big-boned horse in a little body. She stayed fat on low quality feed, part of her wild horse inheritance. She was smart, intelligent and sensible. Stupid horses don't last long in the arid wastelands of the western states. I can't say I fell in love with her but I was sold by the confidence all those around had in her, as a horse, as my coast-to-coast horse and companion.

Smoking Spear. *Smokey.*

The following days were a jumble of time consuming tasks. I needed a saddle, cheap. There was still the problem of the horse trailer. Liability insurance had to be found, with no companies being too keen to offer it when they learned of the use I'd be putting Smokey to. A hundred other things. All this while Pat, like an irritating case of prickly heat, was driving me crazy. I rode Smokey a few times, my lack of skill obvious compared to Vickie's eldest daughter, Tori, on her Supreme Horse Hall of Fame Spanish Mustang, *Titus Unlearning.* This horse, rescued from starvation by Vickie and a group of others, was so small and weak when found it was lifted and taken home in the back of a pick-up truck. Others weren't so lucky. Many dozens were dead or had to be destroyed, all because the price of horse meat dropped, and hay rose. Now Tori's little pony is one of the most respected endurance horses in the central states, winning many rosettes, cups, classes and the much coveted American Indian Horse Society's Supreme Horse Hall of Fame. One of only nine.

By the 1st of April, everything was settled. We were on the road. Pat's rusty old pick-up truck, towing a trailer bought off the Paul family. Smokey inside. With best wishes from the many people we'd met the last few days, and calls of 'Good luck!' we started off on the thousand mile drive to the east coast.

I studied the countryside as each mile sped past, knowing that before too long, we'd be crossing this country again, east to west, just Smokey and me.

The first night we spent in a fairground. An empty collection of arena, pens and yards, suitable for horse shows or cattle auctions. Smokey was very nervous, hardly eating all night, pacing around her twelve foot pen. The train tracks passed behind the buildings, the lonely howl of engine horns startled everyone from fitful sleep. She refused to be loaded into the trailer the following morning despite pleading, feeding, beating and begging. Neither Pat nor I had the remotest idea of how to get the stubborn old mare in the wretched thing, until after four extremely irritating hours, Pat left to enlist help. After a couple of minutes he returned with a middle- aged man, still chewing his breakfast, and a few seconds later, she was in. Red-faced and exhausted we drove on.

The day had started badly, and little improved as we passed through Louisiana and into Mississippi. We were more fortunate with a place to stay that night. One of the National Parks in central Mississippi had a horse camp. Everything was designed for the enjoyment of camping with your animals, in a beautiful leafy setting. I rode a little to stretch Smokey's legs after all those hours in the trailer, then she tied well to the pre-erected picket posts, and munched away contentedly on the sweet fresh hay we'd brought from Texas. As the light faded and the camp was set, the sound of horses and riders returning home broke the evening silence. Tired but full of high-spirits, many riders rode into the campground after a long day on the trails that criss-crossed the park. Horses were fed, a fire built, beer brought out of ice-filled coolers, and hamburgers and hot-dogs were thrown on the barbecue. Shouts and laughing filled the warm night air.

We were adopted and it couldn't have come at a better time. With spirits off the bottom of the scale, irritated with each other after a stressful day, a party with a rowdy bunch of beer-touting horse lovers was exactly what the doctor would have ordered. It wasn't until late that night, when the warming fire had died to an easy glow, that Pat and I crawled back to my little green tent and the white horse. All friends again. Smokey greeting me in the morning with a welcoming nicker.

Pat always drove. I didn't want to, had no experience of towing a trailer and didn't want the responsibility. But he didn't drive with confidence, and so the many hours we spent heading east in that truck were pretty nerve-wracking. He never crashed or came close, but it was always in the air and, rather unfairly, I was irritated with him until I exhausted myself. He was working hard, too hard, trying to please, and with his obvious obsession for me (which he took every opportunity to tell me about) a wedge has driven between our friendship which spoiled by enjoyment, and no doubt, his, of these early days on my long adventure. I also felt a great amount of strain over being a first-time owner of a horse, knowing my equine knowledge to be dangerously insufficient. I needed to be on my own, with this new and strange animal, to make my own mistakes. In private. However, Pat was an excellent cook. There is no better camp cook than Pat and he was generous too, taking the bigger share of gas and motel bills. But somehow I couldn't like him. We couldn't get along together. He was too adoring and I was too cruel. Sorry Pat.

We were on the road three more days after the park party. The first being a broken night in another city fairground. My allergy to horses kept me awake, with a dry, irritating, tickly cough. I knew before I started the trip I did have an allergy, but with typical ostrich in the sand attitude, I hoped I'd outgrown it. Now it was worse than ever. My eyes itched, my chest itched, my ears and throat drove me nearly insane, my nose ran continuously but the dry, persistent cough that made sleep impossible was the worst. Once it started, it wouldn't stop. I started taking off the shelf medicine for hay fever, which helped enormously. It eased my chest and sent me comatose for five or six hours.

The following night passing through central Alabama I directed Pat to take a little dirt road to our left after seeing a tatty, half falling down sign advertising a

Tennessee walking Horse Farm. Half a mile later, we drove into a multi-million dollar enterprise. The five times world champion walking horse had come from this farm and money didn't matter. Even the horses looked rich. In the green luscious pastures, black grooms rode black horses. With all that wealth, they probably also had white grooms for white horses. Very expensive horses, their front hooves fitted with platform shoes and weighted chains to give them the high stepping walk they were famous for. Again I was amazed at how many different disciplines Americans put their horses to, from these remarkable looking horses to the trotters and barrel racing riders. To endurance and cattle work and jumping and trail riding. Horses here were for fun and for everybody. They rather reluctantly agreed to house Smokey for the night in their outside exercise arena which had a grass center. She was delighted. A night off from hay and free to run. We watched the beautiful black horses a little longer, then ran off to the nearest town for a motel, feeling like two school children let out early from school. It was great to be free of the responsibility of Smokey for one whole night. And the tent. And the effort of cooking outside. I paid for the room so we had two double beds, rather than the one Pat always asked for if he paid. We showered, rang for pizza, and watched television until two o'clock in the morning.

On the 5th of April, we covered the last few miles from central Alabama to a thoroughbred farm four miles from the east coast, in Brunswick, Georgia. For fifteen dollars a day, they boarded horses, and we booked Smokey in for two. We were here. We had arrived at the start. No more truck or trailer. What a relief. Against all the odds, Pat had pulled through. From now on, the responsibility was mine.

We stayed at the youth hostel almost opposite the ranch. The buildings hidden in what seemed a humid jungle. Black soil and coal colored still rivers. Moss hanging from trees dense with spring leaves. Dogs and ducks and young trendy travelers. I loved the new conversation and company of the young arty types, was able to talk about books and journeys past and planned. Pat was very out of place and hated it, was possessively jealous.

That afternoon, we drove into Brunswick, and did the tourist loop of that pretty part of the coastline. We visited Saint Simons Island, bought a T-shirt and a hat. The day was wonderfully warm, about eighty degrees and the relief of finally seeing the grey-green water of the Atlantic made us both chatty and good humored. The well restored shops and white clinker built houses with their faultless lawns were a much visited tourist spot, making Pat and I feel, that despite everything, we were, after all, supposed to be on holiday.

The following day was filled with letter writing, reading and relaxing. We looked at the maps, selected a route, then followed it in the truck. A dummy run. Early to bed. Early to rise. Tomorrow would be 'Day 1.'

I was in the saddle, finally. After two and a half years of preparation and trepidation, we were on the road for the first time, heading west. The sun was low in the sky as I urged Smokey past the green fields of the thoroughbred farm, and onto Route 82, the American equivalent of the A4. The four lane highway was bordered on each side by wide grass shoulders, climbing and dropping with gentle gradients of rolling hills through swampy woodlands. Smokey was doing brilliantly. An energetic trot saw the miles slipping quickly beneath us, and the heavy trucks and speeding cars didn't alarm her. By the time the sun started to climb above the tall softwood trees, we'd covered six wonderful miles. I felt all the stress of the last few weeks fall away with the heavy fall of Smokey's steel shoes on the grassy banks. I began to sing aloud, thrilled to be on my flawless little pony.

It didn't last long. The brakes went on at the first bridge. The hollow sound of her hooves on the concrete sent her scurrying backwards onto solid ground. No big deal, I thought. Just wait for a break in the traffic, a little encouragement, and we'd be over. Smokey didn't see it that way, and time after time shied as her front feet hit the bridge. It was only thirty feet or so to the other side, the water underneath, thick and dark. As the sun climbed higher dispersing the fluffy morning clouds, the road became busier, and Smokey more stubborn. Defeated, I asked for help from a good humored middle aged man gardening in his small acreage, a few yards back. He pulled, I kicked, and we were over. Embarrassed, I thanked him, and sent Smokey again into her ground-covering trot. Bridges were going to be a problem. I wondered what else I would add to that list.

We trotted on but the singing stopped. I had failed to win the first round with Smokey. She was a stubborn as I was but a hell of a lot stronger. It was now obvious that, with her, trust and respect had to be earned. She wasn't going to give anything away.

Maybe this whole idea was mad. Maybe a holiday should be lying on the beach in Bali, not stressing out on a Georgia road. What was I doing here?

After seven miles we turned right into a smaller farm road, leaving behind the roar of logging trucks and big eighteen wheelers. Within a mile we were going through the same circus ride as at our second bridge. Pat passed us in his red pick-up truck, parking on the other side of the bridge. He watched as one after another of my techniques for stubborn horses failed. He finally took her bridle and she allowed herself to be led, snorting her dissatisfaction to the other side.

We set off again, only to be stopped a few seconds later by the man from the first bridge, checking to see we'd made it across safely.

Pat had kindly agreed to spend the next few days with me, before heading back to Corpus Christi, Texas, and his job as a landscape designer. Many times during those early days, he'd pull over with hot coffee, cold drinks, or something to eat and reports of his efforts to find a place to stay for the night. I started to enjoy his company more after having the freedom of the hours in the saddle. Everything was made so much easier by his tireless activity on my behalf.

That first night he'd obtained permission from an elderly couple to put Smokey in with their grandchildren's horse in a large grassy paddock behind their old Georgian plantation mansion. Led by Pat, I rode between handsome stone posts crumbling and weed covered, along a stony driveway bordered by ancient American oaks hung with long trails of Spanish moss. It led to a handsome, once-grand colonial style house dominated by climbing plants and old trees. Though a little uneasy, the grey haired Mrs. Bright allowed us to camp under the trees next to a small pond. What a wonderful feeling it was to watch Smokey roll in the long spring grass, knowing she'd be safe for the night in the well fenced field. I watched her graze for a little while before walking, a little stiff-legged, the short distance to where Pat was unloading the truck and setting up our first camp on the road. End of Day 1. We'd covered 14 miles.

An early start in the morning, busily scratching new red welts of mosquito bites. I fed, then saddled Smokey, climbing aboard

about seven o'clock, my feet and hers wet from the heavy dew. It was a beautiful sunny day, but spoiled early when I turned her head towards the stony driveway. She locked her knees and refused to move. She didn't want to leave the company of the grey horse she'd spent the night with, and, as with the bridges, she tested my patience with her obstinate will. When Vickie Ives Spier in Texas had described her as "quite a character", I should have read the hidden meaning. "Stubborn old mare" more like. I kicked and kicked, tried reverse, tried to lead her and then remount, but she'd always end right back at the paddock gate, gazing at her amused companion. I made a fuss, kicked some more, shouted at her and pleaded. She started to rear. High wild mustang type rears, tottering dangerously on her hind legs. Then she started jumping in wide head-throwing circles. Pat donated five foot of his holiday fishing rod he'd never used and that did the trick. With the fiberglass tickling her heels, but her head high, she walked reluctantly back to the road.

I foresaw a difficult day ahead. We were on Highway 32, a good road, not too busy with a decent width of grassy shoulder bordered with the dense woods, plenty of water in the roadside ditch, a road that could take us almost all the way across the state. If we made it that far.

Pat and I had planned on a short day to rest Smokey, but after covering seven miles in the first hour, she didn't seem to want to take it easy. However, the next four hours she dropped to a discouraging slow walk. More problems with bridges, though now I'd dismount and she'd crawl tentatively across. For much of the day she tested me, my patience and skill. This horse had an attitude problem, or was it just horse sense? New things. New places. I look back now and appreciate and understand her caution but then I was red faced with frustration.

We saw two snakes. One writhing, half its five foot body stuck to the tarmac, a victim of the traffic. The other watched us from the black water as Smokey bent to drink. The more threatening risk was the many broken bottles hidden in long roadside grass, any one a lethal edge to a blood filled vein and an ugly early ending to the ride.

Pat spent all day trying to find a place for the night's stop, but had to settle for the loan of an unfenced, unused field, half a mile off the off the road.

A twenty-two mile day. I slowly dismounted, stiff kneed, stiff legged, my back and shoulders crying out with overworked muscles. I had a curly metal stake which I screwed into the soft earth, securing Smokey on a sixty foot rope from her head collar. She stood square footed, her head hung in exhaustion. The first and last time I saw her too tired to eat.

As Pat created his usual culinary wonders on the two-burner Coleman stove, we had our first visitors. The shy, round Pam Robinson came over from her house across the road, bringing her three year old son, Darren. A small plastic freezer bag containing neatly sliced apples and scraped carrots hung from his eager fist. He was dressed in his fancy dress cowboy outfit and was completely fearless of the horse towering over his little frame. I traded the apples and carrots (which Smokey didn't like) for a stationery ride for Darren on Smokey's back. She just stood there, too tired to object, while the little three year old laughed with pleasure. As Pam led him back to their plain one story house, I could hear him excitedly talking of his three year old wishes. I don't think he was the type to let his mother forget. He wanted a little grey pony of his own.

We had already met the second couple to stop. Only a mile or so earlier I had ridden onto the forecourt of a gas station where Pat was parked, deep in discussion with two happy-minded Georgians. They were amazed at the daring of the adventure which Pat was relating to them in grandiose fashion. I was rather embarrassed. It was much too early to start bragging but they didn't seem to think it premature. With handshakes, back-slapping and enthusiastic exclamations over Smokey, they lifted my battered spirits as the dusk faded into twilight. They also bought the horse trailer from Pat and we parted in mutual admiration, the best of friends for a night at least.

I was tired, exhausted really, but slept badly, concerned about Smokey becoming entangled in her long lead rope. I tied a little brass bell to her head collar, the tiny tinny ring telling me each of her movements. When I heard it, I worried about it being caused by her struggling with the rope. When it no longer rang, I was convinced she'd pulled up her stake and left, a fear that one day would prove to be horrifically justified.

Day 3 started off with the same rodeo performance from Smokey. Rearing, charging around, misbehaving. She was testing me, seeing what she could get away with. Also, she was pretty lonely, making me feel guilty for snatching her away from her four-legged friends at Karma Farms. At the sight of any horse, she'd call across the fence in her high-pitched, frantic whinny, and be very resistant to my efforts to push her on. Horses are happier in a gang, and now she only had me.

By midway through the day, there was a noticeable change in the scenery. The dreaded bridges were becoming less frequent and woodlands, still crowding us on each side of the road, were a little less sinister. The swamps with their alligators and snakes were drying up.

Smokey was still tired from her long day yesterday, but did well the first hour, then a slow motion walk for four. We broke briefly at a little country fair but the sounds of chain saws and tractors in competition kept her alert and jumpy, so the time out was wasted. Despite her obvious hangover from the day before, she put on a fabulously energetic performance when we crossed Route 84 a little later in the afternoon. We had six lanes of traffic to cross before reaching the continuation of our quiet country back road on the other side of this major east-west highway. I stopped her at the lights, waiting for our turn at the green, a little nervous myself about how she'd handle such a busy intersection. Finally the cars to our left and right slowed to a stop, and our light changed to green. Smokey set off perfectly, trotting across the first three lanes of stationery cars to our left, across the traffic islands in the middle, past the first lane to the right. Then, without warning, she reared and twisted, leaping into the air. It must have been spectacular. As I fought to control her, our light turned red and despite the entertainment, the impatient traffic started to edge forward. Shaking, I slipped out of the saddle, and hauled her to the safety of our old road. Furious, scared, upset. When was this silly mare going to give up? When was she going to at least cooperate with me, even if we couldn't be friends? Her one good point had been her flawless behavior in traffic, and now I couldn't even count on that. This is now how it's supposed to be!

Each night was different. Some were creepy, some strange, some exciting, some pretty wonderful and some weird. Day three was definitely weird.

Pat had struggled to find a spot for the night, and had finally accepted an offer of an empty backyard in the small settlement of Bristol. The owner, with his stained and ripped tee-shirt stretched over a massive belly, enthusiastically welcomed Pat, truck, me and horse to his bottle strewn quarter of an acre behind his one story house. We roped off a corner for Smokey, discreetly clearing the area of wire, glass, torn metal and plastic waste, and fed her some of the remaining Texan hay. After setting up camp, Pat and I joined our host and his equally round and relaxed wife for a hazy, out of focus showing of an old Burt Lancaster film on TV. I could hardly understand the conversation between the three Americans sitting around the thickly carpeted room, the broad Alabama accents seeming to render the language completely foreign to English, but I nodded and laughed, hopefully, in all the right places. This friendly couple were right at home with two strangers in their house, belching and worse, without a blush. The lady of the house soon fell asleep in her brown corduroy lean-back chair, drowning out Burt Lancaster with her big scale snoring. Pat followed suit, and nodded off beside me, leaving me without a translator. My host didn't seem to mind me laughing in all the wrong places, probably passing off my confused looks with me being an eccentric English person. At the end of the film, everyone seemed to wake up automatically. After a good scratch, belch, and a bit of healthy flatulation by our hosts, we were walked back to the tent. Nothing snobby about those people!

Day 4 began with the usual pantomime from Smokey, but she gained a few Brownie points later in the day when I tried out the saddlebags for the first time. Pat would be leaving us in a few days so she needed to quickly get the feel of the leather backed canvas bags. I put them on gently, only half full. A couple of half-hearted little bucks later, and it was all over. It was a big relief. From the way things had been going, I had predicted a furious Smoking Spear bucking rodeo fashion down the highway, trying to rid herself of the new equipment behind her saddle. Her walking pace improved too, though it cost me a foot off the end of the fishing rod. I made a mental note to try to control my temper.

One of my luxury items, bought in Houston, was a Lo-Fi, ten dollar radio.

On day four, as we walked along more of the same wooded road, I hooked it over the saddle horn for the first time, and listened to the scratchy music stations. It was a welcome distraction from watching the ground for snakes and broken beer bottles.

The old songs and local news stories gave me something to think about besides what an old cow Smokey was proving to be. I knew it was early days, and no doubt she'd improve, but all these fun and games each morning were wearing me out. Everything was supposed to be wonderful. We were in beautiful riding country, a lovely quiet road through miles and miles of shady woodland, the weather was always perfect, a little chilly in the morning, but warm and sunny by nine or ten. I had Pat's support, with hot coffee and chocolate at almost hourly intervals, so I should have been in heaven. I was not. Instead, I was continually irritated and impatient. Always anxious to move a little faster, pass another mile marker. I needed to relax. I was supposed to be on holiday. When I looked at the map of Georgia hanging around my neck in its plastic case, my heart sank at how little we'd covered, and how far we had to go. How I longed to be out of Georgia!

That evening we had our first really good nights stop, which helped a great deal toward improving my attitude about this ride. Nancy and David Moore, a young farming couple, lent us the use of the mobile home they kept for visiting relatives a mile or so off Highway 32. A hot shower, clean clothes, a big field for Smokey, no tent. Artichokes and steak for dinner. I sat on the porch that surrounded the front of the little self-contained building, my feet up on the wooden railing, brushing clean hair, thoroughly enjoying these most welcome luxuries. It was a little holiday from my holiday! If only every night could have been like that.

The 5th of April, Day 5 was hot and humid. The radio reported temperatures of eighty-five degrees, then gave a higher reading with the humidity factor. I wasn't sure what that meant. In the saddle it was sticky, my tee-shirt and trousers pasted to my skin. The heavily wooded countryside was starting to give way a little to small green pastures and poor looking farms. Small settlements of houses had scraped clearings in the oppressive woods. The change was welcome. It made me feel we were actually getting somewhere.

Smokey reared again this morning, but instead of using my voice to try and control her, I resorted to a hefty whack with the fishing rod between her ears. She was shocked. A second or so later, she tried another rear, with a little less confidence this time, and received the same heavy handed treatment. She didn't attempt a third. I was thrilled at the progress.

Alma was a challenge. Our first decent sized town, with plenty of intersections and junctions, traffic, road work, factories and shops to ease Smokey past. As it was her first time through such a large place, I jumped off and led her through the worst. Her head was up, and her ears alert, her big black eyes anxious. She shied at a few things, but gingerly crept round them, encouraged, I believe by my soothing words. Passing one shop window, she saw her reflection in the glass and froze. In the middle of the busy street, she let out her high-pitched whinny, calling to the grey horse looking back at her. It was a funny scene, and I laughed, apologizing to the shocked shoppers as I pulled her away, but again I felt a little guilty for her loneliness.

I was tired after the stressful city miles, so when Pat pulled over in his red truck mid-morning, I handed over the lead rope to him, and slept for an hour under a tree, on the side of the road.

Pat left us on the morning of Day 10. I was enormously grateful for the essential part he played in those early days but it was time for him to go. Smokey and I had come to an amicable agreement as to who was in charge, (sometimes me, sometimes her!) and we'd settled into a daily routine. We were half way through Georgia, 130 miles behind us. As I watched Pat's old red truck disappear into the distance for the last time, I felt a genuine loss, but also, what a thrill it was to be alone. Freedom. Real pioneer-spirit freedom sent me cloud high. Just you and me now Smokey, you old cow.

I'd been given the directions to an empty field for a camp spot for that first night alone. With only thirteen miles to go, we were there by mid-afternoon. I put on my wrinkled shorts, giving my florescent white skin a chance to catch a little sun. I had never really camped alone before, but didn't feel alarmed or worried in any way. Just very peaceful. Rather than set up the tent, I unrolled my sleeping mat in a musty, half derelict stable, took my allergy medicine and slept well. I was awakened in the very early morning by the cold, the mice running over my hair, the lice over my skin irritating my skin. One of the many sacrifices I'd made to lighten the load Smokey was carrying, was in Pat's truck, my wonderful Marco Polo down sleeping bag. I was sleeping under my smelly, sweaty horse blanket and my Australian stockmen's coat. By two o'clock that morning, I was frozen. Curled in a tight ball, it was too cold to stretch out a leg or arm from the limited warmth of my poor bedding, and cramp became a new sleep-robbing factor. These nights, broken with cramp, would last for many weeks yet.

I was up early the next day, April 17th. It was a Sunday and the morning fine and quiet. I groomed Smokey thoroughly as she ate her breakfast of crushed oats and grain from the blue folding bucket, her winter coat coming away with each stroke of the hard bristled brush. She ate slowly, as she always did, chewing each mouthful carefully, which gave me time to saddle her without rushing. First the Navajo horse blanket, with its pink and grey geometric designs, followed by the five dollar Mexican rug, folded into a cushioning pad. The saddle next. A tree-less barrel racing saddle, bought from the five times world champion barrel racer, Martha Josey, in Texas. It was made from soft orange suede with neoprene padding. Very comfortable for me, and seemingly for Smokey, too. The packs went on behind the saddle, but I loaded them with all my camping stuff when they were in position. They were too heavy to swing over her back when they were full. The last to be tied in place were the tent, coat and spare horse feed, all behind the saddle and fixed to the top of the bags. As soon as she took her last mouthful, I folded the bucket, looped it under a saddlebag strap, and we were off. All this took about forty minutes.

On that early Sunday morning the first day without Pat's help, there was the normal little fight with Smokey, the first fast mile, then a more peaceful rhythm through the deserted streets of the Victorian town of Fitzgerald. An attractive brick built central area, glowing red in the early sun, gave way to the sleepy white wooden houses of the suburban district with its laid out walkways, small parks and pretty gardens. By eight o'clock we were back into the countryside with the heavy scent of honeysuckle drifting in almost visible clouds from dense banks growing wild along the roadside. It reminded me of England.

Three miles past the town, we took a right turn onto Highway 107, a stretch known as "Ten Mile Road". The solid borders of trees were back, edging the arrow straight ten mile stretch that faded into the heat shimmering distance. No bends. No curves. Just the rolling road. I hooked the radio over the saddle horn and rationed myself to two hours of distraction from the increasing heat. Water was still plentiful in black, still, swampy looking ditches, but so were the bridges. For the first time, after encouraging words and lots of praise, Smokey allowed herself to be ridden across her first bridge. From then on, each one became a little easier. A bond was starting to grow.

By lunch time we were maybe half way along Ten Mile Road. The scenery was the same as at the start, which made those hot long hours in the saddle seem wasted, the only evidence we were moving were the green mile markers on the side of the highway, each one passed was a mile less to go. We were over halfway through Georgia, and already I was looking to Alabama. However, there would be two major challenges before we'd see the new state: an interstate to pass under, and the Chattahoochee river to cross at Fort Gaines. That bridge, I dreaded.

As I sat there in the shade at the side of the road, drinking warm water out of the plastic canteen and thinking about the problems ahead, a large pick-up truck pulled over, and a slim, grey-haired man climbed out. A little shyly he came over to find out about the horse and rider taking a break. He introduced himself as William, and I recognized him as passing us several times that morning on his tractor as he went from field to field. I had waved to him. I always waved to anyone that waved to me, or slowed down, or was courteous. Within a few minutes, I knew his life history: his marital problems, an unsympathetic wife, the pointless struggle trying to farm the clay rich southern soil. He was a little too friendly, telling me things I didn't want to know, so after a decent period, I began to saddle Smokey for the afternoon shift. He gave me his address and I promised to write.

William caught up with us several times that afternoon. He started to become a bit of a bother. I began to be a little sharp with him, a little ruder. I didn't stop Smokey when he pulled his truck onto the grass shoulder to talk. I had planned on a short day, but with William starting to be a bit pushy, I thought it wiser to put some extra miles in before picking a camping spot. I didn't call it a day, until we'd put nineteen miles behind us. We came upon a small collection of farms and horses, well kept and expensive looking, almost all with the same surname painted across the mail boxes at the end of each driveway. I tried the first, riding along a grass sweep between two man-made ponds, grass high in the shady dips. No one answered the door so I tried the neighbor. After a short delay, an old, bent over lady came to my knocking, a little hesitant, but with a friendly smile. This was the first time I had to face finding my own accommodation, and I was rather worried about the reaction I would receive. Pat had painted an ugly picture of how hard it was to find a suitable spot, predicting nights wondering the lonely roads with no camping place in sight, a long line of rejections behind us.

"Hello, my name is Emma Crosby. I'm from England and I'm doing a bit of traveling in the area with my horse. I wondered if you'd be kind enough to let me stop in the field in front of your house?" This was my standard line which hardly changed for nine whole states. Usually the reaction was, "What horse?" and this led to easier conversation about the white pony tied to a tree or gatepost, the load she was carrying and the area we were traveling through.

Despite having to find accommodation almost every night for eight months, it never became easy for me to walk up to a strangers door with my request. I'm not very good at asking for a favour, and it always surprised me when the response was positive. The walk up the selected driveway was always a lonely one. A bit nervous. A bit pessimistic about the reply. A little anxious as to the character of the landowner. But what a huge relief when the answer was,

Yes! Apart from a handful of rejections on our long journey, the answer always was, YES!

The lady I asked that night lived alone, the retired matriarch of the family that worked most of the surrounding farmland. She had suffered a stroke and her speech was affected. She stammered out her frustration at losing the ability for fluent conversation, but her eyes sparkled with excitement when I told her of my adventurous trek.

After she saw I had erected the tent, and Smokey was fed and grazing peacefully in the long shadow of a tall tree, she walked cautiously through the knee high grass with a bag full of cakes and biscuits. Also a tall jug of refreshing iced tea. She turned down an invitation to join me for an evening meal of beans and crackers, but flushed with pleasure when Smokey tried to follow her to the house.

Night started early in those days, and as the light faded, I caught sight of her a few times looking out across to the pasture to her unusual guests. Her old body was maybe a little younger that night.

We approached the Interstate in the early morning of Day 12. I expected trouble from You-know-who, but she was relatively

calm, just a little unnerved by the "DoDo...DoDo..." noise from the

heavy traffic passing overhead. I lead her, as I always did with these new challenges, and talked encouragement in a calm, monotonous tone. For a brief moment, there was a break in the traffic, and with nostrils flared, we were through. It hadn't been too bad, but she got lots of praise and a chocolate covered Granola bar, her favorite.

By mid-morning the temperature was in the upper eighties, with the humidity draining our energy. Smokey was losing her winter coat in big handfuls of white hair. We were back on Highway 32, a few less trees and more farmland, planted with early crops. As the temperature increased, the heady scent of the honeysuckle lining our path faded, and the smell of the horse sweat became stronger.

"Stop! Stop! Please stop!" A young woman came running, hands waving. She'd seen me through her kitchen window and was too curious to let such an unusual spectacle pass by. Her name was Carrie and she was a horse lover. She had a whole collection of much handled animals behind the house and invited us to rest a while and have a cold drink. I unsaddled Smokey, letting her graze on the green lawn, while I sat under a shady Pecan tree talking to Carrie and her husband about horses and travel, and America and Americans. She longed to do such a ride, and we talked about meeting up in a few months. That day, she had to make do with accompanying me for five or six miles along the highway, until her husband met us with cold drinks and she had to turn for home. I promised to keep her informed of our progress, and we rode on.

As the heat of the day began to ease to a comfortable evening warmth, I started to look around for a campsite. We were tired, but I had the satisfaction of another twenty miles behind us. As I crossed the road to a likely looking disused farm building that seemed hidden enough for a safe nights stop, William turned up. He followed me to the little used track, and parked. He'd bought some cheesy crackers wrapped in cellophane, and a bottle of Jack Daniels whisky.

He began to drink. And the more he drank the more lecherous and personal he became. It was getting late. Already the sun had dropped behind the hills, and the light was fading. I was trapped into staying where I was, not knowing how nearby another good spot would be, and whether William would follow us there anyway. I was uncomfortable. Just as his talk turned to the chances he had of sex with me that night, Carrie turned up in her white jeep. I whispered my worries to her about my unwelcome guest, and allowed her to persuade me to come back to her house for the night. Within half an hour, she was back with her understanding husband and the horse trailer, and we were heading back down Highway 32, and away from trouble. I was embarrassed and a little ashamed that I'd let myself be caught out like that, but I tried to ease my conscience with the thought that I was still learning. I was still learning as I rode down the mountains into San Diego, eight months later.

Carrie dropped Smokey and I off on a dirt road close to Highway 32 the following morning. I'd had a wonderful night in a real bed, with hot food, shower, and my seedy looking clothes were back in the packs, fresh and clean. I looked forward to the time when Carrie would be able to meet us for a month or two of shared adventure, but shortly after I left, she found out she was expecting a baby and travel plans were put on an indefinite hold.

I stayed on the dirt road a little way, enjoying the soft red surface in the early morning sun. It was going to be another hot day, but for the first hour or two, riding would be perfect pleasure. Smokey was easing off from her early morning tantrums, starting to settle into the daily routine. She seemed to be as eager as I was to get on the move each morning, enjoying those early cool hours. Once the heat set in, about nine-thirty or ten, the fun was over.

I settled, in those early days, into a daily routine of early starts, ride until the heat became too much (around 11.30 or 12), then pick a shady spot for a couple of hours siesta. Smokey would graze a while, then stand motionless under a tree, her eyelids half closed, a back foot resting, and her bottom lip hanging in lazy relaxation. She became so used to this routine that within a few weeks SHE would tell ME when it was time to pull over!

I was usually ready to sleep by lunch time after a cold cramp filled night under the horse blanket and stockmen's coat but often the small red fire ants would find me and bite so ferociously sleep would be impossible. However, the red swellings from their wicked bites gave me something to do in the evenings. Scratch. Scratch. Scratch! Our noontime break usually lasted about three hours, though later in the heady temperatures of West Texas in August, it was sometimes seven or eight. I would pass the time by sleeping, if possible, then reading or writing. I would read a cheap paperback, tearing out the finished pages to use as toilet paper. In Georgia, I started with *War and Peace* — good, cheap quality paper, very absorbent! And, thanks to Tolstoy, plenty of it! I also wrote letters to my parents, sisters and friends back home, probably painting a more idealistic picture of the little adventure I was on than it realistically deserved. I wasn't exactly having a wonderful time, though as Smokey improved, and my relationship with her strengthened, things were getting easier. I didn't really start enjoying myself until we crossed over from Alabama into the wonderful Edenistic state of Mississippi, thirty-six days into the ride.

The day we left Carrie, Day 13, we had an almost non-eventful crossing of the big bridge spanning the Flint River, eight miles into our day. This gave me a little relief from the worry about our crossing the big bridge over the Chattahoochee River in maybe five days time. Each person I asked gave a different account of what to expect at this bridge. Some said it was old and covered, rising in a steep rusty arc over the muddy water. Others said it was new and half a mile long. Others even advised a police escort. Only one to two people thought it would be easy.

Almost every night we were somewhere new, and on Day 13 we were lucky. On the advice of a lady motorist who stopped to talk I rode Smokey into the Coney Lake Plantation after a nineteen mile day. It was no longer a real plantation, but a farm in the business of providing holiday hunting. A man's place. Dogs and mules and wagons. Deer horns and wood stoves and hunting prints. I was made welcome by the owner, Big George, his right hand man, Clarence, and the other workers, both black and white.

They saw Smokey housed in a green pasture, already home to three of their own animals, then fixed the water and electricity into a small mobile home for my use for the night. They wouldn't let me carry my heavy packs but became very gentlemanly, moving them for me.

It was nice to be treated as a guest and as a woman. We drank beer, and they talked about their horses and hunting trips, showing off their long-limbed Tennessee Walking Horse, and their unbelievably huge wagon-pulling mules. The barn housed forty or so sinewy English Pointer dogs, and we did the tour, shouting questions and answers over the noise of forty barking hounds.

While Big George, a large, slow talking but respect inspiring man, cooked up a delicious spicy fish stew, Clarence took me for a thrilling ride on their four-wheeled motorbike, driving crazily through the oak woods. Three young English Pointers raced with us. With tongues flying and wild-eyed, they'd overtake us, then disappear into the undergrowth, led by their powerful, bird-seeking noses. We'd fly past, losing sight of the dogs until a few seconds later when there would be a flash of white and black across the path ahead, another flash as a young bitch overtook, veering off into the bird-hiding shadows. We all flew and I laughed aloud, one white knuckled hand clutching Clarence's shirt, the other balancing a cold can of American beer. Within half an hour, as the sun sank behind the knotted trees, the young dogs were drained, trailing the motorbike with drooling mouths and cramping limbs. We slowed down and turned for home, exhilarated and flushed from the beer and the ride.

The fish stew was the best thing I'd eaten in America, as everyone told me it would be. Hot, spicy and interesting, with a real salad. I was missing good food and green things and ate several portions. That evening we watched videos of the Pointers on field trials, and listened to a year's worth of stories from Clarence, Big George and Dennis. I drank too much beer, sitting outside on the picnic table, fields of horses and mules to each side, and reveled in the luxury of the evening: good company, good food, good fun.

Clarence waved us off early the next morning after hot coffee and cinnamon rolls. If I had then had an ounce more sense, I would have stayed another night, but by then I was obsessed with the idea of leaving Georgia. I don't think Clarence, Big George, Dennis and the others were quite sure why I would choose such a way to see America, but they were determined for me to leave Georgia with good memories. And that, they did.

We had a wonderful ride that day, leaving behind the tarmac road for a winding dirt track. The overhanging trees provided welcome shade from eighty-nine degree temperatures. Deer were numerous, Smokey was fascinated by the rustling leaves and breaking twigs as they ran from us through the dense woods. I caught a brief glimpse of an otter before it dived, leaving a widening ripple on the surface of the dark water. A little green lizard basking on a road in the sun, scuttled away as our shadow passed over, and the bendy tracks of snakes in the red dust of the road kept me on the lookout for their glistening coiled bodies and flicking tongues.

We spent the night behind a disused, tumbling down barn, in shoulder high grass. A tin of Ravioli made a most welcome meal complemented by my treat at the end of the day - a cup of tea. I sat in the door of my tent enjoying the solitude of the picture perfect spot, Smokey eating the seed heads from the tops of the long grass. Slowly things were improving. We had a workable routine. Smokey wasn't such a bad old thing really. It was still cold at night, but my allergy to horses was easing a little. Soon we'd have a whole state behind us, with a mere eight to go, and when an interested passer-by asked where we'd started, I would be able to say " Brunswick, that's on the Atlantic coast, in Georgia!"

Day 15 was refreshingly wet. Normally a fan of sun, over the last two weeks I had learnt to appreciate rain. Heavy black clouds kept the temperature down, the occasional shower settled the dusty road. We made twenty miles with little effort, having only a short break at lunch time because of the welcome cooler weather. We followed the dirt roads through sleepy towns. Chickasawatchee. Herod. Deverel. Singing along to country songs on the radio. Thinking about home, the bridge ahead, people we'd met, Smokey. Around four o'clock, I turned Smokey in through the gates of a poor looking cattle farm, an old wooden house to the right of the yard looked unstable and unused with a collapsing roof and peeling paint.

The owner walked unsmilingly towards me, his blue working-mans dungarees stained and torn over a heavy paunch. He was tall, about forty-five, plain and looked a little slow thinking, but agreed to me setting up camp in a corner of the overgrown yard. I kept the six inch knife, I carried on my belt, unbuckled in its leather sheath.

After he'd finished the chores he'd been working on when I rode in, without comment, he left in his old pickup truck. I set up camp. Cleaned, fed, watered Smokey. Tied her to a large mossy tree to graze. I explored the yard, the much-repaired out-buildings, the falling down house. Rain was predicted that night, and I picked out a couple of dry looking places in case I needed to run for cover. Back at the tent, I filled a bucket with water from a trailing hosepipe, and began to strip for a much needed bath and hair wash. I shampooed my hair, cleaning several days of dust and sweat from my hat-shaped hairdo. As I began to rinse, using my little tin cup, the farmer turned up with his son.

He was very different from the father. Full of conversation, lively, very interested in knowing all the details of my trip and life back home. He proudly showed me the competition cattle he was raising in the barn. Big black-eyed beasts. After a very intensive whirlwind visit, he left in his handsome new pick-up truck.

I went back to my bath. Rinsed my hair and began the uncomfortable experience of cold water bathing. As I pulled the grimy tee-shirt over my head another truck pulled in. Quickly, I covered up and went over to meet a neighbor who had heard I was here. He wanted to meet me. He was a big, fat guy, driving a telephone company vehicle. Very friendly. Very amazed that a woman would have the courage to travel alone in an area where everyone had some sort of firearm hidden under the front seat. He was even startled when I eagerly accepted his offer of a cold beer. He was thrilled to meet a woman living such an un-womanlike life. Unheard of in those parts.

By the time he left it was getting dark, lightening flashes visible over the distant flat landscape. I hurriedly stripped for this much needed and delayed bath. As I stood there, naked, in the old cattle feed bucket, washing my legs with an old pair of knickers and horse shampoo, a pair of headlights pulled in through the driveway, sending me diving for the cover of the open tent door. Again, soapy, and slimy, I frantically pulled on jeans and tee-shirt . The farm owner, his wife, son, daughter in law, children and friends piled out both doors of the old truck. The older woman carried a foil-covered plate of hot chicken, french fries and coleslaw. Someone else had a jug of iced tea.

I closed the buckle over the knife hanging from my hip.

Day 17 was our last day in Georgia. With clothes still wet from heavy rain the day before, I rode Smokey through Fort Gaines and down the hill towards the Chattahoochee River. Our first state, with all its early day worries and teething problems was almost behind us. 251 miles with no broken bones despite Smokey's best efforts. No sickness despite changing diets for both of us. No trouble, despite being alone. There was just the dreaded bridge between Smokey and me and our second state, Alabama.

As I strained my eyes towards the river and caught sight of the bridge that had been worrying me for so many miles, a smile slowly caught in my sunburned face, widening to an overjoyed beam. The bridge was nothing. Hundred feet wide, flat, wide shoulder. No trouble.

I jumped off and led Smokey, delighted with the day, the horse, the country, over the muddy brown waters of the swelling Chattahoochoo River.

Welcome to Alabama, a sign read, Heart of Dixie.

Chapter 3

ALABAMA On the. Western bank of the Tombigbee river, /, *she, her, me,* turn into we.

"Welcome to Alabama," the sign said. "It's really really great to be here," I said.

I was leading Smokey. She was developing a couple of sores on her back where the treeless saddle was sitting on her spine, and another where she took the weight from the saddlebags. They weren't serious but catch these things early, and avoid trouble later.

The road was busy, noisy and hot. Route 10 across Alabama. A major highway used by the many logging trucks heading out of the eastern camps to the paper mills and treeless states to the west.

My Reebok tennis shoes were wet from a rain-filled Day 15, and before long the inside of the heel had worn down to the plastic lining, eroding first my thick socks and then my heel. I began to develop blisters. The slipping action of my feet in the wet shoes brought out blisters on the soles too, and by late afternoon, after an eighteen mile day, I could hardly walk.

There were few places to stop on that busy road. The houses we did see had burglar alarms and barred windows and big dogs. When I could walk no further, I turned into the driveway of a pastel shaded one story house and tied Smokey to the fence. A large car was parked in the carport.

An elderly and still beautiful black woman answered the knocking on her green porch door. I asked about camping in her back yard.

"Well, there's no way I should be scared of a little thing like you!" she barked out. She must have been over eighty, but fitter than I was right then with my crippled, swollen feet.

I saw to Smokey's needs, set up the tent, then drank ice-water with this eccentric widow, swinging on the porch seat, watching the traffic. When her confidence grew to know that I was harmless, she invited me in for a shower, and supplied rubbing alcohol for my ugly feet. She was very religious, drawing strength and companionship from her love for Jesus and the Bible. She was outraged I wasn't carrying a copy. She told me all about her beliefs and family and dead relatives as I sat at the kitchen table in the fading light, eating cold hot-dog sausages and crackers. I was dehydrated from the eighteen miles walking, and drank glass after glass of black current 'KoolAid', listening to Irene with her stories, appreciating her kindness. Violence, burglary, trouble were common on those big Alabama roads and it took quite a bit of courage to let a complete stranger into her home. I couldn't have walked another hundred feet.

By the time I pulled myself away from the comfort of Irene and her little house, passing Smokey grazing in the moonlight and got to my tent set up in the shadow of an outbuilding, I felt sick with exhaustion. The throbbing in my feet was passing up to the back to my head.

Irene fed me 'grits' in the morning. A tasteless, white, porridge-like mush made from corn, a truly Southern states dish. She also gave me a small much worn Army copy of The New Testament, which I'm afraid I had to abandon later, because of the extra weight in the saddlebags. We exchanged addresses and promised to write.

By six-thirty, I was back on the road, pain from the blisters making each step an agony. It was good to be in Alabama though, despite predictions of an unwelcoming, dangerous and aggressive people.

Within a mile or two, we were passing through the big town of the area, Abbeyville, quiet and peaceful in those early hours. A small mongrel bitch caught Smokey's scent as we walked past her yard and she followed us through the town. After a minute or so, I worried about her obvious fascination with Smokey leading her too far from home and tried to scare her off. She stopped and cowered as I threw small stones her way, then scuttled back down the road.

I walked on. After a while, I looked over my shoulder to see her fifty or sixty feet behind, her eyes fixed on Smokey, her sandy brush tail wagging nervously. For the next sixteen miles, every time I'd turn around, she'd be there. Every time I stopped to rest my swollen throbbing feet, she'd be there. On her belly, with anxious glances at me, she'd crawl to the horse, fascinated. When

Smokey, dropped her head to graze, she'd wag her foxy tail in submission and lick the corners of Smokey's black mouth and her warm big nostrils. Like me, this dog was lame. Part of the big cushioning pads on her front paws had been removed, (maybe to stop her straying!) and like me, each step was painful. All day, I tried to turn this little dog home, but within a minute or two, without looking, I knew she'd be following again, walking each painful step on the cooler white line at the side of the road.

I became so furious with the little dog's persistence and her close calls with the main highway traffic that when a hunting lodge came into view in a clearing in the woods, I turned Smokey up the driveway. The dog followed. We all rested from the scorching afternoon sun, and waited for the owner to return. After sitting there for over two hours, I tied the little dog to the mail box, leaving a note as to why and where the dog had come from.

I heard that dog's desperate whines and cries for over a mile up the tree lined road, and for many months after.

There wasn't much in the way of pasture or grassy backyards on that long, straight stretch of Highway 10 so when the opportunity arose to take a smaller road heading south, to the small village of Clopton, I turned, hoping for better luck there.

It was a pretty little place. All white wooden houses, well kept gardens and small orchards, made all the more idyllic by the warming tones of the afternoon sun. I had to try several houses before I could find one occupied, but finally a wheel-chair bound old man agreed readily to the use of his overgrown pecan orchard alongside the house.

I went through all the evening chores that had become routine after eighteen days traveling: setting up camp, feeding and cleaning Smokey, finding water. I began to write, catching up letters and notes long overdue. Shortly after everything was settled for a comfortable night, the wife of my host came to visit. We talked a while, then she returned to her husband.

Within a few minutes, she was back again, this time much less hospitable in her attitude. She wanted me out. For some reason, despite my being polite and respectful to her, she no longer felt my company desirable on her property. She felt we would be "more comfortable" on the exposed, manicured lawns of the community center at the corner of the Clopton junction. I tried to point out to her there was no grass at that spot, I would be easily visible from the road, and it was getting dark. She persisted, refusing all pleading and reasoning, even the offer of money. In record time, and in a furious temper, I saddled Smokey. I knocked at the door to ask for water for my empty canteen, they wouldn't answer. I left.

I turned Smokey away from those white wooden houses and away from the village. The sun was sinking behind the pines, and I was worried about being out after dark. We passed several spots, tried a couple, but no answers. Finally, seeing a huge pasture to our left, I trotted Smokey up a grass driveway. She stumbled with exhaustion. I tied her to the fence, a respectful distance from the house, and ran over the lawn to the front door of a Spanish style house. It seemed like forever before a woman in her late forties, well dressed and made up, answered my knocking. I told her who I was, where I came from, what I was doing, and would it be possible...

"I don't think so!" and she slammed the door in my face. Amazed, I turned and jogged as fast as my blistered feet would allow towards Smokey.

"Hey! Hey you!" The lady of the house called after me. She'd changed her inhospitable mind no doubt, I thought, and turned, all smiles. But she didn't stop to offer an apology or a camp spot, she wanted to satisfy her need to talk about her love for horses. The tension of the day was too much.

"You talk to me about your love of horses, and there you are, sending a visitor to your country and an exhausted horse out at this time of night when if ll be dark in a few minutes! I think you've got a bloody nerve!"

I apologized, in her hearing, to Smokey for the unfriendly nature of the Alabama people, and again, turned and left.

We found an unlocked gate a little further on at an entrance to a disused field and, shaking from anger and disappointment, I wrapped my arms around Smokey's tired neck, and cried. I was too tired to eat but made tea for comfort, sitting in the door to my tent under the full moon, rubbing horse liniment on my swollen feet. I swore I'd never forget that pretty little village of white wooden houses. Clopton. Clopton, Alabama.

On Day 20, the 26th of April, we passed the three hundred mile mark. Most of the day was spent on the monotonous Highway 10, with ifs noisy trucks and broken bottles. I was still mainly walking, but the sores on Smokey's back were healing nicely with the aid of a smelly green paste called Demoblin which I'd brought with me from England. She didn't like it and would lay her ears back when she became aware of its strong smell heading her way. The blisters on my own feet were becoming a little hardened, but the mixture of sweat and the many miles kept them from completely healing.

We crossed the major 231 highway early in the afternoon, and found peace and perfect country as we left Highway 10 for the minor farm road, Route 6. We were walking through shady woods, derelict farms and green pastures. Crops I didn't recognize were growing in small fields to either side and the old oaks and pine trees gave shelter from the hot sun. The sound of birds and tractors and distant cattle replaced the tiring trucks and things were good again.

I decided to stop early, We hadn't had a rest day since Day 9, and we were both tired and a little rundown. I saw a man exercising a handsome palomino horse in a grassy field through the trees and thought Td give it a try. He was the first person, apart from Carrie, Td seen on a horse.

When he had finished the exercises he was putting the horse through, he came over to the fence where Smokey and I stood waiting. He seemed a little unfriendly, but agreed to us staying, kindly putting his impressive quarter horse stallion in the barn so Smokey would be free to graze.

I sat under a tree for the remainder of the afternoon unsure as to whether I was really allowed to camp, or just rest awhile before being asked to move on. But as it grew late, I set up the tent. By eight o'clock it was dark and I was under the horse blanket thinking about sleep. Just as I began to doze the beam from a torch light shone through the tent walls, accompanied with cries of greetings from the owner, Mike, and his wife, Suzanne. They had some friends too, all carrying beer and eager to party. I was sleeping in clothes, the nights were still cold, so opened the door, glad to see friendly faces.

The evening went by with a trip to Taco Bell in Troy, (how strange it was to be in a car and going at sixty miles and hour!) beer and boozy conversation. The more sloshed Mike became, the more welcoming he was. I had a great evening learning about his palomino Quarter Horses, which he breeds, trains and shows. We talked about what would be the perfect coast to coast horse, (everyone had their own opinion on this depending on what breed they kept in their barn!) and what to expect from the states we had yet to cross. His wife, Suzanne, was one of those lovely, bubbly, lively people who gets on with everyone, and she made me feel really welcome. I refused her offers of stopping in the house though, wanting to be close to Smokey in the paddock and preferring the freedom of sleeping outside.

The house was beautiful. A big, expertly restored, two story wooden house, once belonging to Suzannes's grandfather. They had moved it thirteen miles down the road to its present location. It had wooden floors and high ceilings, done with sympathy for the age of the house and tiles in the kitchen that were the same as my parents kitchen back in Gloucestershire, England. They easily persuaded me to stop another night to rest Smokey's back. I stayed there three.

By April 28th, Smokey's back had improved, and my feet were less sore, with big patches of hard skin where the blisters had been. I left Mike and Suzanne's ranch after three relaxing days and boozy nights, well rested, but anxious to be on the move again.

We stuck to the back roads all day, frequently being stopped by curious passers-by. One visitor, Jimmie Parker from Troy, returned for a second time bringing a metal arrowhead on a piece of leather to take to the coast. He'd had plans for many years of doing such a trip himself, but with mortgages, family and work commitments, he knew his dreams were unlikely to be lived. By giving me the arrowhead to wear, he felt that just a little bit of him would have made that long trip west.

I lost the radio that day. It was in a pack around my waist, along with sun block, throw away camera, and a bandanna. The catch came undone and it fell without me noticing. I didn't go back, but mourned the loss of the radio.

We spent the night on a chicken farm. I was fed and washed by the friendly family but slept on the floor of the barn, Smokey's smelly horse blanket over my nose to hide the stench drifting down from the chicken sheds.

More of the same the following day. To start, small leafy back roads, pleasant riding though hot. We picked up mail at Luverne, took a right and were back on Highway 10. Smokey had settled down quite nicely, knowing the routine and the pointlessness of her old rodeo starts. I was back in the saddle for much of the time, but when she started throwing her head back, I'd climb down and lead her to rest that still tender back. She led better than she rode, walking faster. I enjoyed the variety, too, and the change. I would stiffen up a little if I rode too long, and to dismount and stretch my legs became a pleasure and a necessity.

We had a great night's stop, after an eighteen mile day. I rode Smokey in though the gateway of a small hobby farm. Fat cattle grazed in long grass to one side and old oak trees bordered the other. A huge heavily scented magnolia stood majestically in front of a slightly dilapidated one story wooden house. I was met by a very mixed scrappy gang of twenty dogs, children, and Don and Terri Roman. They were a lovely family, both parents a little overweight, with a lived in look. Very warm and natural, no pretensions, and generous. We put Smokey in with the cattle, but watched her for a while in case of trouble. The younger cows with their curious noses would sneak up behind the strange new creature in their field and Smokey would lift a threatening leg, but never followed through. The nosey youngsters would run excitedly back to their mothers and try the whole thing a minute or so later.

Terri cooked an absolutely great meal of roast lamb (my favorite) though she continually apologized for the poor fare. It was accompanied by creamy cheesy potatoes and green beans. I was losing a lot of weight on this trip, and I'd never had much to spare anyway, but the fatty lamb and garlicky potatoes made me feel wonderfully bloated. For the second night running, I slept in a barn, but had to put the tent up for protection from the many animals that also made their home there.

Greenville was a big town. Loud, noisy, busy, even on a Sunday. Smokey had become quite used to the heavy traffic, but could be unpredictable with sudden noises and alarmed by things such as flags flapping on car-sales forecourts. Whenever we went through a town, I was always on the lookout for trouble from her.

As we passed in, then out of the residential, commercial, then industrial areas of the town, she was being quite good — seven out often type of standard. That's until we came to the approach to our second interstate crossing. Our road dropped steeply to pass under the wide north bound lanes, a gap, then the two lanes heading south. Even as we approached, I could feel Smokey stiffen, her ears twitched and nostrils flared. She'd gone under the first interstate in Georgia quite well, so I was sure she was just being cautious, but as we approached closer, I had the horrible feeling, that this one wasn't going to be quite so easy.

We made it to the level section of road, fifty feet or so from the actual shadow filled tunnel underneath, past the slip roads rising steeply to join the main highway. Even on a Sunday, the traffic was heavy. Interstate 65, connecting Mobile in the south western corner of Alabama with Montgomery, on to Birmingham where roads went in all directions, connecting state with state, and city to city.

I waited for a break in the traffic to try our first attempt under the road, but the "D0D0....D0D0...." of the overhead vehicles was too frightening for the little grey horse who once ran wild in the traffic free wastelands of Nevada, and she twisted, dashing back a few paces before I could bring her under control. We had been on the road now for twenty five days, and one thing I had learned is that to lose your patience with a mustang, was a waste of energy. Patience was progress. Slow, encouraging, calming conversation with this independent thinking breed of horse took you further, in less time, than any amount of force or tantrums. I was leading, as I usually did on these testing obstacles, (though in later months I found I had more control in the saddle, than out of it) taking a tight grip on the long cotton lead rope. With each lull in the traffic, I would encourage her to take a step or two closer to the shady tunnel. We would make progress one minute, then a particularly heavy vehicle would go overhead, and with sparks from steel shoes on hard road, we'd be back at what Smokey considered a safe distance. The traffic also trying to pass under the Interstate was mainly considerate, though more than once, cars had to veer away, or brake, as Smokey turned and plunged back up the road. All the time I talked to her. Calmly, encouraging, reassuring. Only when she turned away from the frightening underpass, did a firm "No!" break the flow.

We had many attempts before she started to yield a little. With a firm hold on the lead rope, I could keep her standing almost in the shadow of the big road, close enough to hear the noise of the trucks, cars, and RV's passing overhead. Then she went. Like a shot she sprang from her defensive position of four feet braced on the tarmac, to a half gallop, across the lane of oncoming traffic, under the Interstate, dragging me helplessly, half running, half scraping along the ground. Cars had to break and swerve as I fought for control. When she was through, in her own time, she slowed to a rapid snorting walk away from that underpass, and I was able to pick myself off the ground, pale, shaking, a little torn, and a lot older. We split a chocolate covered Granola bar. I needed the sugar.

I tied Smokey up to a sturdy post outside a gas station and fetched water for her in the blue folding bucket. It gave me a few minutes for the blood to ease away from my furiously beating heart and for color to slowly come back to my face. When she saw me walking towards her, she nickered in welcome.

"Nearly kill me you silly old cow, then make out you're glad to see me!"

A gentle telling off, then a pat and a hug, and we were back on our way.

We'd been offered the chance of a midday rest on a property owned by Eddie Bush, who'd stopped us earlier in the day for a chat. A good looking, quiet spoken cowboy, who made a living shoeing horses, doing carpentry, and roping cattle in competition. He told me to ride into his big grass paddock garden in front of his house, close the gate, and let Smokey roam where she will. This I did, dropping saddle and packs under a tree a few yards from a large, cool looking pond. As I was sorting through the bags for paper and envelopes to catch up on letter writing, a noise in the heavy undergrowth and bushes in the far corner of this large garden made me jump up in alarm. I scanned the field. Where was Smokey? I ran to where I could hear the thrashing about in the trees, catching glimpses of a field behind with three horses racing around in panic. Broken weeds and snapped branches showed clearly the route Smokey had taken — down a small bank leading to the three handsome quarter horse geldings in the paddock behind. She hadn't seen the barbed wire fence that separated her from these new beau's and she was trapped. One foot was over the fence. The other in it. Wire was caught between hoof and shoe on a hind leg hanging about thirty inches off the ground. She was kicking and in fright. The wire had lacerated her chest and blood ran down her back legs. My hands went to my mouth. A second later, I was down with her in the ditch, calming the frightened animal. I stroked her neck, then along her back. She stopped kicking. I needed her out of there, but how, I didn't know. I wasn't carrying wire cutters (stupid mistake, Emma) I called for help. Then screamed for help, but no one came. These properties were big, and the next one along was empty. With hands shaking for the second time that day, I unsheathed the big hunting knife on my belt, and began to saw. There were seven pieces of wire alone between hoof and shoe, and until those were free, her leg was held high off the ground. She was caught well and good. The steel blade made quick work of the first two or three twisted strands, but quickly became blunt. I tried the blades of my Swiss Army knife: the two cutting edges, the saw, the file. By this time, Smokey's suspended leg was shaking with exhaustion, but she was calm. I talked to her and I believe she trusted me to get her out of this fix. Many horses would have panicked until free or seriously hurt and once again I was grateful for her intelligence and common sense (though it wasn't so smart to get caught up, was it Smokey?)

Twenty long minutes went by, which seemed much longer, before the last wire broke and Smokey's aching leg could rest on the ground. A minute's rest, then she allowed me to pick up her heavy hooves, and one leg at a time, I guided her over the fence. The blood on her chest and legs was drying, so the damage was superficial. I sat on the grass, and cried with relief. A little stiffly, Smokey jogged over to the three waiting geldings and flirted like mad. She was in season.

The afternoon rest turned into a night's stop when Eddie heard the story of how Td spent my supposedly peaceful break. We doctored Smokey's cuts and found nothing serious. Her near hind shoe was half torn off, so he proposed a meal out with family and he'd shoe her all round in the morning. So I set up camp, played football and did a bit of bike riding, ate well with Eddie and Brenda and the children in town, later that evening, and toasted Edddie's fiftieth birthday, though he hardly looked forty. But I went to bed in my little green tent camped down by the pond, glad the day was over. An interstate, and an accident. Please God, never again.

Smokey had new shoes, but she'd knocked the calluses off her back and again I was committed to walking and not riding. I moved the packs to sit on the saddle to change the distribution of weight, and settled down to a lot of ground work before those sore spots would heal.

We were still on Route 10, but a day or two ahead on the map I could see a large main highway bridge. Still not an expert with these pieces of engineering, I thought it wiser to take a longer route, using dirt roads, to a little country back roads bridge a little to the north. We left Highway 10 at Pineapple (not a pineapple in sight) aiming for an old bridge at the bottleneck end of The William "Bill" Donnelly Reservoir.

The next three days were a nightmare of bad sign posting, bad mapping, new roads in places not shown, and old ones disappeared. Rain. Thunderstorms. Graveyard camping. Wet clothes in the morning, all day, all night. Bad cough and back tracking. The only compensations were the quiet and the views. Beautiful sweeping panoramas of pine covered hills, in the early morning the valleys filled with grey mist. The noise of deer racing away through thick forests and tracks of all sorts of four legged creatures laid out on the red dirt roads. Any clearing in the forest was taken over by the fast growing leprous vine, kudzu. An import from China to hopefully feed American cattle, the experiment had failed. The cattle didn't like the huge leafed creeper, nothing did, and everything it touched, it strangled. From trees, to bushes, to houses, to land. It was almost impossible to kill, and throughout the south eastern states, the name of Kudzu was spoken with venomous hatred. It was fabulous to look at. Like a green crawling blanket, it covered everything.

After all this there was no bridge. Hadn't been for seven years. I wanted to strangle the maker of my map. We retraced our route at twice the speed on the return trip, back to Highway 10, to Camden.

I used to live in Camden. Camden, London, that is, with a whole gang of people living in cheap accommodations. I lived in the coal shed. I thought it would be interesting to stop the night in the American counterpart and compare the two.

On the outer fringes of the industrial area, a drive-through restaurant selling fried chicken and double decker hamburgers looked very appealing after only Beanie-Weanies and sweet corn for four days. It was fun waiting in line, sandwiched between a big boat of a car from Georgia, and one behind from Choctaw County, Alabama. I don't think it was a common sight to see a horse queuing up at the drive through; some tourists jumped out of their RV to take photos and people stared open mouthed from the restaurant proper. This is pretty cool, I thought, as I casually led Smokey up to the little box to give my order.

"Hi! Can I take your order please?" The tinny voice jumped out of the box almost indecipherable from the loud static. Smokey freaked. Four feet left the ground, sending her, and propelling me, four or five feet across the forecourt. The weird voice from nowhere had terrified her. When we'd both landed, (her all ears, nostrils, and big black eyes, me red with embarrassment and my right arm four inches longer) I thought it best to make a quiet exit. At least we hadn't landed on someone's car bonnet or dented a door, and with my luck running the way it was, if we stuck around for a second attempt at that juicy, mouth watering hamburger, some sort of lawsuit would have been a sure thing.

Humiliated and hungry, I led Smokey through the outer reaches of the town, down a sharp hill, up a long climb, and into central Camden. Two streets, one crossing the other, made up the shopping area. Lawyers, clothing shops, a dentist, real estate agents, hardware stores, the town hall. Attractive Victorian brickwork and one traffic light. It felt good after my color had returned to normal, to be in civilization after the nights camped in backwoods Alabama.

The sun was out after two days of rain. We passed into the residential area, and began scanning the yards and smaller roads for somewhere to stop. On one street, parallel to the main shopping street, I saw a man working in a vegetable patch adjoining a large field. Two horses called to Smokey over the fence. The gardener wasn't the owner of the paddock, but set off at a brisk trot to find him. Before long, he was back with a tall, middle-aged gentleman, who agreed to our using the field for the night and also offered the secluded garden behind an empty house he owned as a place to put my tent. Smokey didn't exactly hit it off with the one mare in the field, having to defend herself from ugly attacks; teeth and feet. She stood her ground, but was more interested in the long grass than horse company. She was becoming quite independent from the need to be with other horses, which was a big relief after her early loneliness. She belonged to a two-horse herd now — she and me.

Mr. Dunmarr, my kind host for the night, left in his car to catch the feed store before it closed. Td ran out of horse feed, and he was glad to help. I set up camp. Washed hair and smelly body under the hose pipe leading from the house, and put on my one spare tee shirt, my one spare pair of trousers and turned my only sweatshirt inside out to give me the impression of a soft fluffy going-out jumper. For the first time in twenty nine days, I felt presentable.

Mr. Dunmarr returned, refused all offer of payment for the feed, chatted a while before leaving me to my night out. I was ridiculously excited. Normally I camped a little out of town or miles away from anything, so to be right in the center, with Smokey safe in a well fenced field, was a rare luxury. I planned on a sit down restaurant meal, preferably French, half a bottle of red wine, budget be dammed. With a bounce in my walk, and swinging long wet blonde hair, I set out to explore the town, my mouth watering at the prospect of my imagined feast. Within an hour, I was back, sitting in the door of my tent, sucking on the bones of take-out chicken. There had been no restaurant. I was a little disappointed, but, hell, chicken is ambrosia when you haven't eaten for twenty four hours!

Day 30. Smokey passed over the bridge we'd detoured so far to avoid without any trouble. It was her biggest yet; a long sweep of cement over the Alabama River. Route 10 again, with if s limitless supply of logging trucks, the long, red, weeping tree trunks hanging many feet over the back of the trailers. Even when discourteous drivers gave a long pull on their truck air horns, hoping for wild reactions, Smokey would hardly blink. I jumped every time, and cursed the rude interruption to my reveries. She was amazing in traffic, though cyclists would startle her, with their silent approach. That night we spent in a graveyard tucked behind a Baptist church, just off the main highway. Many of the graves were uncared for; long grass and weeds hiding polished marble stones and crumbling statues. Plastic flowers faded by weeks in the sun, in splitting plastic pots. Smokey ate well, walking irreverently over the long dead. It was very quiet. Alabamans belonging to the Baptist Church were usually black, and superstitious, and I was never disturbed after dark be anything other than deer or rodents or owls. I always felt safe in a graveyard at night; the stones and the dark like a blanket to protect us. That one night, I set up the tent, now a task that took under two minutes, next to some fallen branches. A small bird kept returning to a nest hidden in the dry dead leaves, her mouth full of bugs or worms, to be greeted by the desperate chirping of a young family hidden there. I sat and watched as the mist rose, and the sun sank.

I had been told by non-Alabaman Americans that Alabama was a dangerous state. One of the poorest in the nation, riddled by drug crime and poverty. I'd had no trouble, but riding along those back roads after leaving Route 10 at Vineland, there was an atmosphere of tension. I led Smokey through villages all morning with condemnable looking wooden shacks or tottering mobile homes, full of bare-footed children, but with the contrast of an expensive flashy car parked outside. The priorities, to me, seemed wrong. Racism was blatant. The fascist slogans of the KKK were advertised in black paint on white bridge sidings, or in white on black roads. There was always a white neighborhood, followed by a black neighborhood. I was looked at distrustfully by women hanging out washing or old men smoking outside small town stores. It didn't seem possible in these enlightened times. I felt uneasy and unwelcome. I wanted to take a photo of three black children, barefooted, but in clean colorful clothes sitting on a green porch swing, but as I looked in the saddlebags for the camera, their mother fussed them away. I was used to drivers stopping to find out who I was and where we were going but that day I began to watch for cars or pickup trucks passing us by more than once or twice. Several times one would pull over, parking a little ahead on the side of the road, and instead of the normal smiley greetings from the driver, they wouldn't get out of the car. When this happened, I would stop Smokey a few yards behind the back bumper, not moving either. If they wanted to talk, they could come to me. If I was made to wait for more than twenty or thirty seconds, I would undo the buckle to the leather pouch I carried on my belt. It looked like a gun holster. I would sit on Smokey's back, or lean against her shoulder, my left hand playing with the buckle to the pouch. They would leave. Maybe that simple leather case which innocently held my wallet, Swiss army knife and pen, saved my life on more than one occasion.

Riding into Magnolia was like landing in a safe port. It was a town apart in character from the ones we'd been in through the day. I was stopped by a handsome older woman in a car, who gave me four dollars to buy a cold drink. Another man at the gas station tried to give me three dollars but I couldn't take it - he only had five in his wallet. I bought an ice-cold 'Dr Pepper' and two beers for later. Rather than ask about a place to camp, I took Smokey through Magnolia and out the other side, away from houses, farms and people. The land was mainly rolling forested tracts broken up with patches of pasture land. One huge field offered the shelter of trees halfway down its mile long length, so after a glance up and down the country road to check our exit went unnoticed, I urged Smokey to the security of those trees and covered our tracks. We were out of view from both directions. I kept Smokey on a short lead rope until the dark night gave us added cover, setting the tent up by touch rather than sight.

A little after dark a truck with a broken muffler stopped at the entrance to our field. Even from half a mile away, I could hear the loud male voices.

"She's gotta be in here somewhere!"

They hunted around a bit before driving up the road, then a bit later, I recognized the same loud engine heading back in the direction of Magnolia.

I sat in the tent door and finished my beer.

Day 32 began with six more of those back-country miles followed by another six on the major north-south Highway 43. It took us to Linden.

I tied Smokey to a post on the corner at the first set of crossroads, fed her grain, and disappeared into the restaurant occupying that corner lot. I was conscious of the very lived in smell radiating off my clothes as I stood in line to order a burger. But the embarrassment was worth it, as a few minutes later I ate my first decent meal in quite a few days.

The temperature was already in the upper eighties, so a little further into the sizeable town, I unsaddled Smokey on the Library lawn. It wasn't the very manicured type, so I didn't expect that anyone would mind, and the large shady trees promised a good spot for an hour or twos snooze.

As I checked the maps for a likely looking area to stop that night, a sixteen or seventeen-year-old boy came running over. He lived in the house adjoining the piece of land we rested on and he thought that he'd seen a loose white horse from his kitchen window. He hadn't noticed me lying back in a patchy shade. We talked for a while about his life in Linden; his plans for college, his time at school. He confessed to me he never went to class without a gun hidden somewhere ~ in a pocket or a bag, which I thought was pretty alarming. He was an attractive, blonde, blue-eyed ail-American boy, well dressed and intelligent enough. Not what you'd think of as a gun-toting trouble maker. He said all his friends carried guns. Shootings were common.

Before I saddled up at three o'clock, he had restocked the feed bags with grain from an uncle's farm, and seen Smokey watered. I enjoyed the two hours I spent under the tree in Linden.

We hadn't been on the road for more than five minutes, when an urgent voice called us to stop. A dark-haired man in his late thirties had seen us go by, and knowing his niece to be a desperate fan of horses, especially in white, hadn't been able to let us pass. I remembered my own childhood infatuation with horses, so was glad to offer Smokey up for a bit of adoration. The young girl wasn't at the house, so while the uncle hurried from neighbor to neighbor in pursuit, I stood and talked to the family crowded around the white horse.

It always amazed me how interested people were in my trip. In all the thousands of hours I'd spent in England wondering what it would be like to travel across country on horseback, I never once considered the amount of attention and interest my holiday would generate. Invariably, the different people who stopped to talk were amazed at what they felt was courage to do such a thing, being alone and a woman, in a country they themselves were frightened to be living in. They also admired the fact that I was living out my dream, one that so many of them shared, but which for many different reasons, would never, for them, come true.

The niece wasn't to be found, so a few photos had to do. After accepting the offer of a Coke, the kind women, fussing about how thin I was, packed up a plastic bag full of groceries, which I began working on as soon as I was around the corner and out of view!

We had the biggest challenge of the trip so far, on Day 33.

After leaving Linden the day before, we'd taken the smaller road, 29, only going a few miles before sneaking into a big field for an illegal nights stop. I was aiming to avoid another underpass at Interstate 20/59, and I had heard there was an overpass on farm road 12, a deviation from our westerly route of about thirty miles. It seemed well worth the trouble. Route 28 took us to 80. We'd already seen this spot with Pat on the drive eastwards. I had forgotten the bridge I now saw at that junction.

My heart sank, and everything else with it. From half a mile away, all I could see was a wall of cement rising from the muddy banks of the Tombigbee River. Four lanes of demented traffic raced up it's sides, only to disappear immediately after passing the peak. Smokey would never ever do it.

On the approach, I tried to think of every possible way around the impossible, studying the map until my eyes wouldn't focus. Maybe hiring a trailer would work, but the nearest town was a long way back, and my twenty dollar a week budget wouldn't stretch. Maybe swimming the river was a possibility, but that only happens in films.

We were at the base of my nightmare, and there was no other way. Two men were eating a late lunch at a little picnic area on the riverbank. Should I ask for help? I didn't. The only plus about this whole thing, was the good wide shoulder to each side of the four lanes. I waited for a gap in the endless stream of logging trucks hurtling past. They made no consideration for a horse and rider on the side of the road; so we began the long climb.

"Come on Smokey, good girl. Come on, Smokey, good girl..." I talked to her continuously, trying to disguise the quiver in my voice with a confident tone and a lot of patting.

Slowly, very slowly, we were rising over the river. The trucks began again, keeping their speed up to make the climb. Smokey's ears would flick back when she heard the driver drop a gear and put his foot down, and would turn her head to see what was coming. Some people say you shouldn't let a horse see the danger behind, but I always let her turn her head to look at anything that bothered her, and it worked for me on that bridge. When the truck had passed, she'd resume her steady walk up the hill. I couldn't believe she was doing it. With each click of metal shoe on cement, we were climbing, climbing to the clouds, to the end of the world, where traffic was lost over the brow, where the brown, slow-moving Tombigbee River ran a million miles below.

Perhaps two hundred feet from the top, we came upon the expansion bars in the road. Like fingers woven together, they allowed the bridge to expand or contract, depending on the temperature. Today it was hot, and the iron fingers were spread apart, hardly touching. Through the gap, way down below, I could see the brown sluggish water ambling along on its way to the Gulf of Mexico. With a firm grip on the lead rope, and personally terrified, I jumped the six inch gap. I turned to Smokey.

"Come on, Smokey, good girl. Come on..." She froze, four feet braced against the road, and sniffed the air rising through the gap. I could see her thinking, considering this unknown hazard, then she went to turn. I can't say my life flashed before my eyes, but in the fraction of a second it took me to leap the gap and straighten her back up, I had had visions of horse meeting truck, truck meeting horse, in bloody introduction. Unable to disguise my shaking voice and hands any longer, I asked her for a second attempt. Smokey froze at the brink again, sniffed the rising air, waited for a moment's peace from the traffic, and followed my little hop over the hole with the prettiest little hop of her own. I was ecstatic, but we still had a long way to go. We walked on. The middle section of the bridge bounced and swayed every time it took the weight of a big truck. It frightened me, but Smokey just stared ahead with big, black eyes half shaded by her long, white lashes. As we reached the top, she stopped again. I couldn't believe she was going to turn and run after all that effort, and pleaded for her to move ahead. She waited until I'd finished fussing, then like a tourist hanging over the stone walls of Tower Bridge in London, she looked around, enjoying the view. She watched the tree tops swaying on each side of the rivers edge, the fisherman, almost indistinguishable on the banks below, the muddy water, the landscape ahead, before, in her own time, she turned back to me and resumed her steady, easy, plodding walk down the other side of the bridge.

The second expansion bar on the downward side was no problem. She had learned, in one simple lesson, how to cross them. A smart horse. My little, smart, wild white horse. The rest of the descent passed without event, though the tension kept me staring at the road and talking my monotonous encouragement to Smokey shuffling along behind.

When we reached the safety of the western grassy bank, I cried with relief. Only four weeks ago, Smokey had given me so many problems about the smallest of bridges, and here she was, calmly chewing her share of a melted chocolate granola bar, after crossing a bridge I would have detoured to avoid DRIVING over! I was so proud of her. We had arrived. I buried my face in her wiry grey mane, knowing that whatever lay ahead, she'd be there, fifty per cent of a one horse team. We were going to the coast, and we were going to make it.

There were five more bridges within the next mile, but harmless flat concrete types, so no problems there. I led Smokey for the three or four miles we spent along busy Highway 80, still a bit teary eyed over the earlier redrawing of horse and rider relationship lines. She trusted me, and I had a new respect for her.

My soppy reflections were broken by the rude interruption of a flasher in the bushes. Standing next to his truck, in the seclusion of a gate entrance and protected from view from two sides by trees, the lonely character gave me a private viewing of his one man show. I had waved before I realized what he was up to. He waved back in a different way.

We left Highway 80 shortly after, watching out for the man's blue pickup truck before turning off onto 28 again. A two mile walk found us at a small cattle farm.

Smokey looked especially pretty that night, grazing in the long grass. I remember her picking up her head to look at a noise that had caught her attention, grass hanging out each side of her mouth, her big white head framed against the dark pines. We had just passed the five hundred mile mark, maybe in the middle of that Tombigbee River Bridge, a bridge that marked more changes than just another mile. Smokey was fat, and she was happy. I was thin, but I was happy too. I was happy she was happy. Things were working out okay.

We needed to stock up on horse feed, replace Smokey's curly peg that was now too bent to be of much use, and ideally get something else to read. War and Peace had lasted well, keeping me sane after the loss of the radio, but it was days since I'd used the last pages, and in the evenings there had only been endless games of patience to pass the time.

Livingston was a big, university town. Wide streets of expensive brick houses very much on a pattern of grand Victorian England. The store I was aiming for was one and a half miles out of the way, but without horse feed, though Smokey didn't exactly need it, I didn't feel self-sufficient. Every large American town has a road like the one we rode up that day. Wide, straight, four lane, busy, lined with huge stores with their huge parking lots: J.C. Penney, KMart, Dillons, followed by McDonalds Kentucky Fried Chicken, Long John Silver, Pizza Hut. We passed all these and others like them. When I'd almost given up on finding the feed store, there it was.

We stocked up on crushed oats for Smokey, then crossed the road to the massive store that sells everything, Wal-Mart. It was lunch time so I unsaddled Smokey on the rough ground adjoining the big Wal-Mart lot, but I was worried about leaving all my equipment unattended while I shopped. I asked one of the assistants if she'd mind watching the horse and bags while I rushed around. She was terrified of the horse, but stood guard while I raced from aisle to aisle. I bought gas for the stove, a new curly peg and a drink.

Riding back into town, the university students, lounging outside the big

Victorian annexes, did their best to spook the white horse. One young man rode up and down on a high powered motorbike doing wheelies, others shouted and tooted horns. Smokey behaved like a dream. She was invincible.

There was another bridge to cross, on the exit road out of Livingston. An old iron one with no hard shoulder. I didn't know about it until stopped by Alicia Key who lived on the western bank. We crossed with Alicia driving behind, hazard lights flashing, while Smokey for the first time in 400 miles, trotted. We crossed the bridge in safety and on the invitation of Alicia, spent the night camped in her grassy garden.

I had a shower. I did my laundry. I had a wonderful pasta meal, and really enjoyed the company of bubbly Alicia, her handsome teacher husband, Mark, and their young son.

I lay under a clean horse blanket that night, my head on a clean Helly Hansen jacket rolled up for a pillow, looking back on Alabama and the people we'd met. We only had fourteen more miles to the Mississippi state line, and though Alabama had sometimes been strange, we were here, almost at the western limit of the state, alive and well, starting to relax and enjoy things. Alabama's alright, people!

Mark let me select a couple of books to take away, so the prospect of a good read filled the long hours in the saddle or walking beside Smokey on our thirty sixth day, with an air of impatient expectancy.

We had crossed Interstate 20/59 at the overpass on Farm Road 12 early in the morning. It was a beautiful day, warm, and the road was quiet. I picked a flower from a magnolia tree, putting a couple of the fragrant petals under my hat. The rising heat kept the scent circulating around my head for many miles. Blackberries were in season, though only May, and I supplemented my dull, canned diet lunch with their big squashy fruit at a small hobby farm later that day.

While the large, overweight, jolly owner came and left in his almost antique tractor, I gave Smokey a hosepipe bath. She hated getting wet and made a fuss for the whole five minutes or so I sprayed her down, dancing and backing away. As soon as I released her rope, she took her revenge, and rolled in the recently ploughed field. The owner came back with ice-cold sodas and crisps and asked why I'd traded the white horse. She was a mess.

We spent the night at Fred's, a tough old farmer living in the shadow of the Mississippi State Line. He proved to be a real softie. He asked me to stay.

Fred was one of the old brand of American farmer, but successful. Very masculine, very strong willed. Old equipment working small fields, wooden fences and a couple of horses. Pigs and goats and a pretty garden. The house was quite new, and his wife was young and attractive. When I met him earlier in the afternoon on his tractor, I thought him a bit hard. He seemed a little unfriendly, but offered a place to stay. When he'd seen me settled, camped on the grassy land around his farm buildings, my back to the big machine filled barn, he relaxed, and the more affable part of his character surprised me. He bought me food, and drinks, offered me as many days rest as I needed, was very good company, and did my laundry.

I thought about staying. I would be helping Fred harvest the hay before the predicted rain at the weekend, and a day off from the routine of traveling would be welcome. Being so close to our third state, I couldn't decide. As I sat there, going over the pro's and con's of a day's rest, I watched Smokey biting off the seed heads of the long rye grass she was working her way through, the setting sun casting long shadows from pine trees rooted in Mississippi at the edge of Fred's field.

Smokey decided for me. Fred caught her early the next morning heading back down his driveway, dragging the curly peg and sixty foot of rope.

By seven o'clock that morning, we were in Mississippi.

Chapter 4

MISSISSIPPI
Hospitality and generosity all sit most comfortably
on the shoulders of this prettiest, greenest, most
friendly of states. The real start of the ride.

On my researches for this trip all those thousands of miles away in my
little Gloucestershire cottage, I had learned of two possible routes across
this United States of America. They both began at the Georgia coast
around Brunswick, but the first swung north in Mississippi to pick up the
historic Oregon Trail in Missouri and touched the western coast in Oregon.
This route was well documented with hundreds of settler's accounts of the
long wagon ride west. They left Missouri in April, having to average
fifteen miles a day to make it across the Rocky Mountains before the heavy
winter snows. The mountains are at their highest in those northern states
and by the time I started up those big climbs Autumn would be well
advanced. I was worried about our chances of making it across. The second
choice was an almost direct east-west line, aiming for the southern
California coastline. The disadvantage of following this path would be
the heat. Texas in summer, the books said, offer temperatures soaring into
the hundreds with few shady trees.

Texas is followed by New Mexico with its snakes and scorpions and the stretch of land known as *La Journada Del Muerta*, The Journey of Death. Four hundred miles of New Mexico is followed by four hundred miles of Arizona. Arizona, meaning dry place. A state of deserts. Before reaching the sparkling Pacific Ocean on this route there stood in our way the Yuha desert, the sand dunes of Southern California. The second route was shorter, but it would be harder. I made my choice. Like the song says, *California, Here I Come!* I love maps. Never get bored studying their spider-webs of red, black and grey lines. Never tire of the squiggly blue rivers and the circular towns. The names, the counties, the lakes and mountains and motorways. In their condensed inches I could see the state. I saw before us that morning, our thirty-sixth on the road, sixty saddle hours and nearly nine hundred thousand horsey hoof prints before we'd see the Mississippi river at Greenville, looking over the water to Arkansas. So off we start to two hundred miles of Mississippi roads, fields, trees, rivers and sky.

It was a drizzly day, which was welcome, a relief from day after day of glorious sunshine. Last year's rotting leaves softened the sound of Smokey's shoes on the narrow lanes as we rode through miles of dripping forest. Her back was almost healed but I often walked. Two hours on, one off. Two hours on then a break for lunch. It was quiet, only the gentle hissing of the rain falling through the trees, and the thumping of the buzzard's heavy wings as they climbed away from the road kills of armadillo, dog and snake.

We passed through Porterville and across Highway 45, a shocking contrast of noisy traffic, before dropping back once more into the calm of the peaceful woods. Almost every car that passed us that day stopped to talk. Where are you going? Where are you coming from? Aren't you scared? I was given a cold drink and a sandwich by one local, and another cold drink a few minutes later by another. "Mississippi: Hospitality State." So far, so good!

There were few houses on that lonely road. Those southern states were some of the poorest in the Union, and it was clear from the abandoned farms and empty rural shops that many people had been forced toward town, or westwards. However, from one visitor I had learned of a widowed lady, living alone, with empty fields, who might be willing to share a corner of a paddock for the night.

I passed her house in the late afternoon. She was sitting on the porch swing. She waved, I waved, and rode on. The lane ahead was dark from the heavy overhanging trees, so I stopped, paused, and turned back. Opposite the old two storied house, with its pretty garden and tidy lawn was a small, unfenced pecan orchard. I asked the smiling lady about renting it for the night.

" No my dear, I won't rent it, but you're very welcome to use it!" she said kindly. I tied Smokey to the thick trunk of a pecan, a forty foot length of rope allowing her plenty of room to enjoy the long grass. I erected the tent a few feet from the limit of her circle, then returned, wet-legged to the house across the road.

Christine, without a fuss, fed me, did my laundry, ran me a bath, and found two pairs of unused socks to replace my holey ones which by now had entries at both ends. I spent a lovely evening in her graceful company talking about England and Mississippi, its problems and its pluses. Some friends called by and all four of us sat outside enjoying the evening, the late sun reflecting off the day's shrinking puddles. We ate ice-cream. Smokey was very white against the dark green woods, her heavy white belly hardly lessened after nearly five hundred and fifty miles on the road. I called her. She looked up, paused in her chewing for a second, before head down again. She looked happy. Everyone admired her, but I admired her the most.

An animal chewed a hole more than two inches wide in the black waterproof feed bag during the night, which I patched with blue canvas from the saddlebag repair kit before a big breakfast of bacon and biscuits with Christine. My kind host watched from the porch as I rode Smokey away from the house, the fields, and the pecan orchard, into the shadowy tree lined lane. One last wave at the corner, and we were gone.

We were aiming for DeKalb. a short day of fourteen miles, mostly along the quiet country roads but with a short stint along Highway 16 into town. The weather was beautiful, like an English summer's day, with dense blue skies broken by fluffy white clouds. The humidity began to rise though, later in the morning, after all the recent rain, but for much of the day we were sheltered by the trees and really enjoyed ourselves.

DeKalb looked small on the map but was actually a sizeable American country town, with its own newspaper among its boasts. The reporter met us on the outskirts and bought my story for a cold drink outside a gas station. I sat on a picnic table, Smokey in the shade with a bucket of water, fascinated with all the hustle-bustle of civilization after so long on the lonely back roads. Cars and trucks, camper vans and motorbikes all came to fill up at the pumps as I talked to the young man for his article. He seemed to think my holiday was big news for DeKalb! When the notes were finished, and the talk more general, he told me about the legendary 'Goat Man' ...an old, grey haired eccentric who traveled around the southern states with a little wagon towed by his goats. He seemed to have a whole gang of them: some to pull, some to milk, some young, and a few retirees. He made his living by selling postcards of his wagon with the traveling goats. Nobody had seen him for two or three years, and were worried about his poor health and what may have happened to his many animals if he had fallen ill. I regretted I hadn't seen him, I said.

I began dropping hints about finding a place to stay for the night's stop. Different people were considered or volunteered, the local policeman was found and asked for his suggestion, and between a whole bunch of friendly visitors it was suggested I camp at the industrial estate on the edge of town. One of my hosts, Joyce Aust, volunteered to bring out some horse feed for Smokey, and a meal for me, so feeling well cared for I unhitched for the extra mile west.

My little horse was becoming really reliable in town traffic so it had become a thrill to jump in the saddle and ride past the shops, banks, dentists, lawyers and car sales lots, waving to anyone that cared to wave to me. It was a good feeling to be thought of as a picturesque sight!

The industrial estate was empty. The young police officer, Ralph, had the keys to the gate and had obtained permission from the people who were able to grant it, to let us stay. The huge, flat, shoe box type buildings were laid out around a massive car park. A river lay hidden to the right, the banks lined with trees outlined it's meandering route to the south. Gentle hills surrounded us, mostly covered with evergreen trees, which contrasted strongly with the sandy colored factories glowing in the warm evening sun. I chose a spot looking down on the layout, on one side of the square, where the grass was longest and water close by. I tied Smokey to an air conditioner outlet and set up camp. Joyce was as good as her word, bringing a whole bag of fruit, cheese, biscuits and drink, making a feast for a meal. She also bought horse feed, which as Smokey could only carry three days of rations, I was always on the look out for.

Joyce was a widow, working locally as a teacher, and we immediately got on well. She had horses too. She stayed awhile, but anxious not to stay too long, promised to return in the morning with coffee. I settled down to my meal, sitting cross-legged in the tent door. It felt like an ancient Mexican temple, and I was an Incas king looking down on my worshipful slaves (except that I was alone apart from Smokey!) I ate grapes and watched the sun set.

During the night I was aware of a torch light beam scanning across the tent every hour or two. The police officer, Ralph, was watching out for Smokey and me as we slept.

The factory workers began arriving at 5.30 in the morning. The sun still wasn't up though the sky was brightening noticeably to the east. A security officer came to see who we were, politely enquiring what we were doing on his patch, wished us a good trip when I made it sound legal.

Joyce arrived just as I was riding Smokey away from the shorn lawns, bringing breakfast and an American scale polystyrene cup of coffee. She gave me a little gold guardian angel to watch over us on the days and nights ahead, a Bible, and five dollars. She was a very kind lady, saying good-bye with watery eyes.

We were now on Highway 16, another of those main roads busy with logging trucks and commuting traffic. The hills were becoming more pronounced; long sweeping climbs and descents, the black stripe of the tarmac visible for miles at the brow of each hill. There was a wide grassy shoulder on each side, bordered with dense woods.

The day started off sunny, but by midday thunderous looking clouds began to build, promising a wet afternoon. Twelve miles in, the rain began. Big, heavy drops bounced off my plastic map case. A few seconds more and the landscape was hidden behind the slanting downpour, followed by thunder and lightening. Smokey turned her back to the rain and refused to move. I hunched under my sodden hat, the rain running down the neck of my stockman's coat making me shiver as cold water ran down my back. Smokey looked so depressed I couldn't help but laugh aloud. She'd pick up one back foot then the other as the water ran down the backs of her legs. She hated to get wet. Her normally glowing white coat with the dark flecks became soaked to a metallic grey.

We stood there, frozen in mutual discomfort for nearly an hour. I distracted myself with trying to remember the names of the many people that had pulled over to talk during the morning's ride.

The DeKalb reporter had passed on our story to the local radio station, and we were now local celebrities! It didn't feel like it, with my wet feet and dripping nose, but the rain brought puddles, and puddles meant water for Smokey for a day or two ahead. When the rain was at its heaviest, a large car stopped on the hard shoulder a hundred feet ahead. A plastic bag was passed through the open door and left on the grass verge. The car drove off.

A few minutes more and Smokey was plopping big feet through new puddles. I picked up the discarded bag. It held a paper plate with a meal, meant for me. I wish I had thanked them.

We spent the night on Highway 16, in a wet field. The sun conveniently began to shine as I set up the tent, but too late to dry the long grass or my soaking clothes. It had been an eventful day, I thought, as I drank hot tea and ate the donated meal. I can't remember what it was, but I remember it had all fallen into a corner of the bag when I hooked it over the saddle horn. It looked a mess, but it tasted fine! I'd had three meals that day, all given to me by generous Mississippi people. Pretty good going, I think!

Day 40 was spent on busy Highway 16. Long and straight and a little bit boring. The strong sun dried wet clothes, shoes and saddle from yesterday's rain and wet grass camping as we rode thorough the Chocktaw Indian Reservation without realizing it, then through the small village of Edinburg, heading towards Carthage. Smokey's shoes were wearing out fast on the gravely verges, especially the front two which, though only two weeks old, were now worn out at the toes. I would have to think about finding a farrier before too long.

After a completely uneventful day covering sixteen miles, I turned Smokey off the highway and down a small road heading south to a small town with a promising name: Sunshine. We'd had a long break at lunch time so already time was moving on. I called at several likely looking places for permission to camp but either no one was home, or the husband wasn't home, or the dogs would keep the neighbors up all night. I rode Smokey further.

At the end of the mile long side road were a collection of houses, all with large yards, which seemed promising. I found the owner of the largest and asked.

"Why for sure! Help ya self, anywhere ya want." His arm swept grandly over his several acres of unfenced land, a little of it growing early vegetables. We chatted for a while. He was late middle-aged, a bit small and a bit grubby, but seemed kind hearted. He lived alone with his dogs and a horse in the barn. After a little while, I thanked him for his hospitality and excused myself to erect the tent and see to Smokey.

I chose a spot hidden behind some trees, away from the house and out of view of the neighbors and the road. As I put up the tent, one of the alloy poles broke. It was only six weeks old but packing it away wet with dew each morning had caused the poles to oxidize and they were fragile and very brittle. I cursed. My Swiss army knife came to the rescue but it meant one rod was too short and the tent was never the same again.

As I was super-gluing the pieces together, my host sheepishly called me over. Being spoiled by now, I thought it meant a beer or a hot meal so dropped my tent repairs and trotted over. A police car was parked in front of the house. I couldn't believe the nerve as the arrogant, overweight, gun-toting police officer called me over with his chubby first finger. I slowed, trying to give my temper a moment to cool off.

"What's ya name, and what are ya doing here?" No hellos or polite introductions.

"My name is Emma Crosby, Ms, and I'm a visitor to your country from England." I pompously replied. The owner of the land was hopping from foot to foot in embarrassment, though it was he that had called the police' to check me out[1].

"Do ya have any drugs or arms?"

"Yes. I have some Benadryl for my allergy to horses and my six inch hunting knife you can see on my belt. I also have a Swiss army knife which has two blades, and a mace spray for my defense." I said all this in a very haughty English accent, throwing daggery glances at my oh so hospitable host.

"You are welcome to search me." I added.

The ugly mannered officer asked a few more standard type questions tapping his pencil on a standard type pad, before 'allowing me to go.' I wanted to say something really cutting but I was so mad I couldn't think of anything witty quickly enough. I gave a dangerous look to my host, turned and marched off.

If it hadn't been so late I would have packed up and left but it was now almost dark. I sat in the tent door watching Smokey grazing unawares, while I boiled with rage. If the owner hadn't wanted me to stay on his property then he shouldn't have agreed to it. To say yes, then call the police to 'check me out' made me furious.

I spent a sleepless night worried about Smokey's safety on that dodgy man's land, spending the long night hours thinking of things I should have said to the officer and to my rat of a host.

I left early in the morning without the usual exchange of addresses or saying good-bye.

I was still in a bad mood after last night as we rode into Carthage mid-morning. I was sick of Highway 16 with the constant heavy traffic and sun exposed hard shoulder and scowled at anyone that stared without waving. Riding through the outskirts of this typical American town, we were met by a local reporter so I had to change my attitude pretty quickly. One bit of bad luck shouldn't spoil everything. Within a few feet after telling our story, a garden center owner offered water for Smokey and after the hot morning she was glad of a drink. The thirty-something young man did a lot to lift my spirits with his bubbly good humor as he filled, then re-filled Smokey's folding blue bucket. When Smokey had finished slurping water all over the pavement, he took us over to the feed store where he secured us a decent discount on a bag of oats and some fly spray. My almost empty bottle contained spray that was advertised as lasting for thirty days each go, but I was using it twice a day to keep away the awful horse and deer flies, and it still didn't work too well. It was unthinkable to go anywhere in those southern states without a good coating of the stuff as a bite from either of the little horrors was shocking, so a new bottle felt like the equivalent of topping up the ammunition.

We got lost on the exit roads out of Carthage, trying to find the Thomastown exit, ending up on the four-lane Route 25 in the midday heat. My mood again turned sour. When we finally made it, I rode Smokey to the first empty property, staked her out to graze and fell asleep under a shady tree, my head popped up on the saddlebags. For once, the fire ants, with their evil sting, didn't find me and I managed to catch up on last night's lack of sleep, waking after three hours in a better mood.

The afternoon ride was lovely. A little twisting road with shady trees and not too much traffic. A few houses were dotted around in clearings in the woods, mostly small and many abandoned. It was a pretty picture with the shadows lengthening as the hours and the miles went pleasantly by.

"Hello! Hello! Stop, won't you!" An apparition in a pink track suit, with her arms waving, was hobbling with difficulty across the grass towards us. ' Oh God, what's this,' I thought. I pulled Smokey over and into the driveway of a one story brick house. A big white car was in the carport. I was at the house of Annie Waggoner, local eccentric.

"I couldn't let you just walk on by," she said, "I had to know what you're doing with that lovely little horse on our little road with all that stuff!" A sweeping pink arm seemed to include half of Mississippi. I tied Smokey to a tree, and followed the track suit inside.

Annie, with her crooked wig and slipping makeup, lived alone, a widow of many years. She could have been sixty or ninety, it was hard to tell, as her face was heavily made up so she looked quite young. But her chubby body was crippled with arthritis. She poured me a Coke with trembling hands, moving with difficulty from fridge to table, collapsing heavily in her armchair after handing me the tall glass. She adjusted her hair with knobby ringed fingers, pushed her makeup almost back into place and lit a cigarette. I sat opposite her in an identical chair and through a blue cloud of smoke we talked and talked.

Annie didn't want to let me go and on her invitation I didn't need to be persuaded to stay, so at some point I unsaddled Smokey and staked her on the front lawn to graze and set up the tent around the back.

She was a lovely woman. Full of energy though in agony when she moved, full of life though older than most. Carol Foster, her young, good looking, neighbor from across the road was called over, and between them, I was fed a wonderful meal, showered and had my laundry done. It was fun to be three old girls together. Everyone had a story to tell. The evening passed quickly into night with lots of laughs and a few old ladies' tears.

I moved Smokey to in front of the tent, where the security lights drowned most of the garden in continuous daylight. There was one dark patch between a tree and heavy green bushes, which Smokey reversed into when she'd finished grazing. She was a very private horse at night. I slept well under a clean horse blanket, a clean jacket for a pillow, in clean clothes.

Day 42 saw us over The Yockanookany River, almost half way across Mississippi. I never thought about bridges anymore, though there was rumored to be a horrendous two mile crossing of the river into Arkansas at Greenville. That was still over a hundred miles away, so I wasn't wasting time worrying about that yet. We were a few miles north of the Bienville National Forest where Pat and I had stayed with Smokey on the way eastwards. Two more 'driving days* and we'd be back in Texas.

There is a beautiful road in Mississippi, running from Natchez in the south western corner, out of the state in the north east. No commercial traffic is allowed along its three hundred mile length, and no trailers I think. It is a common route for holidays by bicycle. Unfortunately, horses weren't allowed either because of the 'damage' they'd do to the well kept grass verges lining the road, but plans were being considered for a bridle way alongside. Not nearly soon enough for Smokey and me on that mid-May morning, so we crossed The Natchez Trace Parkway, a jealous glance in each direction and on to Thomastown.

I went into the small village store for a couple of cans to top up supplies, leaving Smokey tied to the wooden porch. As I stood at the till counting out change for Beanie-Weanies and chocolate, I saw a white horse walk past, heavily loaded with blue saddlebags. It was Smokey heading east. I caught her at the cross-roads and hauled her back, red-faced, to the shop with its still banging door.

My mail wasn't reaching me. Only one letter at Goodman, from Pat. After racing all morning through scorching heat to reach the Post Office before closing time, expecting a big untidy collection of letters and parcels and for just the one to be passed across the Formica was a gut wrenching disappointment.

I sat under a magnolia tree next to the train tracks, and sulked. A train went by, blowing its eerie call twenty feet from where Smokey grazed. She wasn't bothered.

It was hard to stay in a bad mood after the lovely late afternoon ride along easy Route 14. We were stopped an awful lot by well wishers with one resulting in an address for the night's stop. A young black couple had agreed to us camping on their pretty green acres close to the next Interstate crossing.

Sitting in the door to the tent with a can of sweet corn for my day's meal, I watched Smokey galloping flat out around the fields heading towards a small herd of cattle kept in a far paddock. She had this 'thing' about cows. It was hard to believe she'd just done a twenty mile day.

We crossed the Interstate at the overpass on Route 14 very early in the morning. There was no traffic on our quiet farm road and not too much on the six lanes fifty feet beneath us. We dropped away from the Interstate through an area of small state parks and wildlife refuges, hobby farms and wooded country, the road taking us slightly north west, heading to the Mississippi River.

The day, May 20th, our forty-fourth on the road, passed in tranquil monotony. Everywhere was pretty, everyone was friendly, everything was easy. Perfect ponytreking day. I talked to Smokey, (not much response) sang and read a little, the lines on the page jumping all over the place as I rode or walked along. Mostly I just scrutinized the ground a few feet ahead, looking for the inevitable beer bottles or if I was lucky, the sight of a snake.

As the evening drew closer and with fifteen miles behind us, I was stopped by another of the friendly locals. With all the attention from the people in this state, our daily distance average had dropped from around eighteen to twenty miles at the start of the ride, to little more than twelve or fourteen. I was enjoying things so much more, though. With the decision to take the route south to California, rather than the longer route north to Oregon, there was no big rush to move on. I could even take a few weeks off in Texas and still make it across the Rockies before winter. So by the time we began to attract all this attention in Mississippi, I was very relaxed, very comfortable with what I was doing, very happy with my little white partner, very glad to meet people, and very, very thin from all the exercise!

As I was answering the questions of the first car load of curious visitors, another pulled up, driver and passenger jumping out to include themselves in the conversation. With two cars parked on that quiet back country road, something was definitely happening, and the third and then the fourth car stopped. Now we had a Mississippi country road traffic jam! They began to argue with whom I would stay that night. "I have a spare room!" "I have a T.V. in my spare room!" "Well, I have a lovely big field for the horse!" "Hey, you guys, I have a huge big field, loads of horse feed and a spare room!"

"Now, come on there fellas, I stopped her first!" I laughed. We all laughed. It was agreed that Smokey and I stay with the original friendly bunch, Martha Jo and Robert DeKard, and everyone else come by for coffee later. It was very flattering to be fought over like that, especially at nearly thirty-three years old and make-up free!

Smokey was in season again. Every three weeks this came around and the change in her character was so marked, her new antics would make an east-end girl-about-town blush. She was disgraceful. Robert and Martha Jo had three horses in a lovely big field. Smokey selected the gelding and went to work. She tried it all and her big quarter horse partner loved every minute.

I drank so much coffee that night sitting in the porch swing with a multitude of visitors, that it was amazing I slept at all. It had been a lovely evening, meeting so many people, swapping so many stories, that after a fun ride in a car (they go so fast!) to get hamburgers from the nearest town, all that talking, a shower, a hairwash and a couple of late night laundry loads, it felt like the middle of the night. It didn't take long for me to drift off to sleep, clean sheets around a clean body, to the sound of Smokey still chasing Robert's tired out quarter horse in the field alongside the house. On the invitation of my kind hosts, we were taking the following day off to go with them to a horse show, so I went to sleep with the luxury of knowing there would be no five-thirty start in the morning. Tomorrow I could have a lie in. Yippee!

Martha Jo cooked a huge breakfast the next morning, Robert coming in after feeding the horses. They were a lovely couple with a young attitude. Lively, funny, enjoying life. Martha Jo was in her upper forties but made me feel like a scruffy old frump with her elegant clothes and fresh face. Her husband was one of those rare men which made me yearn for one like that back home. He was always laughing, always attentive, busy working on his projects around the well kept yard and house.

I left their energy behind to catch up on some letter writing down by a catchment pond at the bottom of the horse paddock. Smokey eyed me warily from the safe distance, her three new friends dozing in the shade, tails constantly flicking at the flies. The water looked cool, but dark, the surface broken irregularly by unseen creatures. Turtles dropped heavily under the surface to safety from broken branches from fallen trees around the edge as I walked past looking for a shady spot.

I wrote until lunch time then helped Robert load the horses into the trailer.

Smokey was staying at home.

The horse show, or 'Fun Day[1] as it was called, was a small country town affair, with an atmosphere of everyone being out for a day's good time. Scruffy horses mixed with well-bred and polished animals, adults and children competing for the same prizes: a bag of horse feed, a salt lick, a soda. When we arrived the games had only just begun. There was a competitive air but the biggest applause was saved for those who raised the biggest laugh, usually at a dramatic tumble. In between answering questions from interested riders and non-riders introduced by my hosts, I watched the horse show games.

The riders were broken up into age groups, the youngest going first. Tiny little children would charge into the arena on big patient horses that mainly knew the routine: to race around barrels or bend through poles, then tear as fast as possible out of the arena for a called time, urgently waited for. Some of these youngsters were too small to reach the stirrups, their main grip coming from one soft childish hand tightly gripped round the saddle horn, but they still raced to win. The less able were led by parents, or parents came to the rescue if the horse began to think too independently. No one was frightened of making a fool of themselves, which was just as well as many of the games were designed to do just that!

Robert entered almost all the events riding both his old horses, despite little chance of success against his competitors. Martha Jo picked the sack pull race. A long rope trailed from the horn of the saddle, the loose end tied securely around the neck of a sack. With one competitor on the horse and the other lying anxiously on the burlap, two white-knuckled hands grasping the taut rope, the timer buzzer sounded, and the horse ran. The rider urged the animal as fast as possible towards the barrel at the opposite end of the arena, the passenger semi-airborn on the sack behind. The horse took the turn, spinning the sack and its wide-eyed load water-skier fashion around the barrel. Then the horse dug in his heels to pick up speed for the home stretch, mud and sand flying from the scrambling hooves into the face of the battered sack rider dragged behind. The time wasn't recorded until the horse broke the laser beam at the starting gate what must have seemed like a thousand miles away. It was one of the funniest events, with all the participants being thought of as good sports.

The news over the loudspeaker that called Martha Jo for her turn on the sack was greeted with loud applause from the friendly crowd. She changed her dressy western shirt for a man's white tee-shirt, then settled gracefully on the sack, taking a grip on the rope. Ex-competitors offered urgent advice and horror stories as she wriggled about trying to get comfortable. She was being towed by a young man riding an ugly white mule. Martha Jo did really well.

She held on the whole way: out of the gate, along the bumpy stretch to the barrel, around the barrel bouncing those shapely hips in an arc of dust and flying hooves, down the home stretch, and straight through the muddy patch! Her lovely hair and pretty face were a patchwork of brown blotches and blonde hair, muddy cheeks and blue eye shadow. Everyone was ecstatic, and Martha Jo laughed with them. 'What a sport!' they all called.

Along with Robert, a tall skinny, athletic man, Bradley, competed in almost all the events. He had been doing these Fun Days for a long time and had a reputation to keep up, so always took his amplified times very seriously. He won many prizes, usually the bag of horse feed first prize, mainly from his skill on a horse, but sometimes from raw determination. I remember him being most entertaining at the barrel hopping. This event had the barrel in the same position as in the sack pull race but the second competitor started on top of the barrel. As the buzzer sounded, the horse raced into the arena, the rider using all his skill for maximum speed. Almost without braking, the horse took the turn around the barrel, hopefully picking up the second rider and then hell-for-leather down the home stretch and out. Even with plenty of practice things didn't always work out as planned. Sometimes the horse wouldn't run around the barrel close enough, shying away from the expectant person on top of the barrel, or it might be going down the straight too fast and unable to take the turn. Sometimes the second rider would jump too early for the back of the saddle, miss the horse completely and end up face down in the dirt, the horse heading for home. Many times the crowd would shout 'Jump!', and under pressure the person on top the barrel would make a desperate attempt to leap aboard. If he could hold on until out of the arena, they had a time, so many finger nails were broken by digging into leather to last those fifty or sixty yards of the home stretch.

Bradley competed at this event a couple of times and it should have been his speciality, he was so agile. He reminded me of a lanky American Peter Pan. From an impossible distance he would launch himself from the barrel towards the ever patient horse his second was riding like crazy round the turn. On his first attempt, he made it to the back of the horse, but in the effort to stay on, dragged heavily at his pilot and the saddle slipped. They both ended up in the mud patch. For Bradley's second attempt, he poised himself on the metal barrel rim, and watched eagle eyed as the horse leapt forward at the buzzer and down the straight.

"Jump!" went the crowd (much too early of course), and Bradley spread wings and flew. He made it to the thundering horse but in his enthusiasm, pulled both his partner and the horse into the win-robbing mud. They were plastered for the second time that day. The crowd went mad. Cheering, whistling, laughing.

I was the worst, knowing I wasn't competing, and laughed until the tears ran down my face, my cheeks painful from such a hilarious day. Everyone was having a go and a 'Fun Day' was exactly what it was.

Between events, Robert and friends and I, would sneak back to his truck for a crafty beer, so by the late afternoon, I was flushed both with the pleasure from sharing in the horses and the people, and the effects of a few cans of ice cold 'Bud'.

My turn to be the laughing stock came later in the day after a trip to the hot-dog stand. For a few cents, I bought a juicy, tomato ketchup soaked sausage in a bun, drooling with fried onions, and a cold Coke. Leaning against the arena rails, my face full of food, I became aware of an announcement over the loud speaker.

" .... we sure are proud today to welcome as a guest of honour

to our little Fun Day, a little old girl who's come all the way from England, Europe, and who's riding a little white horse all the way across the United States. Let's give a big Mississippi welcome to Emma Crosby!".

I nearly choked on the hot dog.

The fun went on until ten thirty. A tired drive back with low headed horses and hot chicken wings from the takeout. A blissful sleep in a real bed, able to turn over without pulling off the covers.

The following day, I laughed all over again at the events at the Fun Day, though my cheeks felt bruised from the goofy smile I'd had on my face even as I'd fallen asleep.

Martha Jo had cooked a big breakfast, and relatives, well wishers and new friends had all wanted a few minutes to say goodbye, addresses hastily scribbled on scraps of paper with promises from me to write from the west coast. Almost everyone asked me to stay, not that I'm a particularly amazing person, but they were a particularly friendly people. I could have spent a month hopping from house to house along that little hilly country lane and when I reached the Mississippi river, been quite happy to turn around and head back for a second run!

Finally I was in the saddle, riding away, waving, missing them already. The day was beautiful: warm, little fluffy clouds. It wasn't long before I was singing away, my limited repertoire of songs learned during the radio days. I missed that little ten dollar radio almost as much as my sleeping bag. Without it, I found I was singing about three lines from each song, which would end up repeating and repeating in my brain like a broken record. It would become so lodged there, I'd be unable to shake it, and end up getting fed up at the whole thing.

People stopped me all morning. Joey Upton, with his daughter Kayla, had driven a long way to find me, pretty, twelve year old Kayla nervously passing over an address. Snow, a relative of Martha Jo's tried to chat me up, and big Albert, a neighbour and new friend bought out cold drinks and sandwiches which we ate sitting on the tailgate of his pick-up truck. He wanted me to stop at his house a mile or so further along, for a day or a month, but after yesterday's rest day, I thought we'd better move on.

A few miles into that ride, we came upon the abrupt end to the hills that had housed us for so long. We were standing on the edge of an escarpment, a startling view of the Mississippi Delta stretched away in the distance, four hundred feet below us. The river itself was still over seventy miles away, but over its long history a hundred mile-wide bed of fertile land had been laid, one of the most productive stretches of farm land in the United States. Cotton, rice, wheat, beans and big square ponds full of catfish took advantage of the thousand foot depth of soil.

We dropped down the climb into a very different country. We'd been so long in the hills that to be able to see such long distances along the flat flat road, was a bit shocking. It made progress seem slow in a land that reminded me painfully of the Canadian Prairies. We crossed many bridges that day, over swampy dark water, much more exposed to the hot sun than we were used to. The humidity was very high from the amount of water around, and the mosquitoes were big and hungry.

We camped the night at a cotton gin, a huge processing plant for the locally grown cotton, only open for six weeks out of the year for the harvest. The gentle mannered owner fed me home-made hamburgers cooked on the barbecue outside. She might have been missing the company of Robert's horses, or made uncomfortable by the exposed piece of land we found ourselves on. I became so fed up though, that I shortened the rope to three feet, tying it high up on a telegraph pole. She had to be still then. Finally she seemed to become calm, but it wasn't a good night for either of us.

Day 47 was long and straight and hot. We rode along Highway 12 between fields of ready to harvest wheat, young cotton, and the first fresh green of young rice. Water was everywhere. Many of the rice fields were flooded, fed by immigration channels dissecting the land. Catfish farms with their huge square ponds, a heavy fountain of water jetting out at one end providing oxygen for its ugly crop. Everywhere was farmed. There was almost no land left to sit idle apart from the weed-ridden sections around a beaten up 'or Sale' sign.

Smokey led flawlessly over the big arc of a bridge across the Yazoo River, just outside of Belzoni. I gave a radio interview to a reporter waiting on its west bank, chuckling with embarrassment at the playback of my ridiculous sounding voice. We were in Humphreys County, only Washington County to go and we'd be out of Mississippi.

Belzoni was a big town. We turned right, avoiding the major built up area, onto Highway 49E. It was that wide road that every big American town has: McDonalds, drive through restaurants, gas stations, and department stores. Noisy, busy and interesting. The clover was so sweet and green on the grassy shoulder in front of one gas station that I was unable to ask Smokey to pass it by. We stopped for an hour so she could graze.

There was only a mile of this major highway before a wiggle to the left and we were back on Route 12, a much smaller road. We had just passed our seven hundredth mile and felt fine.

There weren't many places to stop with a horse in the Delta. The land was so fertile and expensive, it wasn't wasted on pasture for cattle or horses. At the first opportunity, I asked. It was a small farm yard with a huge collection of rusted and antiquated looking machinery around wooden buildings, squashed between flat fields of golden wheat. The son and father owners were very kind, clearing a small fenced area of their horses so Smokey would be able to stretch her legs.

Laruth Ashley, a relative of Martha Jo and Robert, stopped by with her family just as the sun was dropping below the horizon to the west. She'd made me a foil-covered plate of catfish dinner, complete with chocolate pudding, which I ate hungrily. The tender white meat of the catfish was delicious. Her son, Rob, who was with her, was obviously aching to do such a trip as mine. He was only thirteen or fourteen, but in a rather pompous way began to offer advice on how I should be doing things, criticising my choice of footwear and bits of equipment. I found that rather entertaining, with seven hundred miles and nearly three states behind us, to be told by such an inexperienced young man how to do things. I knew it was well meant, it always was, but over the next eight months I became 77 - My Kingdom is a Horse a little tired of advice on 'how to do it' coming from a multitude of different people. Even riding down the western slopes of the Vallecito Mountains in California, the Pacific Ocean only a few miles away, people were still generous with their opinions on the equipment I needed, on the route I should take, or, worst of all, on the horse I should be using. It was a good visit, though. Laruth and her family were very easy to talk to, and we spent at least an hour laughing and telling stories. Smokey was still a little unsettled, walking twice as fast from one end of the small paddock to the other than I could get her to do during the day. The area was well fenced though, so I didn't worry about her too much.

The landowner's son called by shortly after the Ashley family had left, so it was a late night for me, crawling under the horse blanket past eleven o'clock.

May 24th saw us saddling up early with the idea of clocking up a few miles on those exposed roads before it became too hot.

The road was unerringly straight, progress seemingly slow, past huge fields, a faultless blue sky, too big.

After our little interview on the radio the night before, we were again attracting a lot of attention. Almost everyone waved from the comfort of their air-conditioned cars. I waved back, envious of their comfort. When one of them stopped to talk, I would dismount and hang my head through the lowered window, the cold air wafting out the car like a dream over my sweaty face. If they were holding a cold drink, I would find it very hard to keep my eyes focused on their faces, my gaze inevitably dropping to the clinking ice cubes knocking against each other in a sea of fizzy cold soda.

Early in the afternoon, a middle-aged couple brought out a huge plastic cup of iced tea, which was wonderful though the cubes had melted before I saw the bottom. They warned me about a difficult narrow bridge ahead and offered their help to see us across. We'd 'done' bridges. They were no longer a problem. Been there, seen that, got the tee-shirt type of thing, but I accepted their offer of assistance. I knew Smokey would be fine but they were so eager to become just a little bit involved in aiding us westwards that I was glad to accept.

The couple, Louie and Sylvia Duke, with a friend, met me an hour or so later at the approach to the Sunflower River Bridge. It wasn't a difficult one: flat, only a hundred feet or so long but it was narrow. The sides were old iron, though the surface was cement. Louie and his wife went ahead, hazard lights flashing, while the friend drove cautiously behind. It was actually more dangerous with the two cars causing a bit of a jam than it would have been with just Smokey. It was kind of them to go to so much trouble though, and I was very grateful and flattered by their concern.

We pulled over on the other side of the bridge to eat a lunch packed by Sylvia, with more of the refreshing iced tea from the cooler. Sylvia and Louie had been married many years and had travelled over much of the world in their younger days. They were still very attentive to each other, referring often to the other for bits of forgotten stories. Louie was very jolly. He loved life, and the air around him became lighter, his energy infectious. After lunch, they left me loaded with cakes and biscuits to return to jobs left unfinished.

I had unsaddled Smokey. Tying her to a tree on a scrap of land alongside the main highway. The grass was long and the tree provided shade. To one side of a dirt track leading from the road southward, four or five metal grain bins towered against the midday sun. I settled down for a sleep in the shade of the tree, my head resting on the saddlebags. Within a few minutes, Sylvia was back. I had moaned a little about losing the radio and she had returned to bring me a little Sony Walkman she'd had for a while but never used. I was delighted! It was ten times better than the scratchy old thing I'd had before. I offered her money for this new treasure, but she refused. She was a very kind lady. That radio increased the quality of my life immeasurably for the hundred and fifty days I still had to ride. In the soaring temperatures of West Texas, New Mexico and Arizona, when the view seemed eternal, water and food an age away, I would slip on the headphones and stride along in time to the country and western rhythm! It was a luxury that soon became a necessity.

I had been planning on another seven or eight miles in the afternoon to add to the ten we'd already covered that morning, but as I sat under the tree singing along to Alan Jackson and his song about the Chattahoochee River (which we'd crossed in Georgia!) the sun was blocked by the owner of the grain bins walking towards me. In a very gentle voice, he invited us to stay.

A few minutes later, Smokey was giving pony rides to three very excited girls, while I drank Coke and talked farming, horses and England to their hospitable parents, Sarah and Will Beebe-Jones.

I had a bit of a lie-in in the morning, wakened finally by the heat from the early sun building up inside the tent, and Smokey's big nose poking through the screen door, an impatient nicker warning me it was breakfast time. She often woke me like this, her big white nose a rounded dent in the fine mesh. Her patience was limited, only using this technique briefly. If it didn't work immediately she began walking up the tent sides. A vision of eight hundred pounds of horse on my head in the early morning always sent me flying out the tent door toward her folding blue bucket lying empty in the grass. She knew how to get her way!

Sarah had been on the telephone to the local television news people last night, with the result that around nine-thirty they'd be here to tape an interview for that night's news. I saddled Smokey as she ate, taking extra care to see she was all brushed. Once, my grooming kit had consisted of two brushes, sponge, shampoo, hoof oil, leather polish, hoof pick, plastic curry comb... only one brush and a hoof pick remained. She looked the part though.

The lady interviewer spent two hours recording the story. Filming Smokey and me riding in, then out, of the Jones's property, talking about the trip, talking to Sarah and Will about what they thought of it all, a few minutes of the children having a go in the saddle, then the glamorous woman climbed up on Smokey and I became cameraman! Everyone seemed to enjoy the T.V. attention.

The local newspaper then phoned to say they'd be there around two thirty, using up the afternoon. William and Sarah invited us to stay another night. I unloaded.

With Smokey staked out on the long grass beside the house, the children's paddling pool for a water bucket, I toured the rice fields with William and his eldest daughter, ten year old Jane.

The rice was still very young, some only just breaking through the rich soil, covering the brown earth in a hazy green mist. Though the land looked perfectly flat, each field was broken by hard mud levees running along lines of equal ground height. A few inches drop or rise in the height of the land, detected by laser, meant the building of another line of the foot or so high banks. This was to control the flow of water from the channel running alongside the property. A plastic sheet was removed at the highest corner of the field, allowing the water to run in, flooding the area contained by the highest levee. When it was full, William would release the plastic gate to the land contained within the next levee and the water would rush down to the thirsty plants a few inches below. It seemed a pretty skilled job, though it looked so simple. It would be easy to over water, or parch the tender rice. Good 'watermen' were paid well.

All over the Delta, farmers were flooding their land to feed the new crop. Much American rice comes from the Delta.

Jane and I watched as William sloshed through the three or four inches of water to check the rice, dam a gate, or repair a bank. The gurgling of the running water hypnotic in the heat.

Besides the rice, William produced wheat. After an inspection of the hard yellow grains in the morning, T.J., the farm hand, received the thumbs up to start harvesting the four hundred acre field using a hundred and fifty thousand dollars worth of combine harvester. We drove over to watch.

In a small, glass sided, air conditioned cab, T.J. controlled the monster-sized green combine, slicing fifty foot widths of golden wheat up and down the heat hazed field. Wheat drummed into a holding tank behind the driver's head. More buttons and it was emptied into the trailer parked on the track alongside.

"You have a go," suggested William, signaling to T.J. to pick up a passenger.

"Ooo....crumbs!" I thought. I'm not all that good at mechanical things.

I climbed up the monster's side, past wheels taller than myself, taking the passenger's seat alongside T.J. in the cool cab. It seemed an awfully long way up but what a thrill to be witnessing the year's American wheat harvest coming in. One of the few bits of mindless information I can remember from geography class at school, was that it takes one American combine, cutting one hour, to provide enough flour for bread, for a family of four for forty years. (Despite knowing an important fact like that, I still failed geography!) I was at school nearly a million years ago so I can't imagine how things have improved.

I chatted away to T.J. about anything to do with farming, him chuckling at my excited nattering. All the while, the wheat falling away beneath the cutting blades. The tank filled quickly, blocking out the sun behind. We returned to the trailer and emptied. I made no effort to jump out, so William signaled for another turn up and down the field. I think T.J. sighed.

Finally, I climbed down, my face a beaming smile. The wiggly bit down the field ~ my combine driving contribution to America's bread.

We all went out for a catfish dinner that night. Will, Sarah and the three girls. The flavor of that fish is so mild, and the meat so tender, I can't imagine anyone not liking it. We detoured to the grandparents after the meal to pick up Sarah's twin baby boys and watch the news piece filmed that morning. It was pretty embarrassing. I turned very red, but I didn't seem to have said anything foolish. It didn't look or sound like me though.

We drove back through the dark, children tired after all the excitement of TV, newspaper stories and pony rides.

I said goodnight as William and Sarah each carried a child into the house. William turned on the security lights to illuminate my way back to the piece of still packed equipment. I hadn't very far before I realized Smokey was gone.

I quickly scanned the area with my small flashlight, sure I'd see her hollow animal eyes illuminated in the narrow torch beam, grass, forgotten, hanging out the corner of her mouth. Calmly, I turned and jogged back to the house.

"She's gone. Smokey's gone, she's gone walkabout." I whispered over sleepy girl's heads. We took a more powerful flashlight and started to look. So began the worst twelve hours of my life.

I felt I knew Smokey so well that I was sure she'd either be close by or trotting back to where she believed Texas might be. We spent until the early hours of the morning looking. Up and down. Up and down the quiet dirt roads and country lanes, back to Belzoni across the bridge we'd been escorted over the day before, back to last night's camp spot, her hoof marks still fresh in the farmyard mud; eastwards, westwards, tracing and retracing any possible route, the powerful beam of Will's flashlight scanning over the fields from the slowly moving car. Only the owls and the bats broke the beam of the light.

I was very quiet. Sick to the stomach, worried that she might be lying hurt in a ditch somewhere - a broken leg from a swerving car, bleeding from cuts from a tangled wire fence. It was the only time I regretted not carrying a gun.

"Let's go home".

I set up the tent, hoping she'd return to the half full feed bowl lying on the lawn. The main tent pole broke for the second time but I was too low to think about fixing it. I wrapped the sagging green nylon around the packs and me, and waited for morning.

I was up again as the first light broke through the heavy racing black clouds. At five-thirty, William lent me the spare car, he went one way, I , the other. Sarah was on the phone. She rang everyone that might be able to help: the TV, the radio, the newspapers, the police. The story of the lost white horse was shown on the seven o'clock news. On the radio the programs were interrupted with an appeal for everyone to keep an open eye. The only sunshine on that cold black morning was how tirelessly my hosts tried to find my little white mare.

By nine o'clock, I was giving up hope. There was no sign of her anywhere. No horse tracks, no manure, no sightings, no luck. I sat on the corner of the sofa in Sarah's beautiful house, holding back the tears as I asked her to phone the slaughter houses. She may have been seen on television by the wrong person. I thought she may be stolen.

I wondered away from the house to let the inevitable tears fall. She was gone. My little white stubborn headed friend was gone. She was gone. I had given up hope.

A horn blasting. Lots of shouting. My name called excitedly from the house.

"Emma! Emma! She's found! Smokey's been found!"

Thank God, I thought.

"Is she alright?" Wiping away tears.

"She's fine, she's fine. She pulled out her stake, she's half a mile away, T.J. found her. They're waiting for you." A policeman, young and sympathetic, drove me to where Smokey had strayed. She was in a cotton field on the other side of the main highway, calmly biting the tops off the young plants, sixty foot of rope trailing behind her.

The police car pulled up behind the four or five other vehicles parked alongside the field. Everyone was waiting for me, not wanting to risk scaring Smokey by trying to catch her.

I began to walk towards her across the field. For the first time in out life together, she came to me when I called her name. I picked up the sodden rope, the curly peg still attached and buried my face in her muddy neck, new tears falling down her wiry mane.

"Smokey...Bloody hell, Smokey."

I couldn't look at the faces of the people around me and my pony but I know there wasn't a dry eye among them. The police officer handed me the bridle and I slipped the bit between half chewed cotton tops and worn horse teeth. I nodded my thanks to T.J. and squeezed Sarah's hand.

I rode Smokey bareback to the house, the warmth, the smell, the sound of her, sweeter, for having been lost, and missed, then found.

Everyone had asked for rides, including Ruby, Sarah's help in the house. Photos were taken, lunch was packed, Smokey loaded. Words of thanks, that meant more, shakily said to Sarah and Will Beebe-Jones. A needed hug and a hurried kiss, and we rode away.

It was our fiftieth day on the road, May 26th, 1994. The sun came out on Highway 12. All along the route that day, people came out of their houses to express relief at seeing Smokey safely found. Drivers waved out the windows of passing cars, blasting salutes on the horns. Watermen and farm labourers looked up from their wet and muddy work to shout encouragement. We were stopped so many times, by so many different people, I skipped our usual break over the midday hours, worried about not making it to our planned nights camp at Leroy Percy State Park, seventeen miles away.

Smokey made good time. With the sun low we entered one of the few wooded areas of the Delta, a pretty state park alongside a tributary of the magical Mississippi River. The green sites of the campground were almost empty despite the holiday weekend coming up. Horses are generally not allowed in state parks but Sarah had obtained us special exemption from this rule.

The rangers couldn't have been more helpful. Dennis, the head ranger, lead us to a pretty green and shady spot along the banks of the slow moving river. The grass had been left uncut, waiting for Smokey's arrival. Water was bought over in a huge barrel on the back of the rangers pick-up truck. Photos were taken for the office wall and visitors center. Smokey unloaded, tied firmly by the dry, mud-stained rope to a well rooted tree. A young, good-looking, dark-eyed ranger took me on a tour of the park in the truck, giving me my first sighting of an American southern states Alligator, the browny grey yellow-eyed creature watching us from the shadows cast by a small footbridge.

I ate hamburgers and salad with members of an RV camping club, but I was still pretty quiet. It had been a damaging day, and I felt bruised and vulnerable. Smokey was back to being just a horse with the responsibility for me to see her safe. The trust had gone and it would be a long time coming back.

I spent the night in the hastily repaired tent, jumping up every hour or so to check Smokey was still there. The moon shone through the canopy of leaves, reflecting off Smokey's white back in patchy pattern. Now and again she'd snort at the noisy, night time river wildlife. It was the alligators fighting over the night's catch.

We left early the following morning at the time when birds sing loudest, colors are clearest. Almost immediately we were out of the state park woods and back into flat farming country, cotton and rice, heading directly west. Arkansas was only eight or nine miles away, on the western banks of the Mississippi River but we needed to detour a further fifteen miles to the north to meet the bridge at Greenville. I put the Walkman on and sang away to country songs, the lovely music and beautiful morning beginning to lift still low spirits after yesterdays near disaster.

Six miles of flat farming land. Low, one story, spreading brick farm houses framed with wind break trees, far apart, to each side of the arrow straight road. In the distance, I could see the hazy green line of more trees growing along the banks of the Mississippi River.

By ten o'clock the tarmac was melting in ninety degree temperatures, the watery shimmer off the surface, hot winds burning my face and cracking my lips. My sunglasses had broken, a victim of being continually caught on the saddle horn as I mounted, and made a sandwich of with good-bye hugs from hosts. To put them away was unthinkable. A quick repair job with loo roll, adhesive tape and chewing gum. It worked well, the tape gripping my sweaty nose but it took a while to get used to the white blob between my eyes.

I was stopped by Mrs. Jo Williams standing beside the road with the offer of a coffee and a bucket of water for Smokey. Within a few minutes she had persuaded me to quit for the day and spend the night with her and her husband on their four thousand acre farm.

"There's no riding a horse over that bridge," she told me. "Best let me trailer you over in the morning." She had horses of her own and she knew the bridge. I was glad of her offer.

"No, No trouble at all! You go back to the house and put your feet up. You need to rest!"

We took a little dirt road short cut to the barn at the back of the house. Horses, bays and chestnuts, came cantering over to meet the white pony coming through the gates. Jo had driven around by the longer route, pulling up just as I dismounted. I unsaddled Smokey, and we watched her trotting away through the long grass, her ears laid back if a nosy host horse came too close. She was fine. She had become very independent of the need to be in a herd. The others stood in a whispering group, watching her, while Smokey, as was her norm, put her big white head down to graze.

We had a party that night. Kelly Smith and his family joined Jo, her husband, Leo, and me, for a barbecued catfish dinner. Kelly, a small, round bubbly man from Arkansas, though he had never met me before, had gone to the trouble of buying a whole bag of things he thought I might need: waterproof matches, foil blankets, insect repellent... I was amazed and flattered and humbled. Jo had bought me a throw away camera to replace the one I'd lost in Alabama. It would have, or should have, felt like my birthday. Why are people so kind to someone they don't know? The pleasure of giving? The pleasure of becoming involved in something they feel is special? Because they can make a difference? People amazed me, especially those in Mississippi. So dammed nice!

The evening went really well. My bruised mood faded under the influence of these lovely people. They all seemed to think I was amazing which helps to pick you up when you're feeling a bit low! Kelly's almost grown up children sat next to me, fuelling up on the stories I had to tell, staring open-mouthed at the pictures I painted of early days in Georgia and tension filled Alabama. Jo leaned against the stove, her eyes sparkling with possessive pleasure in her unusual guest. I felt appreciated and admired, and I felt better for it. The food was wonderful, my clothes were washed, my hair clean. I didn't have to worry about the bridge, the people were great. It had been a good day. The night would be spent between clean sheets in a real bed. Yes. Someone up there was looking after me.

Day 52. Smokey had been bitten. Several wounds along her back, though superficial, looked sore enough to cancel any attempt at loading her up. She must have been cornered by the five horses in the field and rather beaten. There were probably a few sore teeth from her defensive flying hooves but I'm afraid she had been outnumbered and was looking a bit poorly, four or five hairless patches and a couple of weeping wounds just where the saddle would sit. Jo and I decided to give her the day off, Jo's horses being confined in the barn.

What a luxury! A whole day of lazing about. I packed away the Mississippi pages, studied Arkansas and Louisiana. I watched the big screen television and read *Western Horseman* magazine. I wrote letters, and dozed outside. I did nothing. Just what I needed.

We loaded Smokey in the back of Jo's son's horse trailer on the morning of Day 53. It was the 29th May. We had covered seven hundred and thirty five miles and three states. Today we would leave Mississippi, and the people that had shown me how it could be, behind: Christine, our first nights stop; Joyce Aust and Ralph the police officer, in DeKalb; Martha Jo and Robert and all those people at the horse show; Louie and Sylvia Juke, their Walkman now a fixture around my neck; Jo and Leo, Kelly with his family; my heroes, William and Sarah Beebe-Jones; T.J. I probably wouldn't see any of these people again, but I will never, ever, ever forget them and what they did for me and my little white horse. They made the heat and the cold, the wet and the sweat, the days and the miles all worthwhile. They made Mississippi. I will always think of that state as the real start of my ride.

Within an hour I was sticking my head out of the truck window, my hair whipping my face in the wind. I could see the sparkling, unstoppable river ahead! My heart beat faster at the approach to one of the most famous waterways in the world; The Mississippi! Smokey was behind, her big black eyes staring out first one side then the other of the speeding trailer. I threw her a thumbs up. We're here, Smokey! We're here!

The bridge rose, turned, then turned again for two miles over the water. Two narrow lanes of heavy traffic, no hard shoulder. Jo had been right, no place for a horse. We parked on the far bank, took photos, Smokey framed against the metal structure dominating the skyline. Me, glad to be here, but sad to leave. I loaded her. Said good-bye to new friends and old ones all across the state.

Welcome to Arkansas the sign said, 'Land of Opportunity.'

Chapter 5

Arkansas
A small sampling of the President's home turf leaves a Grade A impression

We were still in the Delta but no longer in Mississippi. For a brief three or four days, Arkansas would be our home. The Land of Opportunity. It really didn't get a fair chance to make a big impression. I passed through only forty five miles in the south-eastern corner of this state, supposed to be one of the most beautiful, the Ozark mountains dominating it. The state is famous for ex-governor and later President Bill Clinton, an Oxford alum don'tja know.

People were supposed to be a bit unfriendly, I was told, but each state liked to bitch about its neighbors so I took little notice of that. It was also rumored that to pronounce Arkansas wrong (say it Ark-can-saw) amounts to treason and could bring down all sort of trouble. Very patriotic. I'd chosen a little south-east wriggle of the road on the map and out.

I was walking. Smokey's back was still sore from Jo's unfriendly horses so it was going to be a few days wearing out the Reeboks again. I didn't mind, whatever it takes to keep us both happy. The wind was strong, sending my silly little blue cotton hat all over the place, the strings around my neck almost strangling me. I packed it away in the saddlebags and the wind and sun burnt my face to a uniform red with only two white spots from the protective sunglasses.

I led Smokey between flat acres of cotton, rice and wheat, battling the gusty wind coming from the north and the airstreams from the big trucks. We went directly west, away from the river, along busy four-lane 82, south along more of the same on Highway 65, before a turn to the right and peace on the quiet farm road heading to Chicot. It was exciting to be in Arkansas, but memories of Mississippi kept me looking back. We'd be here such a short time and only saw such a small part of the state but I still counted it as one of the nine to the west coast. Country and Western music coming out of Little Rock. Post to collect at Wilmot. On to Louisiana by the end of the month and nearly 800 miles done.

There had been a late start with time taken up by the trailer ride across the big bridge so I began to look around after only a ten mile day. An old man straightened up from weeding a bit of garden in front of a small, white, one story house with barns, cattle, fields and chickens to the back. I asked about the pasture and he kindly agreed. Smokey was unloaded, rolled in the grass, glad to be rid of the cumbersome packs, then left to graze. I was invited inside, sat at the kitchen table and watched the jolly round wife cook, drinking one glass after another of cold soda.

Yvonne and James Jones. A retired couple with a little hobby farm, treated me like a long absent daughter. The glass table was laid with good food on good china, including corn bread and aubergines, a long time favorite. (I can remember pondering the riddle of why Americans called aubergines "egg plant". Eggs aren't plants. They aren't purple, either.) We had puddings, too. Now there's a good English word.

The relatives were called up.

"Hey! You'll never guess who's eating here with us." A little wait.

" If's that little English gal riding 'cross country on that white horse."

We'd been seen on the T.V. news. Everyone came around, three generations of the Jones' family, the younger ones sitting on the arms of the full chairs. Nobody could believe that their little back woods road could be part of a three thousand mile coast to coast trek.

Yvonne disappeared a little later, putting clean sheets on the spare room bed.

Day 54 began a little late too, with a full breakfast kindly cooked for me by Yvonne. James gave me some home-made cure-all ointment for Smokey's back which I gingerly applied to her sore spots before loading her up. I really needed to replace the saddle which didnt seem to be doing her any favors, the weight on her spine not a good idea. I was a little sad to leave the couple that had made my first night in Arkansas such an enjoyable one, but with Louisiana so close, I also felt the need to push on.

By mid-morning, the heat was oppressive, the humidity factor sending the temperatures over the hundred degree mark. Sweat ran freely down my top half, collecting at my waist, and down my legs to soak my socks.

We passed straight through Eudora, the biggest town in that south-eastern corner and on to Indian. The Louisiana state line lay four miles to the south. Farming country again, with small spread-out properties made conspicuous by the wind break trees that surrounded them.

I called it a day at sixteen miles. It had been a long walk in that heat, Smokey feeling the strain more than I did. Most of her winter coat was shed, the government brand along her neck now clearly legible - 82495233, in code.

I had been stopped earlier in the day by a woman driving an old truck, a tanned little boy passenger. We had been talking outside an empty closed-up store for a little while and she'd invited us to stay. As we stood there talking, a car passed, the retort from a gun shot from its window made us all jump, even Smokey. They couldn't have been aiming for us, we made such clear targets, but it wasn't a very friendly gesture. Shooting from a moving car was apparently a regular sport in the south, all the road signs pitted or even holed by the bullets. Some of the favorites were almost illegible. Gun racks were a common fixture in pick-up truck back windows. The lady who was to be our host that night drove ahead, and a little over an hour later we were walking along the driveway leading to her house.

The house, in a state that 'being done up' always tends to throw it, lay to one side of a large, weed covered patch, a big mechanic's workshop at one end, a trailer alongside. There was a wooden shelter framed with red metal post fencing for the animals, newly erected, and a good sized pasture split by a small stream. A small, fat herd of cattle was bunched under a shady tree.

The family was what in England might be termed as 'rough'. Dirty, scruffy, lots of swearing and a bit of abuse. I have quite a repertoire of strong language myself and can knock back the beers with the best of them, but even for me it was a bit strong. The most offensive being the attitude towards the children. The three would fight, the older boy drawing blood from the younger, the adults laughing them on. Dogs and kittens sat scratching in the dust, fleas wriggling away in their patchy coats. I was made very welcome though, even if I was made to feel a bit uncomfortable by their rough and tumble relationships, they were more than kind to me.

Nobody was living in the house being done up, so rather than set up the tent, I was offered the use of a single bed in one of the near empty rooms. Thunderstorms were predicted for some time during the night and I was glad of the chance to have a roof over my head. The mechanic of the family, Donald, the divorced father of the little girl, would stay with me. I didn't really trust him, but I couldn't say no.

Everyone met later that night for a meal at a trailer a few miles away, the temporary home of the lady who had stopped me, and her husband. A young dog barked excitedly, almost strangling his brindle colored self on the long chain outside the Gray's home. Broken down vehicles and pieces of farming equipment lay rusting in the long grass, children's bikes, toy tanks and guns, broken dolls lay in the dust.

We ate late. The sky was darkening, heavy clouds flying past each other on a race to Texas. Rumbling in the distance, the wind gusty and strengthening. Not much after the last plate was cleaned, a big crack of thunder followed by X-ray strength lightening and the electricity failed. I sat at the table while flashlights and candles were quickly found. Big splashes of rain hit the tilted open window, the net curtains beating against the glass. A minute more and the drumming of water hitting the roof made everyone need to shout to be heard. There was a dash to the car, hands, rather pointlessly over already wet hair. It was impossible not to be soaked in the few yards to the old truck, me clambering up beside Donald in the passenger seat for the three or four mile ride back to the old house.

It took longer on the return trip, Donald driving cautiously along a road broken by rushing rivulets of storm rain, the windscreen wipers on super fast, unable to cope with the deluge.

The first thing I did when I finally got back at the house was to check on Smokey. She hated to get wet and the storm may have spooked her. I ran over to the sheds, my stockmen's coat held tightly umbrella fashion over my head, my feet quickly soaked in the deepening puddles. She was fine. She looked at me from under the shelter of the wooden barn buildings calmly standing, one back foot resting. Then the race with wet feet back to the house .

I sat at one end of the sofa, my knees tucked under my chin, and Donald sat at the other. We shared a couple of beers. Earlier in the afternoon he'd managed to find a farrier to come out the next day to see about Smokey's badly worn shoes, so Day 55, the last day of May, would either be a very late start, or another day off.

Donald, at his end of the sofa, was a little restless. He kept running his oil stained fingers over his very short hair, laughing a little nervously at each comment and smoking non-stop. With the thunder and lightening and the rain on the roof, the atmosphere was tense. I was very careful for him not to get any ideas about me. Finally he said it.

"Um.... Emma...", a little laugh, "what if I was to say... well...", little chuckle, "What if I should, just ummm...", light a cigarette, "what if I came with you?"

Oh, what a relief, I thought. It had taken me years to get ready, and he wants to be done in one night. Donald didn't even have a horse! I talked with him about it for the next hour or two, about the heat, the hassles, the expenses and what an unpleasant traveling partner I would make. I didn't say no to his suggestion, but I didn't say yes either. After yawning conspicuously for a few minutes, I excused myself to the empty spare room, leaving him to think it over.

The morning was sunny and clear, the puddles in the yard already shrinking by the time I got up. Donald took me on a long tour of the area in the truck, his daughter sleeping between us on the bench style seat. We went to Oak Grove and the river, Eudora and Wilmot. He showed me miles of flat farming country and pleasant towns in both Arkansas and neighboring Louisiana. Neither of us talked very much but the quiet was easy. Nobody mentioned his suggestion of the night before.

We were back in good time for the horse shoer due late afternoon. Stan Smith had come all the way from Bastrop, forty odd miles, to shoe my long distance pony. He set up under the shed; his small furnace, tools, a heavy metal tripod and anvil, thick leather chaps tied over wrangler jeans. He was about my age, a bit overweight with deep set blue eyes - the spitting image of the actor Kurt Russell! Very attractive! He suggested I have Smokey shod with shoes edged with a slow wearing metal to make them last longer than the three or four weeks of normal shoes. I agreed, and he began the lengthy job of welding Borium rivets onto new shoes. As he was sweating over the task, a horse trailer pulled into the yard. It was Donald. He'd borrowed a horse. He was serious about leaving with me in the morning.

"Oh my God!" I said. We both looked up as Donald, a little pink faced but quite pleased with himself, wandered over after unloading his horse. He asked Stan whether he'd have time to shoe another. Stan nodded.

"Don't do it Stan!" I whispered desperately, as Donald walked back to his horse. "He wants to come with me and ifs impossible!"

I knew that half the reason why I'd been so spoilt by the people I'd met on the trip so far was the simple fact that I was female and alone. I needed 'looking after'. If I was traveling with a man, and a slightly scary looking man at that, all the hot meals, showers and clean sheeted spare rooms would come to an end. And I liked being spoilt. I didn't want my trip to turn into just a long trek.

Stan saw what I meant and slowed his shoeing of Smokey. Donald, to one side of the yard, was busy with his chores, but began to realize as the hours went by and the afternoon wore on, that his horse wouldn't be shod that day. Smokey, having only her fourth set of shoes on in her life, wasn't an easy horse to finish. Stan took three and a half hours. He excused himself from shoeing the bay gelding tied to the trailer. After his apology, he left for Bastrop. Poor

Donald, loaded his borrowed horse back in the trailer and drove him home.

His family weren't quite so friendly that night. I think they knew that I had put a spanner in the works, even though it was really for Donald's own good. (Americans use "monkey wrenches" but British "spanners" also do a good job.) His plan wouldn't have worked, but I felt sad for him. As I rode out the next morning, I turned to wave. There were tears in Donald's piercing blue eyes.

We were on Highway 52. Quiet, hot, flat and straight straight straight. There was a little chicanery into Miller Chapel, then more straight to Wilmot. I'd listed Wilmot as one of my postal addresses. From the maps I'd selected small towns I would be passing through at some point, and sent the names and approximate date we'd be there to the people I was writing to. It didn't work very well. Sometimes there was no post office, other times I changed my route. The postal service would only hold the mail marked 'General Delivery' for fourteen days, so if I was delayed, they would send it all back to where it came from. Very annoying. Wilmot was not like that.

"We've been expecting you!" laughed the friendly counter guy, and pushed over the Formica a huge pile of letters and parcels, some having been redirected from Eutaw and Goodman. I think I probably jumped up and down! With a grateful smile, I left the post office, unhitched Smokey from the telegraph pole outside, and asked a local if we could rest a while in his large grassy garden opposite. He kindly agreed, and I relieved Smokey of her heavy packs, tying her to a large tree to graze. Halfway through the first letter, one from my sister in England:

"Hello." I looked up. A nine or ten year old boy stood a few feet away, hands in pockets.

"Hello," I answered. Back to the letter, but it was too rude, and so I spent the next few minutes talking to the dark haired little lad, one eye on the page. Someone else came over, and, in a few minutes, more, I spoke to them. I managed to finish Harriet's letter, smiling at her present of instant tea, and open the next. The owner of the property came over for a chat, then his wife, then the newspaper lady. There was loads of mail but no time to read it! When the last of the friendly visitors had left, I scrambled for the next letter, ripping it open in my eagerness to news from home.

"Hello! Can we come over?" A whole bunch of white coated dental surgery staff were on the edge of the grass. I put the blue airmail envelope down and went to meet them. They were all women. We had a great half an hour talking about the trip, and me, and them. They were very excited to see a female doing such an adventurous thing, giggled when I showed them my six-inch blade hunting knife, touching it gingerly with clean, nail polished fingers. They were shocked at how little I ate and nodded understanding^ at my ripped trousers and dirty shoes. They laughed at their own conservative lifestyles. I really enjoyed them.

As I was saddling Smokey back up for the afternoon miles, three or four of the women came over with a little box. Inside were miniature tubes of toothpaste, dental floss, toothbrushes, a couple of tiny bottles of mouthwash. I really appreciated the gift. Another gave me a big bag of juicy ripe peaches.

We were heading southwest along main Highway 65 toward the Louisiana state line. That night would see us in out fifth state. Only three nights in Arkansas but I hadn't needed my tent or cooked a meal. Actually, it had been so long since I'd had to feed myself that I wasn't sure whether I was carrying any food! Could be peaches for Day 56. No tent and no cooking in Arkansas, that has to be a perfect record. And no rejections either. I'd like to see more of that state one day. Good people, there. Kind, generous, friendly people.

Chapter 6

Louisiana
The red rose of romance blooms briefly under a big easy sky

Louisiana. Loo EASY Ana — the last of the 'easy' states. We passed the big sign welcoming us late in the afternoon, setting up camp a little further behind some open sided barns housing huge farm machinery. The first night in the tent for a long time, Smokey tied to the fence facing the open door. Peaches and nuts and tea for a meal flavored strongly by the 'Skin-So-Soft' oil I was using as a repellent against the massive horse flies. Nothing would keep them away for very long, I had tried all the advertised brands. Still Smokey's nose would be striped by the red lines of blood from their vicious bites and she'd run from one end of the lead rope to the other trying to escape for the hour before dusk when they were hungriest. After the horse flies, came the mosquitoes; big, fat, mean. No wonder the RAF named fighter planes after them during WW n. They're deadly on the attack.

We left the highway with its parallel train track the next morning at Jones, taking the cut off road to meet up with Route 140, a much quieter and more pleasant road. It was the June 2nd and by nine o'clock, hot.

We were two hundred miles from Smokey's home farm at Marshall, and I'd written to Vickie to say to expect us sometime around the fourteenth. I was eager to get there. For six to eight weeks Smokey could rest under the east Texan pines with her old gang at Karma Farms, while I headed down to Pat's in Corpus Christi for a holiday from my holiday. The time would also be spent in research about the western part of our trek, with the mountains, the deserts and winter equipment, then relax on the beach, put on a few pounds with Pafs great cooking and psyche myself up for the tougher half of the United States. We'd had the easy bit, it would be time to get ready for the rest.

These were my thoughts as I rode along the long flat roads of early Louisiana — thinking ahead to what I needed to do.

By eleven o'clock it was too hot to ride. (By 9:30 really but I had to push on that extra hour or we'd still be in Alabama!) An empty house with a hosepipe and a big shady tree in an almost treeless landscape was too appealing to pass by, and we broke for our midday siesta. Smokey rolled gratefully before settling down to graze. I dozed off under the tree, slapping at the bothersome fire ants automatically in my sleep.

I love the habit of sleeping during the day. Still do now, where I can. With a yawn and a scratch I was awake again, Smokey dozing in the shade a few feet away . When I woke up, she'd stretch too, and go back to eating. She knew the routine: it wouldn't be long before saddling up time so get a bit more grass down.

Not long after waking, a big expensive pick-up truck pulled over, Stan Smith, the horse-shoer from Bastrop climbed out of the passenger side. He introduced the tall, late- middle-aged driver in the white cowboy hat as his friend and neighbor, Dosher Cockrell.

I'm not really sure if I should write about this, it's rather a delicate subject, but I'd just been to the loo. It's amazing how shifty you can be at doing the necessaries on a completely exposed piece of land during a break in the traffic. That day, not expecting any callers on that lonely stretch, I hadn't bothered to be too discreet, leaving under a tree an obvious example of my, so to speak, passing. As I stood there talking to Stan and his lovely natured friend Dosher, I became painfully aware of the ugliness lying just a few feet away. As plainly visible as white flags on green grass were a couple of pages of my latest cheap novel, used as loo paper and waiting to be burned when camp was cleared.

I tried to position myself so it wouldn't be in their line of vision but Smokey, very uncooperatively, kept to that side. I jumped in the way, laughed over-loudly to keep their attention on my face. They must have thought me a little sun-stroked.

Dosher and Stan wanted me to spend a day or two on Dosher's four hundred acre farm south of Bastrop. It was a little out of the way. They pressed me with offers of clean clothes, hot food, showers, a few cold beers, and a horse trailer to take us there. Stan confessed they'd spent the last two and a half hours driving around the lanes trying to find me. I graciously conceded defeat. (Whoopppee!!!I really thought!) The chance of all that luxury and a day or two in the company of good looking Stan, was an un-refusable offer for a single, skinny, smelly, thirsty girl like me!

Dosher, his fun bubbly wife, Gloria, and Stan met me two hours later a little further along on Route 140.

Dosher and Gloria lived in a small red wooden house on a narrow lane, the four hundred acres of pasture behind dotted with fat horses and cattle, trees and huge water troughs. Smokey was turned out in a big field all to herself and I was given adamant instructions not to worry about her at all during my stay. Dosher would see to everything. Fine by me!

The afternoon and evening went by quickly, sitting on the wooden deck surrounding the Cockrells house, talking, joking and telling stories. Dosher was a very tall, gentle, man with an unshakeable smile on his sun lined face. His wife, Gloria, a quick witted woman quite a few years his junior. They treated Stan like a son, and he treated them with respectful teasing, answering man and wife's playful banter with rib digging of his own.

Stan lived a few hundred feet away on the same road, on a little patch of ground fenced off from the fields. An old mobile home stood on bricks in the well kept yard, the excited yapping of eight Rottweiler puppies in a pen behind. We returned there in the dark after eating out in town, a six pack of beer in the cooler sliding from one side to the other on the pick up truck.

The inside of the trailer was pretty cramped. Like camping out, but Stan kept it pretty tidy. Cowboy hats and bridles, lariats, leather saddles and horse blankets, a patchwork quilt over a wooden framed sofa. Plastic-wood cupboards and an unmade double bed. A big old black and white television was in the corner of the bedroom, a long barreled loaded gun under the open window. The shower was wonderful, powerful, even though the bathroom was in miniature. I wiped a space on the misted mirror and put on some make-up, relaxed after the hot water and cold beer, not quite sure where the late evening hours would take me. An hour or so later, I found myself, a little disappointed, alone in the big double bed, Stan took the couch.

There was a horse show coming up at the weekend and Gloria was to compete in the barrel racing. I was invited along and feeling in the need of a little more of that young, single, male company, I was glad to take the extra days off.

I woke up late to a hot Friday morning (even during the night the temperatures hadn't dropped below 75 degrees!) Stan had left to shoe a horse, planning to be back by ten to pick me up.

I borrowed a baseball cap and a tee-shirt, took extra care over a bit of make-up, played with the puppies, read, checked the face, then waited. Stan pulled in shortly after ten, changed his sweat soaked shirt and we left to see to a horse with bad feet. After I 'd watched Stan laboring away over the split feet of a high-dollar competition quarter-horse, and then another, after that, he called it a day. It was too hot to work. We picked up a few beers and headed to Doshers.

I fancied Stan. I liked his cowboy image and his wrangler jeans, his attention to the horses he shod and the way he drove the little white pick-up. I hadn't had any sort of relationship since Adrian, two and a half years previously, and felt the cravings of a lonely single woman.

We sat on Dosher's porch; Stan, me, Gloria and Dosher. Smokey way off in the pasture somewhere. Stan and I had been paired up but it didn't seem to be moving too much in what I thought would be the 'right direction.' I resolved, after the numbing affects from a couple of beers to push the point. I was sick of being single.

Back at the trailer, country music playing quietly in the background, the smell of leather and dogs and shampoo. Talking. It became late and I talked about bed, booked the couch, had it rebuked, yearned for a bit more and went to bed, alone. Oh well.

The horse show was the following day. Dosher was up early, hosing down the ugly grey horse Gloria rode around the barrels. Stan had to check the horse with the bad feet, doing what he could to make the sore animal ready for its nineteen seconds in the arena. We set off separately. Dosher and Gloria in the blue air conditioned pick up truck, Stan and I in the white with the windows rolled down. It was hot but with the wind on my face and Smokey resting, the sunshine was welcome.

Stan set up under a shady tree to shoe any horse that the hours allowed. The sore horse arrived with heavily bandaged legs, pretty, alert, a big heart. The young girl rider needing the winning points for a high school scholarship.

Gloria was very casual about her involvement in the quite tense atmosphere of times, penalties, wins and losses. She was a very popular woman. So many people were introduced to me that day through her and through Dosher. Nothing wrong could be said about either, they were such a kind-hearted and loveable couple.

I shared the time between taking to the Cockrells and their many friends, and watching Stan. I'd sit on the inverted tail gate of his truck and watch his bent over body shoeing bays, chestnuts, duns and greys. He was a perfectionist. He'd shod Smokey. First class job. I had a lot of respect for him, which made him more appealing. I took the money for shoeing off satisfied owners, stashing it in the glove box of the truck and feeling at least a little useful. No alcohol allowed at these family events but somehow I was being a little intoxicated with the horses, the people, the sneaked beer or two, Stan.

Gloria made a good time at the barrels but no first prize. I won a cake on the cake walk, but I think it was fixed. Bless them. They were so welcoming.

The drive back, with the cooler full and the beer lowered out of view from patrolling police cars. (It was illegal to have an opened beer bottle in the front of a car, hence the many bottles on the side of the road.) The warm night air was like a drug. I stuck my head out of the window, letting the wind take my hair in contest with the band that held it back. We were back at the trailer too soon. To travel so fast, at night, with the lights and the speed, and knowing Smokey was safe, was so intoxicating. The beer had something to do with it, I suppose.

We collapsed on the couch. Me leaning against it, and Stan full length. I lay my head on his legs and we laughed about the days competition, talked about Dosher and Gloria and how special they were. About country music, about dogs, about horses, about everything. It was late. It turned half rising to go to bed. Stan looked at me and I kissed him. Game over. That night we spent together. Late. Not much rest. Hot and cold. Loving. Exhausted sleep.

I left on the morning of Day 6, a little sad, but with an open offer of a place to stay when Smokey was safely back at Karma Farms. I'd almost forgotten about poor Smokey over the last few days. Dosher had fed and cared for her. The only time I'd seen her was for a photo session for the local newspaper, and as a distant white speck, way off in the pasture, a cold beer raised to toast her. All I'd done was to rest, follow Stan, eat, drink, sleep, play at being in love. Or lust. It was time to go.

There was a bad bridge past Bastrop on Route 2. Dosher had kindly offered to trailer us over so I left the packs with him to hand over later in the day. With Smokey unloaded I was able to trot away from the comforts and contact of my short lived romance. It was the only time I wanted to turn back and put the saddle and bags away.

It was a pleasant ride as far as the main highway: leafy and quiet; suburban houses on a Monday morning. It ended at 165, a four-lane, exposed, hot.

We almost made it to the turn-off for Route 2 when Dosher and the horse trailer pulled up ahead. Smokey picked up her ears and loaded easily, stepping over the packs and full feed sacks in to the cool trailer.

The bridge was pretty bad. Metal floor, narrow, with continuous traffic and no hard shoulder. It was the metal floor that would have been the problem. Smokey would have gone over but it might have taken all afternoon to persuade her. With only two lanes, we would have been an accident waiting to happen.

I was sad to see that blue truck head back towards Bastrop. We'd been so spoiled by Dosher and his wife over the last few days: meals and trips out, new clothes, Smokey cared for and laundry done. They couldn't have been kinder. I wanted to race back to Texas, turn Smokey out in the field, and get back here! All afternoon I felt melancholy, the soppy country and western songs fueling my dreamy mood. I kept the radio on all day, rolling in the luxury of this half forgotten emotion. A lady met us at about the nineteen mile marker. She had seen us plodding along in the heat and offered water for Smokey and a coke for me. The brief stop turned into a night's stay, the camper van behind the house, mine for the night, Smokey tied to a big tree in the garden. I excused myself early from the friendly family, not feeling very sociable. I pretended I was tired, but I wanted to be alone to think about Stan.

I felt a bit cheered up by the next day. It was our sixty-second day on the road, the Seventh of June . It wasn't much more than a hundred miles back to Karma Farms and with over eight hundred done, it felt like a stroll around the block. We were heading almost directly West, the early sun already burning my back, a humid 95 degrees by midday, country and western music lifting spirits whereas yesterday it had been a pleasure to keep them low. Oh well. It probably wasn't undying love!

We were stopped so many times by people who'd read the article in the Bastrop Daily Enterprise that I didn't take any time off for the traditional afternoon sleep. One of our visitors was the familiar blue truck, Dosher and Gloria out to see how ' their little English gal' was doing. They bought me sodas and food and tried to give me money. They wanted to take me back. Old friends.

We passed through the small town of Farmerville late in the afternoon aiming for the Lake D'Arbonne State Park. At the gate I asked if they'd object to a horse as an overnight guest and gained permission to ride in. It was getting late, the sun lowering on a clear blue sky. No grass. We had to leave, apologizing to campers who wanted to talk, racing against the oncoming night to find a greener spot. A fast four miles found us at an empty field just in time.

Day 63 saw us back in the routine of early start, ride, rest, ride. We left Route 2 for the Alternative Route 2, a quieter road but a little longer. The hard shoulder wasn't as good, dropping away steeply around sharp curves, disappearing altogether in some places to make horse travel more dangerous. We were out of the Mississippi Delta area finally, hills and trees, pasture land and cattle farms replacing the flat fields of cotton and rice. The first signs of the oil fields coming up in dotted groups; twelve- to twenty-foot high nodding derricks. Their slow metal noses dipping to the ground to pause a fraction, followed by the steady climb. A heavy metal cable fixed between their iron ears pumping the oil along an invisible pipe to field-side tanks. I thought many of them were broken but I learned later that they only start up their slow nodding when the pressure underground builds to a measured degree. They seemed almost alive with their varying sizes and family groups. I'd watch them a little uneasily, the plot to 'War of the Worlds' could have been hatched in the oil fields. Passing through wooded areas the squeaking of the older machines made Smokey alert and snort a little, her ears twitching to locate the source of the noise.

A twenty-three mile day; our record. It was Texas being so near that pushed me on.

We came across a small collection of buildings on either side of the road around a big pasture framed with trees. I pulled Smokey over, letting her graze on the long roadside grass and thought about the prospect of asking to stay. Within a minute an old pick-up truck pulled over and a young guy climbed out.

We talked a little, me asking advice for a spot for the night and suggesting the paddock on the other side of the red post fencing. He drove off to ask the owner who ran the local shop a mile further west. While I waited, another car stopped with Larry Haynes from Arkansas asking the usual questions. He offered a Coke and a big, round, sticky pat of peanut brittle. Both were good! The first young man was back quickly with permission from the landowner to house Smokey in the field and also with the offer of the use of a shed converted into living accommodation. Wonderful! We unloaded Smokey, hauling the heavy packs into a large square room, once a shed for metal working equipment, a huge table dominating the center. A kitchen area ran along the northern end, a stereo, a couch and chairs, a small bathroom. Butch Bays, the owner arrived. He was in his late forties, single, hardworking and successful, and delighted to be able to be able to help. My melancholy of the Bastrop days had lifted and I was in fine spirits. The previous night spent in a field made me glad for company that night.

Smokey was let out in the pasture but the horse and deer flies were horrendous. Nothing seemed to work to keep them away. She raced around, panicked by their vicious bites, blood running down her legs and the tender black skin around her nose. There was nothing I could do for her. White horses seemed particularly vulnerable.

The evening turned into a bit of a party. Jed, the first young man and his chatty wife, Mandy, turned up, and half their extensive family too. We went to Jed's property to pick up fresh supplies of horse feed, meeting more of the friendly and kind family. Back at the farm, Butch emptied the fridge of all sorts of home cooked dishes, piling my plate high. We had a couple of beers, and that set me off. Chat, chat,, chat! They were very impressed with me! Not a usual sight I suppose in back roads Louisiana, a lone female rider heading west, and they all seemed to enjoy the novelty and took obvious pleasure in my stories about the people and places we'd seen so far.

When I returned to the shed later that night, well fed, with my laundry clean, and me, showered and fresh* a big mattress lay to one side of the central table. One of the best things I'd seen all day! Twenty-three miles and I was tired out. I slept well; Smokey was safe, no tent, and Texas one day closer.

I gave two newspaper interviews in the morning, sitting around the big table in the shed, the two women reporters jostling each other for the best photo angles. It meant a late start but under the saddle blanket I found two twenty dollar bills, a donation from Mandy and Jed's Dad, and another two were given to me by Butch. A morning for 'two's!' They were too kind! I was always short of money, the trip very under financed, but it was difficult to accept donations from people who'd already been so kind. I always tried to refuse their offers but was very glad when they pressed me to accept! Eighty dollars in one day. I was rich! I rode away from that little leafy corner of Louisiana amazed again at the unconditional support and generosity of the American country people.

By Day 67 we were almost out of our fifth state, approaching the home run back to Karma Farms. The previous night had been spent at the Sheriffs house, Smokey sharing a field with goats, an animal that not many weeks ago would have scared her silly. A big bridge across the Red River, a take-out Pizza from Pizza Hut in Vivian and our last night in Louisiana. We spent it at a roping family's house, only six miles from Texas. The trip nearly ended for me that night. Everything nearly ended for me that night. It was June 12th. I'd unsaddled Smokey in a small pasture adjoining a larger one containing three or four of the owners horses used for cattle roping. A barn connected the two lots. It was feed time and the owner opened the gate for his horses to enter the barn for their ration of oats. As the horses raced towards their usual places to feed, I closed the second gate to prevent them running on through to the smaller pasture where Smokey grazed close by. She heard their hooves thundering over the hard packed earth down the central aisle, thought they were after her, and with her head between her knees, sent both back legs in a flying kick in their direction. She hit me in the back. I paused, expecting to fold in an agonized pile on the grass, but with the blessed life I was living, she'd kicked me an inch or two above my tail bone, and though the force has winded me, there was hardly a bruise to show for it. A little higher and she could have broken my back.

Tragedy can happen so quickly. A few seconds. A couple of inches. I learned a strong lesson without having to pay the price. Every day is a bonus, precious, a prize. Don't waste them.

"You are now leaving Louisiana," the sign said. "Come back soon!"

I looked back into the shadowy woods, said good-bye to the east. Texas lay a hundred feet to the west, the biggest state we were to cross. Over six hundred miles of easy, hard, hardest, but it felt like coming home.

"Walk on Smokey."

Twenty seconds. Thirty seconds. Thirty five seconds. Just the sound of Smokey's steel shoes on the road, her slow rhythmic plodding taking us, step by step, on. Closer. Birds and a plane flying way up there in the hot Texan sky ahead. Forty seconds.

"Whoa, Smokey."

We were out of No Man's Land, parallel with the huge sign signaling the start of our sixth state. I took a photo of Smokey irreverently grazing around the base. We were winning.

I mounted up, smiling, sun burnt, skinny and happy, blowing a kiss at the solo white star on the background of red and blue.

"Welcome to Texas, " the sign said," The Lone Star State."

Chapter 7

Texas

Meeting up with "The Lady With The Wagon" rounds off a six-hundred mile crossing of the heaven-made Lone Star State. If you're a Texan, you're a friend of mine.

"My name is Emma Crosby, I'm from England doing some traveling in the area with my horse and wondered if you'd be kind enough to let me stay the night on your field?"

"I don't think so!" A slammed door.

Our first rejection in many, many miles was our welcome on our first night in Texas. What a disappointment. After looking forward so much to a Texas homecoming, we had been turned away. It was a shock.

The neighbor was almost as unfriendly but grunted assent to let us camp in a huge open grassy area alongside his house. No invitation to use his glorious looking swimming pool.

I was up early the next morning, awakened by Smokey's big nose pushing against the screen of the tent door. It was five-thirty, the sun not yet risen through the trees to the east. In the half light I fed Smokey from the almost empty feed sacks, loading her up excitedly for our last day of the first leg. Today we would ride through the gates of Karma Farms.

As Smokey chewed her last mouthful, I folded the bucket, tucked it under a saddlebag strap, and swung into the saddle.

"Walk on, Smokey."

A couple of miles on Highway 49, still too early for the quiet to be broken by much traffic. Only the birds with their morning song accompanied us away from the woods and into a very pretty and historic looking Jefferson, a town supposedly boasting one of the highest counts of millionaires in the country. Oil money. We didn't stop to admire the handsome wooden buildings, but crossed over the lights to pick up major Highway 59 heading south towards

Marshall. It was one of the busiest stretches of highway Smokey and I had traveled; logging trucks, commuter traffic, hauling trucks heavily loaded, speeding sales reps, pickups, cattle trucks and livestock haulers, motorbikes. All sped by a few feet to our left. Two lanes up, two down. Fifteen feet to our right, the polished parallel steel tracks of the tram lines.

About five miles away from the ranch where Smokey had spent ten years of her captive life, she realized where she was. She stopped in her tracks. Immediately her head went up, her ears, her tail. She'd recognized her home turf and was like something possessed! For the next five miles she danced a pretty quick step, all head and tail and blowing nostrils. It was all I could do to hold her to a reasonable pace, with the bags flapping and me laughing so much at the pretty picture she made. I could see it would be pretty disastrous now to fall off, so close to home, and Smokey ready to run. Eighteen wheeler trucks were hurtling past on our left, the freight train was blasting away only fifteen feet to our right, just about every dangerous hazard you could think of when on top of a horse. I thought if I could handle her with all this, then everything else would be easy. But she wasn't interested in trucks or trains, she was on her way home and had eyes and ears for nothing else. We turned in the driveway after she'd made known to the horses racing along the fence line that Smoking Spear was coming home. Sixty-nine days, 970 miles behind us, Smokey, fit, fat and well and I could have gone on for ever.

Later, I was in the arms of my Louisiana horse-shoer in a Monroe motel.

We spent quite a few enjoyable days and nights together, but I felt a little out of place without my big four footed security blanket. I was glad she was having a rest, she deserved one, but I missed the role having her around put me into. Also I couldn't wait to see the dramatic west Texas landscape and find out how we coped there. Following Stan around, people often embarrassed me with 'You back again?' so when the time was starting to drag, I bought a ticket for the Greyhound bus down to Corpus Christi, heading to Pat's place. Pat hadn't changed at all. He was still considerably besotted with me even though I let him know, very clearly, that all his adoration was wasted. Alcohol and frustration made him unpleasant and he threatened to kick me out several times in the five weeks I spent with him. By the morning, he would be apologetic and would beg me to stay but I knew it wouldn't be long before he'd have another alcohol induced spat and I made ready to move on.

I found the maps I'd been looking for, very detailed, showing each road, path, every water source including windmills, every tiny settlement, every building, Texas to the Californian coastline. I changed my worn out Reebok tennis shoes for some black leather English jodhpur boots and my irritating floppy hat for a cool looking Australian Akabra. I sharpened my knives and made a serious assessment of the value of each item in the saddlebags. With the hot summer riding ahead, I needed to drop the pack weight by a good third. I made the agonized decision to sacrifice the stove. No more hot food and, even worse, no more of those end of the day stabilizing cups of tea. I cut down Smokey's veterinary supplies to under half and the grooming kit dropped to only a brush and hoof pick. However, I still kept the make up! Even us road rats like to feel a little feminine sometimes! All the winter equipment, sleeping bags and thick clothes, went to Dosher Cockerall in Louisiana. He had kindly agreed to post it on when the weather cooled.

For five weeks I studied the maps, became addicted to Country music television (twenty four hour country and western videos!) ate Pafs wonderful cooking, drank loads of beer, and craved the company of my little white horse, and the solitude of the open road. I was trying to think of our crossing of the arid deserts after the scorching summer months and the mountains before the winter snows. Eight weeks of lazing around and putting on weight should do it, but five weeks was all I could stand. On the 18th of July I was, once more, heading up to Marshall.

r d never seen such a fat horse! Could have been twins the way her white belly sagged to her knees! Smokey was standing in the dappled light of a tree's shade, watching me approach with her big calm black eyes. She stood quietly while I checked her for sores or scratches, her feet and back. When I slumped down in the shade beside her, began talking about the trip yet to come, she walked off.

Never was a very affectionate pony. I laughed as her big fat rump swayed from side to side as she set off to join the rest of her herd around the pond. When she'd disappeared from sight, I turned to walk back down the hill through the scorching Texan sunshine to the house.

For five days Vickie Ives Spear, friends and family, generously gave their time to setting us on the road again with renewed health certificates, inoculations and shoes.

At first light on the 23rd of July, after only three hours sleep and with a roaring hangover, Smokey, my little white American Indian pony, and I, were once again, saddled up and heading west.

I thought Smokey might make a bit of a fuss about leaving the ranch but she walked away at her standard two and a half miles an hour, back up the dual carriageway, left at Woodlawn, her big fat belly forcing the packs to swing out at weird angles every time she took a step forward. There hadn't been enough money to replace the treeless saddle which I knew would mean trouble later but there was nothing I could do about it. If I had to walk to the coast then that would be the way we go. I was just glad to be traveling with my horse-friend again, a sense of calm and Tightness washing away the irritability of the last five weeks. I loved what I was doing. I felt right and at home in the saddle, all I needed was in the two blue canvas packs. And I had no better partner than the little white horse plodding away beneath me. It was good to be together again.

'Real good!* as I so often heard the Americans say!

The first night back on the road was spent in an idyllic little cemetery fifteen miles away from Karma Farms. It was a big place completely hidden by trees from the road with long grass and working water faucets, a shed to pitch the tent under. With no stove, there was no hot tea, only warm thinned down 'Gatorade', an orangery energy drink that I learnt to like, sort of. For a meal, I opened a bag of nuts and raisins. Sitting cross-legged on the table in the open-sided shed, I ate and watched Smokey graze, her long rope tied to a handsome old tree, the darkening shadows moving across the headstones, welcoming. There would be no visitors after the final light faded. The start of the second leg was so different from those early days in Georgia. Now I wanted to savor every mile, every night and day, every ker-plop of Smokey's shoes on the roadside. Georgia had been a frustrating race westwards. This was so much better. Smokey was the same but I had changed: more patient, more relaxed, more experienced and able. A better person. I think.

I had been warned that Texas was a barren and desolate place over-run with snakes and spiders. I didn't' know. I'd never been to the west but I'd picked out the route so carefully from the detailed maps that I didn't foresee any major difficulties for a few miles yet. We were swinging Northwest to avoid the huge metropolitan areas of Dallas-Fort Worth, then we'd follow a fairly wiggly route from town to town, from water to water, into New Mexico at the Lubbock end. The thought of crossing New Mexico did make me nervous, and Arizona, I wasn't even thinking about. For the time being, I'd just enjoy my ignorance.

Smokey was sore. Only two days and a worrying swelling had appeared on her left back hip. She stumbled a lot and seemed a little jerky in her movements. We'd just passed the thousand mile mark but this new worry overlaid any feeling of achievement. I called it a day at eleven miles, turning Smokey up the driveway to a pretty little property surrounded by pastures. Without pause for thought, the Dupree family welcomed me into their home.

After a relaxing hour or two chatting, I confessed my fears about the swelling on Smokers back hip which by now was the size of a dinner plate and tender to touch.

"We have a vet in the family" offered my friendly host, and went off to phone. An appointment was made for the next morning, and I was amazed again at the unseen hand that had guided me up this gravely driveway. With something being done, I felt a little better, but dreaded a bad diagnosis. At least it came up early on, we were still so close to Vickie's place that if necessary, I could turn her around and rest her there.

The young, good-looking vet was much respected in the area for his ability with horses. They were his specialty. As soon as he ran his hand down Smokey's neck I was sure his advice would be constructive; no grandiose dramatic statements just to show off his skill and scare the life out of me. He was very quiet and gentle and though a little unsure what may have caused the swelling thought I'd be okay to carry on for a bit. "If it doesn't go down with the liniment I give you , we may have to send a probe into that sore spot and see what's happening there, but it's pretty unlikely."

He gave me a bottle of clear, strong smelling liquid called DMSO. Once used as a miracle drug in the treatment of arthritis, it had later been banned because of the unpleasant side effects. Veterinary use only now. The vet also gave me a paste in a big plastic syringe-like tube to be squirted into the corner of Smokey's mouth morning and night. Horse aspirin he described it. The kindly man refused my offers of payment for his time and for Smokey's medicine.

"You just have a good trip. I'm glad to help in any way I can." We shook hands.

There was a quick whiz into town to my favorite store, WalMart, to replace my Swiss army knife, which in my disgraceful hung over state, I'd left on top of the feed sacks back at Karma Farms. Without the knife I had no tin opener, an essential item. Mrs. Dupree bought a couple of things, then it was back to the house to saddle up and move on. How lucky I was to have stopped with this wonderful family with the relative vet. I'd been fed, washed, laundry done, and enjoyed the luxury of a real bed. Smokey had had a lovely pasture to graze on and medicine freely given for the soreness in her hip. I was humbly grateful.

I deduced several weeks later that the swelling had been a result of Smokey walking crookedly after an uncomfortable set of shoes were fitted in Marshall.

By Day 75, we had passed through the big town of Winnsboro, named after an early settler, John Ewynn. The spelling was supposedly changed by a newspaper editor in the 1870's because of a shortage of Y's' in his type. The whole area is famous for the dramatic autumn colors from the extensive tracts of forested land surrounding the town, and much of West Texas was as pretty as my own English Cotswold countryside

We left the northwestern route of highway 11, for the direct north of farm road 69 to skirt around Sulphur Springs. With my fabulously detailed maps I could tell whether the road was big, small, crowded or not, where the bridges were, and whether the road would lead us over an interstate or become a dreaded underpass. The 69 east of Sulphur Springs went over.

Without effort we crossed Interstate 30 late in the afternoon and began to look out for a night's camping spot. The swampy area after the Interstate, with the bridges over White Oak Creek, Rock Creek and ifs tributary, gave way to the lush green of farms and tree-rich ranches. I tried a couple of places before asking at a cutting horse farm on the left. We'd just completed a twenty-two mile day.

The owner was rather cool in his welcome but agreed to housing Smokey in the barn shared with his expensive quarter horses. Their well bred lines and muscled bodies had bought him success as a raiser and trainer of cutting horses, the most elite of American Equine Sports. It was fascinating to watch. The cowboy would select a steer from the herd, either to doctor or brand on the range, or the judges choice in competition, and *cuf it out from the crowd. The horse's job was to keep that cow away from the rest; the border collie of the horse world. The horse's reactions were very quick, jumping to left or right, ears and eyes intent on the separated animal. Crouching down like a dog, a good cutting horse would need no guidance from its rider. I found 'cutting horse' people a little less welcoming than the normal run-of-the-mill horse lovers.

The guy that allowed me to stay that night belonged to the Mormon religion. No coffee, tea, alcohol, tobacco. Very disciplined. In Canada I'd lived in a Mormon community on the wide open Alberton prairies. They had been very friendly and an honest, family oriented people, but I'd made the mistake of taking a bottle of wine to a dinner party. Big social blunder! I hadn't known. Now I know their traditions a little better and appreciated their way of life.

Despite the coolness of the young owner, I was invited into the house and offered a room for the night. The wife turned up a bit later with her sister and child, standing on the doorway to the sitting room, struck dumb by the scruffy looking stranger in her armchair. I introduced myself. They became quite amenable but the atmosphere was so tense I denied being hungry though I hadn't eaten in twenty-four hours and excused myself for an early night. I can imagine the husband received a bit of a beating after I'd gone! I was glad of my early start in the morning with no addressees being asked for or exchanged. They were kind to let me stay but I was glad to leave!

That day, Day 76 of our trip, we really were in the sticks! With my new maps I could cut corners using tiny dirt tracks which was completely luxurious. Rather than having to stick to the right hand side of the road, I could wonder from side to side depending on where the most shade fell. It made me feel much more like an explorer! I was picking up Dallas radio loud and clear on the Walkman, and my new boots were proving really comfortable. Dave, a friend of Vickie's at Karma Farms, had given me a lovely pair of handsome spurs, tiny silver four-leafed clovers on the wheels. They made a lovely little tinkling sound as I walked along and made me feel tough! They didn't make Smokey walk any faster though! Since we'd started back on the road Smokey had seemed to be on her best behavior, almost as if she'd been told she couldn't go on a trip and at the last minute she'd been allowed to go. Maybe in those five weeks off, she'd missed our journey as much as I had.

Those little Texan back lanes were some of the best riding in the whole country, maybe partly because of the beautiful scenery, but also maybe because of the tougher country soon to come. They felt like the calm before the storm.

The smelly clear liquid I was using on Smokey's hip was doing a great job. The swelling was gradually easing away and she was stumbling less and less. I started to ration the Bute, the horse aspirin, to when she felt a bit under the weather. With her improved condition we docked up another eighteen miles that day, stopping for water finally at a dairy farm in the middle of absolutely nowhere! A tall blonde young man was busy in the milking room but saw me tie up outside and offered any help he was able. I asked about places round there to stop and he suggested the grass alongside the buildings. He had an almost new looking trailer parked close by and with rain expected that night recommended I stay in there. I was glad to accept.

Smokey was unloaded and tied to the trailer steps. She grazed a little but was quite unsettled, maybe by the cows close by or the storm clouds building away to the west. Glen returned later in the evening with oranges and to see if I was okay, and, shortly after he left, the rain began. Smokey hated to get wet and there was no shelter for her. It made me feel very guilty listening to the heavy drumming on the trailer roof knowing that outside she'd be miserable. At least it wasn't freezing. The nights rarely dropped below eighty degrees even at three or four o'clock in the morning, so she was unlikely to catch cold.

The milk truck woke me up at five-thirty. It was hard to leave the dreamy comfort of sleep and saddle up but with the temperatures usually soaring over the hundred marker at midday, the earlier the start, the better.

I saddled up Smokey and said good-bye to my kind host, Glen, before setting off westwards under a sky heavy with threatening black clouds.

The morning was wonderfully drizzly, such a break from the normally oppressive heat, but the insect life was so noisy in the breaks between showers that I could hardly hear the approach of vehicles from behind. Six miles and we were back on the hard surfaced farm road. The rain began in earnest. Smokey was miserable. Her normally gleaming white coat was soaking up the water, turning a silvery grey, and despite my long Australian stockman's' coat, I was getting wet, too. A church to our right boasted an open sided shed full of tables and benches for outside parties, so I pulled Smokey in to wait out the storm.

After a few minutes the wet weather seemed to be settling in for a bit of a spell so I unsaddled Smokey, tied her to the sturdy corner post, and fed her a little grain to keep her quiet. She was just glad to be out of that downpour. I laid myself down on one of the picnic tables and went to sleep.

"Hello! Hello!" A funny looking old man was standing a few inches away peering into my face.

"Here, d'ya wan' a beer?"

"All right mate, cheers!" I was never one to refuse.

A few minutes later another guy arrived and he waved his arms about for a while cursing the weather, predicting worse and offering to fetch his horse trailer to take us to his place for the night. We'd only covered six miles but these details no longer bothered me. I drank his health and agreed to his plans.

While I waited for the horse trailer, I rummaged around in the packs for the Super Glue. My front tooth with a replacement cap fitted after a bicycle accident, kept falling out and I was worried about completing the trip with a big hole in my face. A couple of drops of the powerful quick setting glue and my tooth was safely set; I could smile with confidence!

Smokey hopped up into the trailer with no trouble at all, a very different story than the hours it had taken in those early days. Dean lived a few miles away in a lovely little property on a quiet road. His wife and two children were equally friendly and the afternoon went quietly by in chatting, playing and drinking good cold beer.

Some friends turned up later in the evening and we all sat around outside, listening to the car radio and drinking rum and coke. One of the girls, a very pretty young woman who's name I've unfortunately forgotten sang a wonderful accompaniment to the Reba McIntyre song, 'Fancy.' She knew all the words though the song was complicated and despite being completely drunk, was so fascinating to watch as she threw her lovely slurred voice heavenwards, a half finished rum and Coke dangerously at risk of being spilled (though not a drop was lost), that I can now never listen to that excellent song without seeing her in my mind, her pretty face with the red rimmed eyes, her lovely blond hair escaping from the band that held it back. I can't remember how that evening ended. By then, I was completely gone myself!

By Day 79, the first of August, the trees were starting to thin out. They were still tall and respect-inspiring but they were beginning to be spread a little further apart.

I had a mail pickup at Wolfe City, a lovely old western style village with one main brick-paved street lined with typical American stores. Hardware, grocery, fabrics and crafts, dentist's doors, a doctor, a bank set back a little from the rest. The sound of Smokey's shoes on the bricks reverberated against the flat facades attracting attention from the shoppers; old men sitting outside the garage tipped their hats and remembered back to the days before cars. There were quite a few letters and I greedily read them while sitting on the side of the road, Smokey under the shade of a pecan tree. The postmaster came out for a chat, offered help and congratulations. We didn't stay very long because of lack of grass for grazing, so headed west out of town, picking up Farm Road 816 towards Leonard. Not more than a mile further a frail looking old black lady stopped to offer a place to rest. She seemed so fragile and so gentle that I was quite taken aback at her offer. I was glad to detour a little out of the way, normally unheard of by me, to spend a few hours with this unusual lady.

Tidy Johnson lived in the nicest property I'd seen for many a mile. An old colonial style wooden house set in many acres of lush green grass, fat cattle enjoying the shade. I could see the pretty white painted house with the big windows, tumbled old barn and pond through the trees as I approached up her gravel access road. Tidy was waiting at the entrance.

"Will she go over the cattle grid, dear?" Oh no, of course she won't, that's what cattle grids are for, I thought.

"Maybe." I replied. I dismounted and led Smokey up to the metal cage-like grid that kept the cattle in without having to use a gate. Smokey dropped her nose and took a good look. One hoof touched the grid and a loud metallic ring rang out. She scuttled backwards.

"I don't think she likes it," I said.

"I've got a bit of a board in the car," Tidy offered, "Let's try that."

She lay the flimsy sheet, the sort of wood that goes to make up tea chests, over the bars. I could see all that lovely grass, imagine that cold drink and tasty lunch and a peaceful few hours rest in the company of my very relaxing host only five feet away, on the other side of the cattle grid, all as inaccessible as tea at the Ritz. Fortunately, Smokey was on the same wavelength. She knew it was break time too and she could see all that lovely grass too, and her friends, the cows. Like a dog that doesn't like the water, she stretched out a stocky front foot, tested the wood, backed, tested it again, and using the board as a stepping stone, leapt to the riches beyond. She amazed me. Horses are usually so unreasonable and stubborn, but I'd never met one like Smokey. What a woman!

The afternoon was worth the little bit of stress at the gate. I had a really lovely time talking to Tidy and I think she enjoyed the company of a scruffy little English girl. Her quiet strength was quite remarkable in such a small frame, living alone as she was.

Smokey passed back over the grid without any pause about four-thirty in the afternoon. I would have liked to stay the night but I think Tidy assumed I'd like to move on and didn't make the offer. She stood waving at the entrance as I mounted up and headed back in the direction of Route 816. For some reason Smokey was breathing fire. Her head was up and her eyes wide open, ears forward and a high stepping walk back up the gravely track. Horses were in the field alongside and though I couldn't see them I think she could feel them there. She was picking her feet up so high and slamming them down so hard that it wasn't many meters before she'd bought the tender part of her hoof down on an unforgiving piece of gravel and bruised herself. She became lame instantly. Good grief, I thought, but carried on. As soon as I was out of sight of Tidy still waving at the gate, I dismounted and led my hobbling mare.

We joined up with the road, crossed a couple of bridges and about a mile and a half out of town I pulled her over and slumped down on the grassy verge. Smokey dropped her head to graze while I thought how unfortunate I was and what to do next.

In under a minute, I'd had two separate offers of a place to stay. Behind me, back from the road, was a quarter horse stud farm. The owner suggested we quit for the day and rest Smokey there. Absolutely, I thought!

The owner was a tall, imposing looking, grey headed Texan, but a kind and generous nature underlay his booming voice and domineering stature. By 'rest' he meant stay as long as I wished; for as long as it took Smokey's foot to heal and for as long as I felt I needed. His small round homely wife backed him in all his offers and his newly married daughter and husband offered a bed in their little house in Wolfe City. I felt swamped by their kindness - it just wasn't English! Texas and Texans were proving to be the most remarkable combination of un-self conscious interest, generosity and kindness. I had to get over this English hang up of feeling I was imposing on people and it was hard to get used to. Americans are different from us Brits! I stayed with Heath and Tina and their little baby for two nights, spending the extra day writing letters in the shade of a tree, watching Smokey graze in the pasture. Tina picked me up late afternoon and we bought a few beers on the way home. It was lovely to be in the company of two such well suited happy young people, Tina's face glowing with health and pride in her perfect family.

Theirs was one of the stops where I could have stayed longer but Smokey's foot was now fine and I had no further excuse to hang around. I saddled up and rode away from these new friends with an offer of always a place to stay and a phone number in my pocket in case I needed help in the next couple of hundred miles. It was Wednesday, the third of August.

The scenery was definitely starting to change. Rather than the comforting coziness of the heavily wooded dirt roads, the hills were becoming more austere, more rolling and less densely populated. The fields were becoming larger and farming was giving way to the famous Texan cattle ranches. The new country was impressive and scary and exciting. It felt like we were getting somewhere. Smokey and I were becoming more exposed to the burning sun and having to travel further for water, less selective about a midday spot. We were still in east Texas, not yet past the sprawling metropolitan area of Dallas-Fort worth. I was hearing a lot of gloomy stories about the impossibility of taking a horse, unsupported, across the sandy, barren, stretches of the west.

Just when I'd think the green country was past, we'd drop once more into a leafy lane and revel in the luxury of a shady ride. We rode away from the kind quarter horse farm people and on to Leonard, tying Smokey up next to a stall selling 'Snow Cones,' a favored cold drink made of crushed ice and chemicals. The portly owner of the store whose parking space we occupied came out to offer water for the horse. She was glad of a good long drink on that hot afternoon. Seeing he was a good natured sort of man, and feeling a bit cocky, I invited myself to stay.

"Don't fancy a visitor plus horse tonight do you Lou?" He didn't mind and I jotted down some directions.

Lou's little house was off our road about half a mile on one of those idyllic Texan country lanes, trees almost touching overhead. His was almost the last property, an old wooden house with a perfect pasture laid out below, an almost overgrown stream running through its center. But it wasn't the long grass, or the fat healthy horses, or the friendly people coming out to meet me, or the pretty view that caught my attention and held it, jaw hanging down. It was one of those amenities that I'd so often dreamt and fantasized about on those recent hot hot days. Lou had a POOL!!!

I sat in that pool a little later, my white skin turning blue with the cold, and loving it. Lou was there hanging against the side and a long snake like plastic thing weaving around cleaning the bottom. It was wonderful. I hadn't been so cold for ages, not since those early Georgia nights curled up in cramped agony at two or three in the morning, unable to stretch out from the miserable warmth my coat afforded me. It was a bad sort of cold then, but the sitting around in the deep clear blue water with Lou, I reveled in the luxury, saving the memory for the hot days ahead.

By Day 84, we were traveling through some of the most desirable ranch country in Texas. White fenced paddocks full of expensive shining horses, thoroughbreds mainly, lined the road across rolling plains. I felt a bit out of place on my stocky little mustang but wouldn't have swapped her for any of those high class horses. We rode into Aubrey and stopped with Pud and Billie Wilson, me sleeping in their little camper van next to Smokey in a field full of cows. Billie spoilt me with a breakfast in the morning before we pushed on out of Aubrey along the back roads towards Sanger. We were directly north of Dallas heading towards the next interstate crossing.

Clouds began to build up again, threatening another wet night ahead, so before I had the chance to be soaked in the first downpour I began to look about for a stop where I would be undercover. I thought I'd give a try to a small hobby farm a few feet away from the overpass across interstate 35. We'd go over when the traffic was quiet.

An old couple lived on the property. They were rather shy and nervous about agreeing to us stopping but could see the rain was about to start and let us stay. I could see they were worried so suggested I camp in the garage but little by little their confidence grew, and by the end of the evening we were quite good friends and I was offered the use of the sitting room floor. Being close to the busy motor way had bought them and their neighbors bad experiences from strangers knocking at their door, so to let me stay inside was quite a brave thing for them to do. I slept well while the rain beat against the windows, dreaming of Smokey tucked under the garage overhang out there in the rain.

By Day 87, the trees were becoming fewer, more and more stunted, the sharp spiky bushes of mesquite covering the red, stony, sweeping hills. Water was becoming hard to find and I knew it was going to get worse. I started limiting the amount of times Smokey could drink to encourage her to fill up when she could. Occasionally, I'd see a line of cattle walking single file, their route bendy and twisted around the thorny mesquite, heading to the watering holes. I'd watch them, follow their tracks, find water for the horse. For myself, I was carrying a two pint canteen, adding a tiny amount of Gator Aide powder to cover the taste of the water. Sometimes it was so sulphurous I'd need more of the orange powder to make it drinkable. But, hooked over the saddle horn in the sun, a black slimy coat of mold would spread quickly inside the plastic canteen, so the water would not only be warm and un-refreshing, but foul tasting too. Often I went thirsty rather than face drinking the poisonous stuff.

The next major problem after water, was shade. Without the trees to protect us from the burning sun during our 11.30 to 4.30 lunch break, there was no point in stopping. Our days were becoming very long; 5.30 a.m. until I could find a place to stay, maybe five, six, seven, eight in the evening. The temperatures were regularly around the 105,106,107 degree mark with the sun burning down, melting us in its unforgiving glare. My new Australian hat was black and very hot but the protection from the wide brim was essential. My Ray Ban sunglasses had been broken across the bridge so many times by hugging hosts good-bye and from being caught on the saddle horn when I mounted that I no longer dreamt of replacing them. With the chewing gum and tissue repair job, the sweat soaked into the paper and kept them in position on my nose. I couldn't have left them off. The stark pale glare of the burnt-out landscape would scorch my eyes with its intensity. Only in the earliest hours of morning and in the easy evening hours could I stand up straight and look around. Smokey didn't care for the heat. Her face was almost completely free of hair because of it's strength. Fortunately her skin was black so she didn't burn, and if I could, I'd wash her off at her watering spots, morning, noon and night.

To me, the heat was just another challenge. I'd wear loose clothes; an old pair of cotton trousers made in India that had become so fine I had to be careful when lifting a leg to climb into the saddle. The bum was paper thin! A long sleeve shirt hung down over the pouch and knife around my waist, allowing the sweat to run freely down my back and make if s tickly path down my front. It was no use going "Oh bloody hell, it's flipping hot". It would just make everything worse trying to fight that sort of discomfort. I just absorbed it calmly, letting the sun feed my bones through flimsy clothes and thought about other things. Mind you, I was very glad of a cloudy day! Even to watch the progress of a fluffy white cloud across the uniform blue sky was a thrill. I'd wonder whether, for a few seconds, the sun would be hidden away behind its gentle changing shape or would the poor little cloud be another victim to its heartless glare and have evaporated before it had the chance. I'd think about a lot of things like that. Firstly, to distract myself from the heat, and secondly, to avoid thinking about the shimmering road disappearing way off into the distance through mile after mile of house-free landscape.

We made it through Decatur on day 87, taking the 1810 on the west side which looked like a quiet road from the map but was dangerously narrow and bendy with the constant roar of gravel trucks bearing down on us from each direction. After a couple of miles the quiet of a pasture to our left was very attractive and I was given permission by Ben Muir for its use. Ben was a strange sort of man, late middle aged, rather stiff and a bit unfriendly I thought, but my first impressions were shown to be completely false when he came over to where I was unsaddling Smokey a few minutes later, and offered me the use of the dance studio alongside rather than set up my tent. His wife, Dixie, had been unwell so I never met her, but grey-haired Ben on his quiet and very un-Texan way, made my stay that night one of my most memorable.

Staying in a dance studio was a first for me. A big square room, half surrounded by full length mirrors, posters on the other two walls advertising makes of shoes or a performance long gone. Somebody had left a towel draped over the piano in the corner. There was a little reception room and a small bathroom, air conditioning and a tape player. The water smelt awfully of bad eggs. The studio, normally full of the banging piano keys, children's voices, parents picking up, women trying to lose a bit of weight or gain a bit of poise, was empty and dead quiet tonight.

While there was still light to see I sat on the doorstep drinking a warm beer I'd been carrying for a couple of days and watching Smokey. Once her white body had become a ghostly blur in the shadows, I went inside and locked the door. I hadn't seen myself, full length, in a mirror for ages. It was fascinating. I made a little bed of cushions from the chairs in the reception room, spread my coat over the top, watching myself in the mirrors as I walked across the room. It was so quiet. I practiced a few exercises at the bar, laughing at my lack of balance and clumsiness, my chuckling sounding loud in the hollow empty room. I was very thin; ribs poked out through my back as well as the front, each part of my back bone countable. Blue swollen veins ran down both sides of thin arms. My hands and face were brown despite using Factor 15 face cream every day, and everything else was a pasty white. My legs were strong, thin but very sinewy, my best feature. My hair, un-brushed for ages hung down my back in a congealed lump. I thought I looked alright! I sang and danced and talked to myself until late (that's nine o'clock to me!) Then I slept well on the crooked cushions.

Ben bought me out breakfast in the morning, and coffee, too, which I missed more than anything with the loss of the stove. Though it was still early when I mounted up, the gravel trucks were already thick on the road, heading to the gravel factory east of Chico. I turned and waved to Ben as I left. It was Wednesday, the 10th of August. Day 88 of our ride.

Smokey was completely flawless in traffic, not taking any notice of the noisy speeding trucks. Not many of them slowed or gave us extra room. From the maps I could see that Chico was on the eastern edge of a huge, sparsely populated area dotted with oil wells. It meant dry, hot, exposed cattle country. Names such as Wizard Wells, Runaway Bay, Lost Creek, Truce and Friendship, all gave me clues as to what to expect. We crossed bridges over dry river beds, with names like Big Sandy and Dry Hollow Creek, picking up an address for the night from a lady we met east of Chico. We pulled into her place mid-afternoon after a fifteen mile day.

The lady, Jeannie Palmer, lived to one side of a huge oil refinery a little south of the 1810 road we'd been traveling on all day. She had a tiny, scruffy, overgrown area fenced off where we put Smokey, and a cafe-store which she ran with the help of her big, strong friend, Tom. Jeannie was a short woman in her late fifties with a little American Indian blood giving her heavily lined face a graceful appeal. She had long, thick, straight hair, once black, now almost completely grey. I liked her immediately. While Tom sharpened my knives, Jeannie cooked a wonderful hot meal, not allowing me to help, but ordering me to take full advantage of the fridge full of cold drinks. Both she and Tom lived in little camper vans in the garden, a very basic hosepipe shower rigged up behind a home-made partition. There were few supplies in the store part of Jeannie's place, she was tying everything up, trying to sell to be free to travel, follow up parts of her heritage and see the country. She loved my talks of life on the road with a horse, the problems and the pluses that the companionship of an animal will give you. Jeannie was an experienced horsewoman and had a dog, a blue-eyed stray Malamute she'd named Spirit Dog.

We talked until late. Tom made me a really comfortable bed on some packing foam on the floor of the store and I went to sleep with the stars shining down through the open door. The gentle breeze and the monotonous humming of the oil refinery sending me to sleep.

Haifa mile past Jeannie's place the 2127 cut off to the north, taking most of the traffic, leaving the 1810 much quieter and easier for me. We left Mise county crossing into Jack County early on, heading towards Jacksboro. We were finally west of the Fort Worth area to the south and in a few more days could officially announce ourselves as being in West Texas. Jacksboro would be where our westerly line became much more wriggly. I planned on swinging north to Seymour to avoid a long barren stretch between Throckmorton to Haskell, turn south to avoid an equally lonely looking stretch between Seymour and Dickens, the same sort of roundabout route to avoid a thirty-five mile stretch on 380, then hopefully we should arrive safely in the flat farming area around Lubbock right on the western side at the end of August.

It was now the eleventh, hot, with very few trees, a planned day of twenty miles would take us to Jacksboro. After eight, we passed a tiny little settlement of white houses, a church on the hill, no store or gas station, called Cuncliff. At one house I pulled Smokey in to ask a couple of guys standing around a pick-up talking if I could water the horse. The conversation must have been important they were completely uncurious about this stranger riding into their yard. I stood to one side, Smokey's nose in the bucket, me drinking a cold beer they'd given me while she filled up on the cool water.

When Smokey was finished, feeling I was intruding a bit, I mounted up and said thank you and good-bye. The two men lifted their beers in salute and carried on with their absorbing talk.

It wasn't very many yards before I realized I was enjoyably drunk. The effects of one beer on an empty stomach in the midday heat was to make the day suddenly all that more enjoyable. I slumped in the saddle, a silly grin on my flushed face while the burnt grass, mesquite bushes, and occasional tree became more and more like old friends. The rhythmic plodding of Smokey's worn-out shoes on the road set the tune for little ditties I made up as we ambled along.

"Here we are," *cli-clop, cli-clop* "riding along," *cli-clop, cli-clop" on* top of old Smokey," *cli-clop, cli-clop "singing* a song,"*c/z-clop* "could do with a pool," *cli-clop, cli-clop,*"could do with a drink," *cli-clop, cli-clop "Mm* a silly old fool," *cli-clop, cli-clop,* "and my face is all pink," cli-clop, cli-clop, cli-clop.

No comments from Smokey who often failed to appreciate the finer things in life.

I tried to find water again at Maryelta but the deserted houses had had the water cut off and none of the faucets gave so much a trickle. We headed on, a little behind schedule, towards Lost Creek and Jacksboro. We crossed over the dry river beds of Hell Creek and the Trinity West Fork, long flat concrete bridges, late in the afternoon, needing to push on before dark.

On the western bank of the second bridge, a flat bed pick up pulled over in front of us. It was one of the men we had met at Cundiff. On the pick up bed sat a huge barrel of cold water. Smokey could smell it. Buster, his wife Donna, and their two twin girls climbed out of the truck, Buster all apologies for being so unfriendly when I'd stopped by earlier. It didn't matter a bit I said, I was just glad of the water for the horse, and thanked him again for thinking of bringing out the barrel of water which Smokey was gratefully drinking. Donna had packed a carrier bag of goodies for me too; sodas, crisps, sandwiches. We all had another beer. After the third, Buster enthusiastically suggested taking Smokey and me back to stay with them for the night. By then,

I was relaxed and reluctant to move on, it was late now, too, that I was only too pleased to agree. Using the mobile phone Buster made arrangements for a friend to bring out the horse trailer, and a few minutes later it was parking in a lay-by a few yards behind us. Smokey loaded up easily and we all retraced our steps back to Cundiff.

The evening went by in the relaxed company of Buster and his family, Smokey in their pasture with two little ponies. Smokey's shoes were so poor now that Buster suggested I join them for the weekend, the farrier not being available until Sunday. The steel had worn so thin that I really couldn't have gone much further. I was grateful for the offer and gladly accepted.

I spent the night in the air-conditioned office, a cosy bed made up on the cool floor, country and western discs playing on the stereo. Waiting for the farrier meant two whole days off. What a lovely feeling!

The next day, being a Saturday and school holidays, Buster and Donna had planned to take the twin girls and their eleven or twelve year old son to a roller coaster theme park in Arlington near Fort Worth. I was invited too, and we all set off quite early for the hundred-odd mile drive southeast.

The day was, of course, gloriously sunny, the long drive passing easily by in the air-conditioned cab. We made it by lunch time, Buster kindly paying my entrance fee as well as the others. We were into the famed two hundred acre theme park, *Six Flags over Texas,* a park boasting the *Texas Giant,* voted the world's top roller coaster ride,.

The place was completely packed and the queues to the rides were often an hour or more long but with TV to watch in the line ups, and delicious frozen lemonade, it didn't seem to matter. We all started off on the easier rides with Donna and I opting out of the more scary ones like the 'Texas Cliff-hanger', where the cages drop like a falling elevator from many many storeys up. We'd sit at the tables laughing at the pale shaken faces walking away from the exit end of the ride, waiting for Buster and his two brave girls. They were no less pale than everyone else when they made their quiet shaky way back to where we waited.

Another ride we opted out of was the huge 'Flashback', a roller coaster ride that drops from a 125 feet tower and careers through three loops at speeds of up to fifty-five miles an hour and just when you think it's over, you relive the experience ~ this time, backwards! That was too much for Donna and me, but Buster and his son rode it, saying it was great. Donna stood down also on the 'Shock wave', a big double loop roller coaster which twists so steeply over water, you're sure your carriage will skip the rails and plunge you all to an ugly end. 'Roaring Rapids' was great though. Well landscaped white water ride with a huge drop in the final turn. Lots of everyone getting a refreshing dousing. There were plenty of food stands and souvenirs, shows, music and fun.

By the end of the afternoon, our courage had built up enough to try the breathtaking 'Texas Giant.' The line up to this ride was longer than all the others, each rider becoming more and more anxious the closer to the ride they became. Horror stories from people already broken by the experience were banded around in glorious exaggerated color to the novices nervously pacing in line. Three boys ahead of us, veterans of fifteen runs, warned us and gave advice on how to ride 'the Giant.' The only one I remember on the 143 foot climb to the clouds was, 'don't look down!'

For what seemed like ages, the seven cars crawled their way seemingly vertically up the wooden roller coaster, rattling its nerve-wracking path to the summit where Bugs Bunny held a wooden sign. I think it said, "Too late now, Folks!" or something like that. I had one of the twins beside me who'd gone worrying, quiet and pale. We both held onto the bar holding us in with white knuckled sweaty hands. Everyone around us was either talking in hushed whispers, or was dead quiet.

There was a pause then the first car was over the top, followed by the second pulling five others in speeding pursuit. Everyone began to scream! All those people boasting in the queue, or people who'd ridden the other rides with hands arogantly in the air now held desperately onto the metal bar, and screamed with fear and exhilaration. The vibrations of the cars as they reached 62 miles an hour over the wooden structure was tremendous. I had an instant headache after leaning my head against the head rest. For what seemed like an eternity, the seven car train sped by, twenty eight screaming passengers hurtling up, down, round the Texas Giant. Just when you'd think the ride must be ending, it sped it's way towards the next climb, allowing a few seconds of moderate speed as it slowed towards the peak. As the cars in front of us dropped away, the passengers screaming unrecognizably, my twin rider and I got to view the drop before us, the track disappearing away at an horrendous angle, into a dark corner or an impossible looking bend. We'd add our screams to the others! I was making all sorts of noise and laughing hysterically too -1 always laugh when I'm scared, and by the time we finally slowed and pulled into the blue roofed exit, tears were rolling down my flushed face and my voice was hoarse. As soon as it was over, everyone began to talk excitedly, exclaiming how good it was, how scary, about the bad bends and big drops, about how much they screamed and how much they loved it! It was really, really, brilliant!

I slept well that night, with the sound of Six Flags over Texas in my head and ringing in my ears.

For our second day, Buster had a party planned down by a nearby lake in the evening. For the hot hours of the day, I read, wrote, relaxed. Excited about the party, I washed my hair and put on a little make up. It was a bit of a wasted effort really, because within a few minutes of pulling into the woody, lakeside park, everyone was in the water, swimming and splashing around. Loads of people turned up later and a barbecue was laid on. Big coolers full of beer quickly disappeared as the sun went down, all the drunken guys flirting like mad with me. I probably encouraged them a bit!

Buster had to be back quite early so Donna drove us home for a fairly early night, all of us a bit sloshed and glad of a comfortable bed. The horse-shoer would be here in the morning and then if d be time, yet again, head back down the road. With our two days of with the Moody family, I felt I'd had a real holiday from the trip, making getting back in the saddle that much more enjoyable. I'd met some really kind, though often pretty earthy, people like Buster and had a couple of addresses tucked away for use further west.

By the end of Day 92 we were halfway across Texas.

Day 93 was our longest so far, twenty four miles over eleven hours, a slow steady pace broken by short rests and made possible by the flat landscape and the cool cloudy day. The temperatures fell down into the low nineties giving a welcome respite from the pitiless heat of the previous few days. Apparently Texas was having an unusually cool summer.

We stopped the night with Jo and Stormy Echois on the outskirts of Megargel. A comfortable bed, good food and the welcome company of the friendly couple made for a good nights stop after such a long day.

We were definitely in West Texas now, the country we'd been warned about, given advice, encouragement, discouragement about. John Wayne country. Long sweeping grand vistas of dry sandy and rocky ranch land, the tallest thing being me and Smokey and the occasional thorny mesquite, now and again, a creaking, rusty, old windmill. I'd ride Smokey up the gradual inclines of these grand hills to stare amazed from the crest along the long rolling road heading west and to eternity. For as far as the eye could see the barren land stretched, if s wealth deep under ground, until like a tiny long legged bug on the horizon, a painted white or striped water tower indicated a settlement or small town. When I first saw the tower it meant a twelve mile ride. If I could define the legs, it meant five. If I could read the name of the town painted on its swollen side, it meant we were there and the day's ride was over. Ten to twelve days of this town hopping should see us at the fertile flat lands around Lubbock.

Day 94. We stopped early in the afternoon for water at the property of John Herman Harr and his wife, Marjorie, and ended up staying for the night. Their old ranch house was at the top of one of those long, dry, climbs with a view to the west of Seymour in the very far distance. It was another lucky night for me and for Smokey. The pasture hadn't been grazed for a long while, John retiring from farming some time back. The tough wiry grass, the only sort survivable in the tough climate, looked un-appetizing but was very high in protein and Smokey seemed to like it. I spent the afternoon around John's son David's lovely cold pool drinking lots of lovely cold beer! Certainly a much more recommendable way of spending those long, hot, hours.

There was a big family dinner in the evening, Marjorie going to all sorts of special efforts to provide a wonderful feast. They were a lovely older couple, and their family too, making me feel relaxed and welcome in their ranch house on the hill. Clean sheets and a comfortable bed made up the end to another perfect evening in Texas.

We were stopped by the Seymour newspaper reporters as we passed through the town the following morning, delaying us on the side of the road for a little while as I told our story. We rode right through the center of the town, Smokey drawing plenty of attention from shoppers, ranch people and oil men. I could now take her anywhere, never having to worry that she'd fool about. Even at the traffic lights at major junctions, she'd stand stock still, one back foot resting, waiting for the familiar words 'Walk on, Smokey.[1]

Seymour was the limit to our northern trek. To avoid sparsely populated country further west we were swinging down southwest to take advantage of the more regularly spaced towns. It was a longer route, but not knowing the country, safer I thought. We were now on busy Highway 277. The Walkman came to the aid as a distraction from thinking too much about the grey shimmering road disappearing off into the distance.

Just a mile or so on the 277 and a familiar old looking camper van pulled into a little rest area ahead. It was Jeannie Palmer from Chico. It was wonderful to see her. Knowing the priorities, she pulled out the cooler from the van, offering up its load of refreshing cold drinks. With Smokey unloaded and grazing on the short grass, we caught up on the news and Jeannie's revised plans.

While I knocked back can after can of cold soda, Jeannie told me about how over the past week she'd become obsessed with the idea of buying up a couple of cheap horses and joining Smokey and me for the remaining two thousand miles to the coast. I laughed, told her she was mad and then we went into detail about the possibilities. I thought Jeannie would make a good traveling partner. Though she was older, she was prepared to do things 'my way', because, after all, it was 'my trip.' She also had more money and a packhorse would maybe allow me to carry the much missed stove. Winter wasn't all that far around the corner and I had no idea where I could pack the cold weather gear on Smokey. Yes, it might work out with Jeannie. I agreed to her plans readily, but she still had land to sell and property too, horses and equipment to find. I thought it unlikely that she'd pull it all off. She stamped and addressed some postcards and I agreed to drop one in a box every few days so she would know where to find me.

With Smokey saddled up and on the road, we enthusiastically said good-bye full with excitement at, for me, the prospect of traveling with someone else, and for Jeannie, doing something that had long been an ambition.

All afternoon I thought about what the new trip would be like. Harder in some ways, easier in others. Safer, too, probably though I'd had no trouble so far. The third horse would be handy and Jeannie wanted to bring Spirit Dog, too. He might be good though it meant extra food to carry. Jeannie having more cash than me might be reassuring but I had become used to living on a twenty dollar a week budget and couldn't afford to keep up if she wanted to be more flashy. I was sure it meant more trouble in finding places to stay. Say good-bye to those clean sheets, hot meals, laundry done and generally being spoiled by kind people thinking I needed looking after. I didn't for more than a fraction of a moment believe Jeannie would get it together, but the thought of it kept me entertained for the rest of the day.

John Hermann Farr had kindly arranged for Smokey and me to stay with a friend of his, Billie Jean Young, at the end of a seventeen mile day. At about the sixteen mile marker, a horse trailer pulled over with a very glamorous and excited young woman running back and asking permission to ride with me a little ways.

"I'm almost where I'm heading." I told her, but she didn't mind for how brief a time it would be and unloaded her impressive bay horse from the trailer. The jolly and attractive young lady had heard about me from somewhere and had had her husband drive her out to find us. We chatted like old friends for the short distance to Billie Jean's. The lady's name was Annette and her husband and son took care of the trailer. Billie Jean was one of those ladies that inspire you to live life fully. She had so much contagious energy, was continuously laughing, always busy. It was hard to believe that her life had ever been struck by bitter tragedy, but Billie Jean lived alone, her husband having been killed by a fall from a horse, and her daughter was also fatally injured after slipping on ice. It was amazing the courage this woman had.

All three of us women stood around the door to the house, laughing and telling stories, Smokey tied to the basketball post. Billie Jean and Annette were near neighbors and knew each other slightly. Everyone knew Billie Jean, she was that sort of lady.

Just as Annette was thinking of leaving, her husband patiently waiting to one side with their loaded trailer, her eight or nine year old son came over, throwing a rubber snake at our feet.

"Ahh!" the two women screamed, jumping back in alarm.

"Lunch!" I said and we all fell about laughing.

Billie Jean took me with her to singing practice in Seymour that night, where she played the piano. I sat, tapping my hand on my knee, grinning along to the lovely songs the all male (apart from Billie Jean) group worked on. They had a very particular style, a bit like a cross between barber shop and old country, I wasn't really sure, but they were always in demand for weddings or parties. They even had made a tape but no one had a copy.

It was late when we drove home. The threatening clouds of the afternoon were now hurtling across a sky illuminated continuously by forked lightening. The wind was tremendous, beating the car from side to side, the two spread-out beams of light from the vehicle seemed feeble and insipid compared to the strength of the savage storm. On the brief moments there was no lightening, green spots danced in front of my eyes and everything seemed dangerously black. We raced home against the imminent rain.

I worried about Smokey during the night. Over the sound of the howling wind I would occasionally hear the plaintive whinny of scared horses calling to each other, then the sound would be lost as the screaming air strengthened. The rain beat down with bitter fury wiping away any thoughts of going out to check on her. In the comfort of the warm bed in Billie Jean's spare room, I shrank lower in the sheets and kept my fingers crossed. I am ashamed to say I slept rather well in Billie Jean's spare room despite the gale raging outside and Smokey out there in the middle of it. The morning shone clear, the sun coming through the open curtains and the smell of breakfast drifting in from the kitchen. I checked on Smokey and fed her, saddling up after breakfast and said good-bye to my new friend, Billie Jean Young.

Out of the driveway and back onto the long straight 277. The normally busy main road was almost traffic free. All along the route electricity pylons and telegraph poles lay in fallen chaos. Company workers had been working through the storm to try and clear the road and re-supply the community with power. One big eighteen wheeler truck had been pinned by a fallen pylon, trapping the terrified driver for hours before help could free him. Cables lay in untidy tortured twists and loops on the side of the road, Smokey and I giving them a wide berth. Last night, we had been hit by the outer edge of a tornado.

This part of Texas, a whole band spreading through the central time zone area was known as Tornado Alley.' From that day, Day 97 of the ride, after witnessing what even the outer edge of a tornado would do I never took the thought of being struck by one too lightly. Always on the exposed stretches with cloud and wind building, I'd mentally note the nearest deep ditch or sheltering bridge.

By the time we made it through Monday, seventeen miles from last night's stop, it was obvious we weren't going to make it to the planned address. Just into the city limits, we were stopped by some friendly locals and the local newspaper. With an invitation to dine at Dairy Queen that night and the reporter offering to find out whether we could stay at the veterinary clinic on the western edge of town, it didn't seem like a town to miss!

The lady vet was just leaving when we pulled in. Already the sun was low, giving the red bricks of the town a warming homey feel. The clinic was brick too, with the outbuildings behind housing recuperating animals and with a big surgery on the left. We put Smokey in a pen between other horses, all victims of panic during last nights storm. Severe cuts and swellings almost completely covered the legs of one once handsome horse. I knew Smokey would never do something so stupid. All those high dollar, high bred quarter horses didnt possess half the amount of basic good common sense that came naturally to my little white Spanish Mustang mare. I thanked, whomever it was, for sending me Smokey.

I had a Togo* at Dairy Queen; a sort of sausage on a stick dropped in batter and deep fried. Loads of tomato ketchup! It was followed with a whipped up white ice-cream full of butterscotch bits. Very delicious and fattening. I was treated as quite a celebrity by my kind host and the staff working in the restaurant, rather embarrassingly asked for autographs! Bit of an ego boost really! With my drawing ability as an illustrator, I was able to do a little sketch of Smokey and me, so that in years to come (probably months) they didn't pick up the signature and say, "Who the hell's Emma Crosby?"

Smokey was a little put out at being in a pen after the spacious freedom of the last few days, especially as on one side a small herd of goats was huddled along the fence line. After checking on her, giving her the usual 'night-night' routine, I made up a bed on the cement floor of the operating room, a young cat for company one side and the ghostly silhouettes of ominous looking apparatus on the other. The smell of antiseptic and bleach was a bit overpowering, and I had to take the first allergy pill in ages because of the cat, but I remember sleeping well on that hard cold floor.

We left early in the morning, traveling along the 222 in a straight unbroken line, a dip to the south with the Jarvis oil field on our right, then westerly again towards Knox City. It was another very hot day with the hot air rising off the road being almost suffocating. To each side of us there were the nodding derrick heads pumping the rich oil to the tanks alongside the fields. Knox City Oil Field, Hackathorn, Jek, Goree, O'Brien, Juliana Oil Fields, the land divided into one mile squares, a section, edged by a dusty dirt road.

We stuck with the 222 as far as Knox City then turned southwest along route 6 as far as O'Brien. There were more crops here than we'd been accustomed to recently, mostly peanuts, replacing for a brief while the dry ranch lands.

Just on the outskirts of the tiny settlement of O'Brien, a battered old camper van (not Jeannie's!) pulled over and I could see a rather scruffy middle aged woman in the nearside mirror waiting on the drivers seat for us to catch up. When we pulled up level, she climbed out the cab and introduced herself as Viola Hurt. She was a friendly woman, a little tatty, and overweight, dark hair pulled back in a tail but with a big friendly smile on her face.

"You look completely exhausted," she told me and automatically my shoulders slumped and I felt ten years older. There was another four and a half miles to the next address given me by John Herman Farr at Rochester, but she convinced me I was on my last legs and offered a couple of nights to recuperate at her little hobby farm only a couple of miles away. I ummed and arr-ed about it being out of the way but she answered all my resistance with the offer of a friend's trailer to take us there, clean clothes, hot shower, good food and a generally lazy day off. I folded. Viola drove up to the store to use the phone and with everything set up for the trailer, I sat on the wooden porch treating my parched self to a cold soda Viola had bought for me.

Before many minutes, her friend, Robert Berryman, pulled up with a large stock trailer used for hauling pigs. Smokey was rather reluctant to climb into the back with the smell of the animals still heavy in the air, but finally did, knowing after all that it was easier than walking.

Robert drove ahead and Viola and I followed in the old van with a little Jack Russell puppy lavishing attention on both of us in the front seat.

We drove the two or three miles to Robert's amazing collection of buildings, housing all sorts of animals in a sort of half-wild chaos. Trees growing everywhere untouched, the house and buildings built around them. Robert even had the silver barked trees growing right up through the floors of the house and out the roof!

As we unloaded Smokey, she caught the saddle horn on a piece of string tied from one side of the trailer to the other and she panicked a bit at this unseen restriction when she was already half way out of the trailer. In a fraction of a second the string broke but one of Smokey's back legs had caught on the trailer door and she was holding it in the air in pain. Everything's over, I thought. A nasty scrape down the near back leg began to bleed and she was reluctant for some time to even try putting the leg on the ground. Accidents happen so quickly and can be disastrous. I felt the sore part over and there seemed to be no major damage to the muscle or bone. I breathed again. Finally Smokey made a tentative few steps *cli-clop* towards the pen where she was to spend the night. Robert very kindly said she could stay as long as the leg took to heal.

With rather a sunken heart and a grim expression on my face, I followed Viola to the trailer she shared with her husband and daughter in a clearing in the woods, on Robert's property. The big open plan room was full of comfortable chairs and cushions, horsey prints on the wall and dog hair in the corners, washing piled up around the kitchen. It was a very sort of lived in place. The huge TV had me instantly glued and with Viola's insistence that I just put my feet up and relax, I was given a free rein to watch, goggle-eyed, film after film. Misty, Viola's daughter, joined me later; an energetic beautiful big teenager with a very confident and loveable character. With John back shortly after Misty, the family was complete and not for one second was I made to feel less than an honored guest.

We all went up to check on Smokey later, and between us agreed to give her the following day off to be on the safe side. I think she had strained a muscle in her hip so doused her with some of the DMSO I still carried and we let her out to join Robert's horses in the big pasture. I was very happy to be spending another day with Viola and her family. They were the sort of people who made you feel as if you'd known them for a long time. Very easy company.

Misty gave up her bed for me, using the excuse of being able to watch TV all night if she took the couch. Viola cooked chicken and potatoes and the evening went quickly by.

Robert was trying to build a new pond behind his house, to fish from, I think. When I was there he'd been having problems with the water seeping away, so much of the day was spent sitting around the almost empty hole eating ice cold water melons and watching the water level rise. Smokey seemed perfectly happy and well now, running around with Robert's horses, then hiding in the trees in the big woody pasture. Pigs, goats, hens, peacocks, dogs, all sorts of birds and unusual animals pecked or scratched away in the dust around Robert's house which, between him and his wife, Dorothy, they'd built from scratch.

John, Viola's very quiet and gentle mannered husband, drove me around to view the area for an afternoon treat. The country was mostly farming, peanuts mostly, with huge half-mile-long irrigating arms keeping the crops watered in the hot Texan summer. There were an awful lot of water melons for sale! This fertile strip was very narrow though, away to the west we could see more of those windswept dusty plains.

I had breakfast with Robert and Dorothy on the Sunday morning, the day Smokey and I were to ride out. What a shame it was to leave that happy sheltered little corner of Texas behind, but there were many more miles of that grand state yet to cross and we needed to make it over the ominous Rockies before winter.

It was Day 99 of our ride. With the day off at Viola's, Smokey and I both felt rested and eager for more. Her leg was fine now, already hair growing over the scrape. She really was a very self sufficient little animal.

We followed the dirt road away, enjoying the soft cushioning dust and the shade from the small trees. For most of the day we ambled along from side to side planning only to make it to Rule, a distance of twelve miles. Away to the west I could see the beginning of the long barren stretch that would last almost as far as Lubbock, a good hundred miles. This would be our last day before knuckling down to the tough stuff.

A guy in his late forties or early fifties stopped me shortly after we made it to tarmacked Farm Road 617. We had a beer each sitting on the bonnet of his car and he offered a place to stay for the night. I thought he might be a bit dodgy but he met us as we came into town, too, and it seemed a bit rude to refuse. He'd already arranged for Smokey to stay in a little pasture belonging to his sister living a quarter of a mile down the road, and his wife seemed kind and friendly so I was glad to be shown wrong.

Lloyd and his wife Leah, lived in a little old wooden house, almost the last in town. The interior was very old fashioned with wonderful wood paneling from floor to ceiling, old furniture and a tiny little kitchen. They had two dogs, one a short haired Pointer cross and the other a Chow. I could never understand why these thick coated dogs were so popular in a climate which is torture for them. We looked at photos and talked about families, then just about dark, piled into the pickup to go to the drive-in movies. For a few bucks we drove onto a grassy patch in front of a large flat, patchy concrete screen, parking between two sound boxes. The film was The Cowboy Way' which I'd wanted to see, but the quality of the sound was a little scratchy and muffled and Lloyd and Leah were having some sort of simmering scrap going on. He kept leaving and heading off to the popcorn place while I sat in the car half being able to understand the movie and half sympathizing about what a poor lot men can be. The couple next to me didn't see much of the film either but for a completely different reason! I think the whole place was a bit of a spot for the guys to take their girlfriends to see how far they'd go. I had a great time but I don't think my hosts did.

With a long day ahead I went to sleep early, in the luxury of the spare room in the little old house. I was sorry that my hosts didn't seem to like each other very much anymore, but my stay with them was still very enjoyable and memorable. That was Rule. Rule, Texas.

The main Highway 380 ran through Rule and we followed it in the morning with the early sun already beating on my back and Smokey's rump. There were road works for many miles, an unfinished new lane fenced off allowing Smokey and me the luxury of a traffic free patch on busy stretch of road. For as far as the eye could see the arrow straight ribbon of black headed westwards, shimmering from heat by 9 o'clock in a landscape of bleached sand and rock. Oil fields to our right and left, dirt roads going off into the scrub.

We took a rest from the sun at a deserted looking village called Old Glory. A post office, a church, a factory-like building but very little activity. I sat under a tree and dozed while Smokey grazed then dozed too. At the first sign of the sun waning, I saddled up again and we followed the 380 further. I thought we might make it to Aspermont by the day's end but after seventeen miles, with our long noontime break and Smokey's slow pace, the sun was already low with six miles to go. A collection of buildings on our left, some of them barns and corrals, a donkey in one, seemed like a good place to try and I turned Smokey up the driveway.

No horses lived there anymore, but it had once been home to many. Now a doctor owned the place and the only equine was his little donkey. He amiably agreed to putting Smokey in with her for the night. We'd seen a few donkeys on route; they were often used to protect herds of goats from coyotes, being defensive animals, but Smokey had never cared for them too much. Now she was in such close proximity to one she seemed quite happy to share the hay we threw out to them.

I spent the evening sitting around the kitchen table with the doctor whose wife was away for the week hence the big pile of plates in the sink. I opted for a night in the tent for an early start in the morning. It was the first time I'd slept in my little green castle since those first few Texas miles and it felt curiously luxurious to be independent again. I went to bed when it became too dark to see, my naked body sticking horribly to the plastic mattress with the heat of the night. It was the end of our hundredth day on the road.

For three days we stuck with the 380, passing through Aspermont, a night in Swenson with a preacher and his family, over the *Brazos de Dios,* a series of rivers named "Arms of God" by thirsty Mexican adventurers crossing this desolate area, and on to Jayton. We'd been on the radio that day and I'd been listening at the time. What a shock it was to hear the lady news reader going on about Crosby did this, Crosby did that! I had a good chuckle when I heard it. By the time we entered the city limits of the tiny town of Jayton, we were quite celebrities - we were even invited to stay the night with the Mayor!

It took nearly an hour to travel down the three quarter mile long high street. Everyone wanted to know in more details what they'd heard about or read in the Aspermont or Abalone papers. I would answer one set of questions, move on a few yards, the answer the same ones all over again to another friendly group. I had a multitude of offers of places to stay and was in little dust-covered, hungry, thirsty travelers heaven. Even the lady at the checkout where I went to buy a drink knew who I was ~ it was impossible to be anonymous, I guess, with a big white horse clue tied to the lamppost.

The lovely old mayor, Ray Smith, met us at the end of the high street and led us to his little white house where Smokey had the run of the backyard. His wife, Kathryn, everyone's idea of the perfect grandmother figure, fussing over my laundry, putting clean sheets on the spare room bed, cooking 'something special' for her appreciative guest. They had to pop out for a long standing engagement in the evening but came back to find me sitting outside with a neighbor looking over the photos he'd taken of his trip to England.

"Isn't it green?" I kept saying.

The Smith's grandson, Michael, came round for an hour in the evening and taught me how to lasso a bucket, much harder than it looks. He was an eighteen year old, very handsome young man with plans of joining the police academy in Levelland in a few weeks time. We all sat round, half watching 'Wheel of Fortune' on TV. Ray told me about Jayton's claim to fame as being the 'Town Where the Elephant Died.' There had been a traveling circus visiting the town with the unfortunate animal being fed moldy old hay, making him collicy and dying. As the mayor, Ray had to arrange for the safe disposal of the huge beast, nobody having much experience in the field of dead elephants. Eventually, a big excavating machine dug a large hole for a grave. The two tusks were removed, the mayor being the lucky recipient of one, the sad owner keeping the other. The elephant was buried.

The police were called out in a couple of days later after reports of strange noises and lights being seen around the freshly covered hole, catching a couple of school kids excavating the carcass, hoping to score a few points by supplying the school with a full sized elephant skeleton. The fire ants were pretty wicked in Texas but not lethal enough to clean the bones in two short days!

Ray also told me the surprising news that there was another lady traveling coast to coast only a few days ahead of me! What a shocker to hear I wasn't the only batty female out in the Texas summer heat. Apparently she was traveling in a home-made wagon pulled by three mismatched horses, the slogan 'Pulling for Christ' in red paint on the white canvas sides. I was quite curious to see what she was like, but she sounded like a bit of a religious crank so maybe it would be better to stay clear. This unusual sounding outfit was traveling along the main westerly route 380, which we were just about to leave for a while, so in a few days she'd be well ahead of Smokey and me.

The 25th of August, Day 103, ended up being a very brief eight miles. Smokey had a bit of a sore back from sweating under the saddle so I was back on the ground full time. It wasn't long before I had a juicy looking blister on my heel.

We stopped for water at the 4-Play Ranch and ended up staying the night, getting pretty sloshed on lovely ice cold beer with Mike and Cynthia Jones. I finally made my rather wobbly way to the spare room bed, having to sleep with one eye open to stop the room from spinning out of control.

We were again heading north to avoid a long dry stretch between Post and Clairmont, aiming for an address in Spur given to me by John Hermann Fair. It was also our next post pick up point.

We pulled into town after a fifteen mile day, the buildings casting long shadows from the late afternoon sun. The post office was set back from the road, with a green lawn, over which hung the Stars and Stripes unmoving in the still hot air. There were letters from home, another from Pat, one from Jeannie. I put them away to enjoy later. As I untied Smokey from the spindly young tree, a voice from across the road called out,

"Hey, d'ya need some oats?" I looked towards the feed store on the other side of the road.

"Sure, that'd be great!" We crossed the road as the store owner slit the neck of a fifty pound bag. Smokey saw the spilling oats and walked right up the feed store steps and into the store! There was nothing I could do to pull her big white head out of the sweet smelling feed, apologizing red-faced to the owner and staff who were rolling around laughing. As luck would have it the newspaper people arrived just at that moment and the store owner earned himself a wonderful promotional article with a front page photo of the staff and me surrounding the little white coast to coast horse, crushed oats falling out of each side of her mouth in the feed store door.

William Ball, the generous owner of the store refused my offer of payment for saddle sore ointment, vitamins and minerals and the oats, quite a few dollars worth. I hope the publicity from the Spur paper compensated a little for his kindness, the story certainly spread enough.

I spent the night at Jill and Neilan Hensley's house on West Harris Street. Unfortunately, but fortunately really, the family had to go to a football game that night which I opted out from because of the late finish. Though I missed the opportunity of a night spent in their friendly company, I was glad just to be alone, relax, watch a bit of TV and raid the freezer! The letters I received that day were answered sitting in the back yard with their old Chihuahua hobbling around on inch long toe nails; the sound of Smokey flirting with a look-a-like horse across the fence.

Day 105 was the last complete day on those dramatic sweeps of arid sand ranch land, the smell of sage in the morning as strong as the intoxicating perfume of honeysuckle in Georgia. As we left Crosby county the next morning, way over in the distance, I could see across the horizon a range of flat-topped high land, marked on the map as the Cap Rock Escarpment, the eastern boundary of the vast *Llano Estacado* or Staked Plains, and the end of the West Texas tough stuff. The town of Post nestled at it's base. I had another address given to me by John to try here and I rang up from the gas station halfway up the historic main street. Delores Redman jumped in her car and drove out to meet us.

Thinking I looked exhausted (why did people keep saying that?) she gave directions to the property, sped home and sent her husband, Jimmy out to pick us up in the horse trailer. They lived not more than a hundred yards away.

I spent two nights with this lovely couple; glamorous wife and rugged cowboy husband. Jimmy spent most of his time with me, sorting out a new system for carrying feed, changing weight distribution on the saddle, altering pads and seeking advice from experienced packers. Smokey was wormed and dwindled stocks were replenished in the saddle bags. Delores took me to Lubbock where I bought a small tape recorder to make keeping notes easier though it blew my budget for over a week, and generally I was fed, cleaned, rested and spoiled, being sent on my way on the 30th August feeling healthier and better prepared. Also, Post was quite a marker on the map for me. We were about to make the climb onto the fertile farming lands of the Cap Rock, the 'impossible' west Texas dust bowl behind, and August nearly done. I felt that soon the intense summer heat would ease into warm autumn days and many of my problems would fade with it. I didn't realize then that I wouldn't witness any cooler weather until almost overnight we were in the ice of the Rocky Mountains many weeks later.

The ascent up the side of the escarpment and onto the farming lands of the

Cap Rock was not nearly as difficult as it looked on the map, only a steep climb for under a mile and we were seemingly back in the flat lands of the Mississippi Delta. Fields upon fields of cotton with hardly a tree or building to break the dead straight line of the horizon. We stuck to the back roads, enjoying the soft dusty track, the quiet of almost non-existent traffic and the easy green of the irrigated fields. With addresses to cover us for the next three nights the pressure was off and life was grand.

The first of these addresses was an exotic bird farm at Hackberry. Ostrich, Emus, Kiwis. The 'in' stock to farm, the birds producing almost cholesterol-free meat. A breeding pair of ostriches cost a small fortune at thirty to thirty-five thousand dollars. Smokey spent the night in a pen next to a huge male ostrich and was not unreasonably petrified. We'd seen quite a few along the way but she'd never become used to the sight of their long ugly necks and heavily feathered bodies on spindly long legs. We always went past them at double double speed. She'd never seen one quite so close as on Day 108. I fed her grain in the folding blue bucket but it was quite a while before she found the courage to relax her concentrated stare at the ominous bird and drop her head to take a mouthful. Normally she chewed her feed slowly with her nose a few inches above the rim of the bucket, her eyes closing in sleepy satisfaction. That night she grabbed a mouthful bolting down the food with her big black eyes intent on the fluffy ostrich on the other side of the fence. She didn't try to run, hide or jump the wire but her four feet were braced firmly on the ground. Only once did she lift a hind foot to give a hearty kick to the family Shetland pony that was trying to attract her attention. The force of that kick sent the poor little guy like a bowling ball, rolling in the dust.

When I went to load Smokey up in the morning after a comfortable night with the McGeettee family, my little grey mare was still standing, rooted to the same spot, though the Shetland was at the furthest possible extremity of the tiny pen. I don't think she'd had much of a rest.

The poor old thing had the same sort of trial the following night when housed next to a pen of sheep, another new and unwelcome experience for Smokey. The day had been spent on more of the luxurious flat soft dirt roads. Plodding along without a worry, country and western music coming out of Lubbock across a clear blue sky. We found an abandoned little house with the porch shaded by a scruffy tree for a few hour's break over the midday hours, aiming for the property of David Wied in Wilson late afternoon.

A mile out of town, with storm clouds overtaking us from the east, Walter, an older friend of the Wied family drove out to guide us, like a south coast tug, into Wilson. All sorts of relations and neighbors were out to meet their unlikely guest, made famous by a front page article in the Post paper. (We were almost always front page!) Smokey was very upset at being housed next to the sheep, quite a rare animal in Texas that time of year, but the pen was well fenced, I was tired, so she had to lump it. David took me to the house of Carolyn Klaus, a lively, funny, middle-aged lady living on one of the main streets of the little town. There was quite a party of people there, too, and I had to put on my entertainment hat and amuse them with stories of our adventurous life and England until late. It was lots of fun, mainly because my audience was so appreciative, sitting open mouthed at the scary bits and laughing hysterically in all the right places. It was such a success that Carolyn arranged for me to give a talk to the school in the morning which served me right for being so cocky.

I hardly slept a wink trying to work out what I was going to say the following day. I found it easy to talk to a small group, especially about Smokey, but the idea of facing a whole class of rowdy kids filled me with horror. By the time the morning came round I knew I was about to blow my Mr. Cool image and make a complete idiot of myself.

Carolyn took me to where Smokey had spent the night. She looked a bit huffy and a shade worn but I think she'd worked through her fear of sheep. The local reporter met us as I saddled up, finishing an interview he'd begun when we arrived, everyone took lots of photos, and unable to delay much longer, I was mounted and heading to school. The day was overcast, threatening rain later, so good riding weather to come, if I only survived the next couple of hours. David drove slowly ahead to show me the way and met me with the head mistress as I dismounted outside the red brick buildings of the school on the manicured green lawn.

"Don't poop!" I whispered to Smokey.

I was led like the condemned through the network of school passageways, lined with pictures painted by young artists, bits of sculpture and montage. The muffled sounds of classes in progress and the creepy smell of school filled me with dread. They took me to a medium sized room where a single chair at one end faced rows upon rows of identical chairs at the other. Almost immediately the first group of youngsters were led in. The teacher introduced me to the class, and the class to me.

I chuckled and waved and felt very foolish.

"Hi! My name is Emma and I'm from England and I'm doing a coast to coast ride across America on the little white pony you may have seen outside."

I was off. I chatted away about the adventures, the horse, the laughs, the equipment, England, the Queen, Di, snakes, bears, rain, my tent, people I'd met, starvation rations. Loads of stuff, on and on. We then had a question and answer bit, my favorite question being, "Are all the castles in England made of sand?" I loved that one. After the questions we all trudged outside to see the real star of the show, Smokey standing quietly tied up to the flagpole. She turned her head to watch with those big black eyes, the noisy bunch of eight and nine year olds heading her way. The children were each given an opportunity of climbing up and sitting on the most famous horse for miles around. Smokey, usually quite intolerant, was a model of docility, with children touching her all over, pinching her nose and putting fingers in her mouth, yelling "Me! Me! Me!" when I asked who was next. I hoped my liability insurance wasn't full of holes. As I answered their excited questions, child after child climbed up, patted Smokey or held the saddle horn, then reluctantly dropped down the other side. The class held about forty five children! Poor old Smokey.

"Back to work! Back to work!" the teacher shouted and the noisy youngsters pulled themselves away, crying "Bye Smokey! We love you!" from across the lawn. I sighed with relief a I watched them go.

"Here comes the next group," the Headmistress said, and I turned to see the second lot heading my way. Smokey and I went through the same sort of ritual for three more groups.

It was early afternoon by the time we pulled out, with a slow drizzly rain falling from low, dark clouds. I was wearing a long sleeved T-shirt, a gift from the friendly school, *I love this place Wilson, Texas* written around galloping white horses on a blue background. One of the saddlebag pockets held a bunch of postcards to send from along the route so the students could plot my progress on a map on the wall. I had also been given a lovely twenty dollar bill by David to help me a little further along the way. He'd also replaced a rattlesnake tail, lost from my hat, victim of a young souvenir seeker! Despite the dread of the night before, the hours spent at the school and with the people who'd looked after us in Wilson, were some of the most enjoyable and memorable of the whole trip. It was quite a town.

We followed Highway 211 all day, heading towards New Home where we were to stay with John and Mary Bess Edwards, a couple with a huge reputation for hospitality and humor. I met them at the hardware store on the main street of the one street town. Everyone seemed to be hanging around inside, mainly drinking coffee, smoking, not buying anything but gossiping plenty. I tied Smokey to a post outside, a white horse in a line of white pick up trucks. Everyone gently teased me about my adventure and made me feel very at home.

John and Mary Bess were amazing. They took me to Lubbock to eat, did my laundry, fed my horse, gave me a warm bed and an evening of good company. I left in the morning after guiltily accepting a crisp fifty dollar bill from John, guilty because they'd already done so much. Some friends of theirs had also donated a twenty, just another example of the good, kind-hearted Texas nature. We'd been in Texas over six weeks with only four nights spent in the tent. I dreaded the thought of leaving the Lone Star state behind.

It was the 2nd September. Day 111 of our ride and heading towards the 1500 mile mark. We were halfway across the country. I decided to dig out the little tape recorder I'd bought in Lubbock and record the day for 'the folks back home'. It was much harder than it sounded; too much giggling, unfortunate gaps, loads of uummms, and the sound of your own voice is nothing like you believed it to be. I sounded like a silly giggly Australian girlie but it was a distraction from the heat an the long straight road.

Mary Bess caught up with me not long after we'd left Farm Road 1730 for the dirt tracks again heading west, and told me she'd obtained permission from some people in Ropesville to camp opposite their property. The religious lady with the coast to coast wagon was already there and wanted to meet me. I thanked Mary Bess and thought about avoiding Ropesville. I'd got to the point on the ride where there was nothing to worry about it, nothing to dread. I trusted my little horse almost 100 % and I was very contented with plodding along, Smokey and me, our own pace, our own company. To meet up with another outfit would change things and I had a rotten feeling, it wouldn't be for the good.

I thought about it all day as I recorded our progress, but with each step we came a little closer to Ropesville.

As we left the dirt road, picking up hard surfaced farm road 41, a car pulled over, a middle aged woman driving, a long-haired, heavily wrinkled man-woman in the passenger seat. I stopped Smokey and smiled down through the open window. The driver introduced herself as Delores Bevers, my host for the night, and her passenger was 'the lady with the wagon.' She cast a quick appreciative glance over Smokey and pointed across the fields where I was to go. I looked up to see a large canvas covered home-made wagon with 'Pulling for Jesus, Coast-to-Coast,' in painted red letters along the white canvas. A smaller trailer hung off the back, equally home-made, banners with passages from the Bible gently fluttered in the breeze along it's sides. 'Could be tricky,' I thought.

As Smokey and I came closer, I could pick out three mismatched horses and a young colt in the area opposite the Bevers' house. It was the grassy yard of the town's community hall. The animals were contained by a fragile electrified ribbon. To one side stood a covered pile of hay.

The 'Lady with the Wagon' came over to help me unload and began to fire traveler-to-traveler questions:

"How far have you come? Any lameness or sores? How many miles a day? Who does your shoeing? Any problems? What do you feed?"

I answered her questions as I undid the straps and buckles to Smokey's equipment, sliding the saddle and bags off her back and onto the hard sun-baked ground. I pointed out a couple of sores on Smokey's sweaty back.

"You've hit the 1500 mile mark and its impossible to get over it," barked this domineering, though obviously very experienced horse woman. "Let me help you," she added. That comment, being rather a negative general sweeping statement irked me some but I smiled at her.

"Sure," I said.

We put Smokey in with her gang of horses and watched for the inevitable getting to know you troubles. We talked more and I learned the lady's name, Finisia Medrano, a poet and story teller from Idaho, a veteran often years on the road. She admired my horse and congratulated me on her condition, marveled at Smokey's flawless feet and strong legs. She told me to do something, turn on the hosepipe or some other little chore. I turned and called her bossy and we both laughed. She was a strong minded woman but I was too. We liked each other for it.

The Beves family owned the property and piece of land the wagon was camped on, facing the community center, now home to five horses. Finisia and the wagon had been there several days already, killing time before she headed up to Lubbock to the annual cowboy Symposium held at the Civic Center in the middle of the city. The house was small and cramped, just room for Buddy, Delores, and their young daughter along with loads of still unpacked boxes from their previous house. They kindly offered to clear enough space on the study floor for a mattress for me. The invitation was welcome. Though it was obvious Finisia planned to keep me around for a while, I thanked the Bevers and predicted riding out the next day but one, which was a Sunday, hoping to find a farrier to shoe Smokey by then.

With everything settled with the kindly family, I sat out with Finisia around a cold camp fire, the sun dropping towards the flat western horizon. I'd laid my packs over the tongue of the wagon next to the heavy leather harnesses of Finisia's. We began to share stories of our adventures.

Finisia was about thirty seven years old though with the hardy outdoor life she'd been living, looked considerably older. Her thick brownish hair lay down her back in a heavy plait, her face rather ugly and mannish, wrinkled by weather, determination and humor. A dusty man's shirt stretched over her slightly over-weight body, broad shoulders and muscley arms leading down to thick fingered rough hands. She sat with her legs relaxed, dressed in handmade deer skin trousers, Indian beading in dramatic leather fringes down the outside seam. Hard wearing and hard working boots were set firmly in the dust. On her hip hung a long barrel loaded gun.

She told me of her travels, her conversion to Jesus, her reason for her way of life. For six years she'd walked, all over. She followed that with three years with a string of horses meandering around the country. The wagon was her latest acquisition. The trip started off in Idaho, had taken her to Florida where the young colt had been born out of her four year old paint mare, and now she was aiming for the coast around Los Angeles. The leg from Los Angeles back to Idaho was often thought about and longed for. She was homesick and a bit lonely. She asked me to travel with her for a while but I was reluctant to break with my comfortable routine and I dreaded to think what my parents would say if they found out I was traveling around the country with a completely eccentric American religious crank!

As the afternoon gave way to evening a sizeable crowd of locals, the Bevers family and friends and neighbors came to sit around the camp fire, sing play guitars, chat and listen to the fascinating poems and stories from Finisia, the Bag Lady, as she liked to be called. With the dramatic lighting from the crackling, burning logs, the wagon as a back drop and the occasional squeal from the penned horses, the stories of her childhood and travels held her audience fascinated. We were soon all addicted to the slightly over-weight, long haired, wild-eyed narrator pacing in front of the fire, arms waving in descriptive emphasis. Now and again she'd break out into the animal sounds of a native American song, which took a bit of getting used to, but we all clambered for more.

I finished the tape I'd begun that morning with a crackly recording of the camp fire songs around the soft guitars. I was pretty sure that something had ended, not just the tape, not just the day. Something else. And something new was about to begin.

I spent five days camped on the floor of Buddy and Delores' study, waiting for September 8th when Finisia and I would ride, together, to the Cowboy Symposium in Lubbock. The days were spent in learning the craft of Indian beadwork, shoeing Smokey (Fin did it herself, and what an ugly job it was!) more adjustments to tack and saddles, relaxing, visiting, reading, generally waiting around, enjoying the rest. Most of the evenings passed by around the big fire, playing guitars, singing, telling stories. It was very comfortable for me to be able to take a back seat to the Bag Lady, enjoying the freedom from the usual questions and the pressure to be Miss Entertainment. I phoned Dosher Cockerell in Louisiana and asked him to send my winter equipment, sat back and enjoyed the break.

Early in the morning of September 8th, day 117 of our adventure, I was saddling Smokey in a drizzly threatening grey mist. Finisia was busy hitching up her three mismatched horses and loading the home-made trailer with the five month old skewbald colt. Two young lads were to ride in the wagon that day, Clint and his buddy, and they were suffering the lashes of the Bag Lady's quick tongue if they did some strap up wrong or got in her way. As soon as they were ready, the loud sound of Finisia shouting 'Click' to her team alerted me they were off, followed by the rattling, banging, squeaking and creaking as the heavily loaded wagon and trailer pulled away from the Bevers' house and towards the highway. The two wagon dogs barked excitedly at the heels of the horses. I could hardly hold Smokey as I tried to climb into the saddle. She reared and tried to run, the bond already strong between her and the smallest of Finn's horses, Shortcake. Smokey didn't want to be left behind. Finally I was up and trotting through the puddles after the disappearing wagon. Fin was carrying the packs and feed sacks, so for the time at least, all Smokey had to carry was me. It was a lovely feeling to be so unencumbered.

We left Ropesville at a full ahead trot taking a right onto 82, heading north-east. Lubbock was twenty-two miles away. The rain set in for the day, falling continuously and heavily, running down my stockmen's coat and filling my boots. We kept just behind the wagon, Smokey trotting whenever she wanted but unused to the fast pace. I kept under the shelter of my Australian hat and coat, the hiss of the rain on the road, the sound of the wheels slicing through the puddles, Smokey's rhythm. Now and again I'd see a worried young lad's face peeking around the edge of the canvas to watch me a while as I rode through the rain. I sang a little:

" Do you want to get in the wagon?" Finisia shouted as I drew nearer the wagon one time. "No. I sort of like it like this!" I shouted back, heavy drops falling from my hat's brim. She laughed. She knew what it was like to cross Texas in August and what a pleasure a rainy day was. The two boys stared open mouthed, and, Finisia told me later, fell in love.

Delores had arranged for Finisia to give a talk to some children at a school in Lubbock so we headed straight there, covering an average of five miles an hour compared to Smokey's and mine of two and a half. We also missed out on our normal noon time break.

By the time we rode throughout the outskirts and on towards the downtown area of Lubbock, the sun was out and the streets were dry. I positioned Smokey behind the colt's trailer as we rattled and banged our way through the city traffic, over lights, through junctions, towards the school. The people in their cars and on the sidewalk stared in disbelief at the outrageous spectacle. I was glad to see the entrance to the school finally in sight, both Smokey and I were pretty puffed out! We hadn't done any trotting at all since crossing the bridge at Fitzgerald in Alabama, and that was over a thousand miles ago! And trotting is very hard work. It is said that if you trot and chew at the same time you are using every muscle in your body! As I slid out the saddle in the school car park, I believed it to be true.

I unsaddled Smokey in the shade while Finisia talked to various classes about her trip and why she was doing the coast to coast thing, about her religious thoughts, finishing with a poem or a story. The two lads and I enjoyed the peace after the stress of the ride through the busy streets, while four horses dozed in the sun.

"This lady's from England. She's come all the way from the Atlantic Ocean on her horse," I heard Finisia bellow out, and for a few minutes I talked to the class about what I was doing and about the Spanish Mustang I was riding, my voice feeble sounding next to the one beside me.

Several groups came out, all of them seeming to enjoy the few minutes out of lessons, then with thanks from the staff and pupils we prepared to leave.

"Click" Finisia yelled, and her noisy clattering and banging outfit made the turn around the car park and back onto the street of Lubbock. We weren't due to be at the symposium until the following day, so with the sun lowering in the afternoon sky Fin selected a piece of unused land at the edge of the highway for the night's camp spot. With a lurch and dangerous looking roll the wagon and trailer climbed up off the road and onto the grassy unfenced field surrounded on three sides by suburban modern housing. The electric fencing was strung and the horses turned out to graze. I was back in the tent for the first time in plain view of the road.

Visitors came and went until late, attracted by the slogan on the side of the wagon and the colorful horses peacefully munching down the city grass. Some sort of official from the city council came over with a complaint about the smell of the horses' poop, though the nearest house was few hundred feet away. He also asked to see some sort of proof that we were allowed to be there. Stuff like that made Fin really mad, one hand on a big hip, the other on the .47 magnum. She shooed him off the campsite in search of proof that we shouldn't be there. He never came back. Mostly people were just curious. Some came with food, some with donations of money for the horse feed. I spent most of the evening talking to an unhappy young man going through an ugly divorce and all afloat mentally. My advice was to find himself a horse, saddle up and head west!

It wasn't until nearly eleven o'clock that night that our last visitor left and Finisia went to her bed in the wagon, me to my unfamiliar little green tent and the two boys rolled up in their sleeping bags next to the wagon tongue loaded with saddle and harness.

The following day began early with the noise from the traffic building as the sky lightened. Finisia and I had arranged for a visit to a car tire place to renew two worn out front tires on the wagon in exchange for a bit of TV publicity. With the help of the two boys, she was ready about the same time I threw a stiff leg over Smokey's back and gingerly lowered myself into the saddle. I was very sore after yesterday's burst of activity.

With the flags flying, the banners waving, everything rattling, creaking, the colt in the back calling to his mother in the traces, we again, headed into the early traffic and westwards. We were at the tire shop as it opened. For over an hour Fin and Delores Bevers worked to synchronize TV reporters with new tires, Smokey and me standing in the shade eating chocolate covered raisins. Finally it was done; two new tires for Fin and a report on the evening news for the happy looking tire place owner.

"We put tires on anything," he told the reporter. I was interviewed too, but my story seemed a bit monotone compared to the Bag Lady's dramatic history.

"Oh, I'm just here on holiday, meeting the people, seeing the sights," I answered. I was quite contented to be a non-celebrity. With the newspaper people also taking a hurried interview, it was a pretty full morning, the wagon and Smokey and me not rejoining the city traffic until almost midday, the sun hot in the flawless Texas sky.

The wagon horses all behaved admirably in the heavy Lubbock traffic, setting a smart pace through the city though some people shouted abuse as they drove past for using up a whole lane in the road. Most people seemed to realize we were heading to the cowboy symposium and were tolerant, giving a wide berth to the unusual outfit. Smokey was flawless too, keeping up well, enjoying the company. With a couple of miles still to cover to the Civic Center, a police car pulled in behind Smokey as we waited at the traffic lights.

"Y'all going to the Symposium?" he grunted.

"Uh Huh," I replied, nodding, nervous smile.

He dropped in behind, blue lights flashing, keeping the traffic back. No more complaints from irritated drivers. I chuckled to myself, laughed at our new importance.

With Finisia's amazing sense of direction we took wrong turns and early afternoon pulled up onto the green lawns of the civic center, waving good-bye and thank you to the stern faced officer in the car.

There were already a load of restored wagons away to one side, hauled in by truck and trailer - no horses. There was to be a 'cook-off all over the weekend; an old cowboy-style cooking competition . Couldn't wait to try them out! Finisia selected a big area of the richest grass, turning the wagon to attract the maximum attention from the passing traffic. The electric fence was put up, the horses released, water fetched, then time to relax. Curious visitors immediately started coming over, attracted by the 'Pulling for Christ, Coast-to-coast' on the wagon. Some of them asked if we did pony rides! Fin went off in her hat and leathers to the square modern Civic Center buildings to find out where she was to do her story telling on the indoor stages, and I answered the visitors questions as best I could.

"Oh, I'm just along for the ride," was my standard response when asked about religious things, "Finisia will be back shortly."

Mostly I just waved people away from the electric fencing and if they took no notice, pass them a told-you-so smile as they leapt back with the kick from the charged ribbon. Some people even had the nerve to climb into the pen to pet the horses, the young colt with his striking brown and white markings was the usual goal.

"Wouldn't go in there, lady!" I'd shout. "Wouldn't want you to get hurt!" A pink faced exit.

Mostly the horses were quite gentle, though unaffectionate, but Shortcake, Smokey's new pal, could be mean spirited and the big black thoroughbred Finisia saved from the slaughter house didn't like to be petted.

Eventually Fin was back with free entry passes for both of us. TEmma Crosby, Coast-to-Coast[1] on mine. She'd also managed to wangle free meal passes and entry to the country and western dances. She had a way with people. With Fin back, I was free to spend a bit of time listening to the poets and storytellers in the cool of the hall and wander around the craft stalls; mostly cowboy paintings, books, leather work and home-made sweets. Some of the afternoon poetry was a bit second rate, pretty sentimental stuff about cowboys and old faithful dogs and the Texas countryside. They were mainly amateurs, somehow there by invitation. The evening's entertainment was much more professional.

Finisia was due to tell a couple of stories and a few poems late in the afternoon both days of the symposium, and another slot was for Mike Lamb from Ropesville, one of the campfire cowboys. He was very nervous, singing songs he'd written himself, and I felt bad for him when he forgot words, lines, notes. Finisia was very different. She woke the half-full hall with a powerful story from her childhood, both sad and funny. She didn't need to use the microphone. Between her slots on stage she traipsed around trying to sell some of her Indian beadwork. I asked her if she'd like to try and sell some of my feeble efforts too. With a big grin she met me later at the wagon, waving a twenty dollar bill. Apparently mine had been the first to go! Over the weekend she gave me much more than that twenty. Living in Fin's shadow I was no longer receiving any donations myself, and my twenty dollar a week budget had been blown by having to buy horse feed and food for myself. The Bag Lady gave me half of any that came her way.

The evening was spent around a small fire in front of the wagon, many visitors wishing to speak to the 'Lady with the Wagon' and also attracted by the two boys and their rope tricks. The taller lad, Clint, could do all sorts of twists and turns and still hook the rope over the plastic cow he's set up on the grass. When it was no longer light enough to see, they scuttled off to try their luck at the Country and Western dance in the hall.

The Saturday passed in the same way, though the crowds were thicker with visitors to see the more acknowledged story tellers and poets. Events also went on outside like horse training and longhorn bull riding, the cooking competitions in a carriage, and the Cavalry. This ageing bunch turned up mid-morning (in horse trailers!) and did a little display; a couple of charges; a few salutes and turns, a shot or two in the air. Rather amateurish but entertaining. Most of them, looking mainly like retired dentists, mechanics and old farmers, seemed a little unsure of how their horses would react with all the activity going on around. When the sergeant yelled 'Charge!' and raced from one end of the Civic Center lawn, half the cavalry followed at a more cautious trot. They were quite picturesque though with their famous blue uniforms, a gold stripe down each leg, the company flag flapping in the breeze.

After the Sunday breakfast the wagons from the cook-off began to pack up. A non-denominational service was held with many of the artists from the symposium giving a reading or telling a more Godly story. One woman, Betty Martin McRae, dressed in stars and strips everything; trousers, boots, shirt, gave a rather moving little recital though embarrassingly patriotic. She was a bit extreme but a great pal of Finisia's and was to join us when we pulled out. She was a bit too political for me, but then I'm not an American and maybe too ignorant of the political arguments with which she was fluent. She was to take the place of the two boys whose turn in the wagon was up. They went home with their parents full of talk about saving up for a wagon and heading west.

Our aim that day was to just get the wagon out of town but it took ten miles of ugly city roads, noisy traffic, and suburbia before we left the Reese Air Force Base behind on the very edge of Lubbock, countryside ahead. Fin picked a rather ugly spot at the junction of 114 with 2378 but it was shady. The grass looked terrible, dry and hard, but as soon as the horses were released it was heads down and they seemed to enjoy it. Smokey was bottom of the heap in the herd hierarchy so she had to wait in line for the water. At feed time I used to stand guard to stop her being bullied away from her food as she liked to take her time, whereas Fin's horses wolfed it all down at double rate, They were all fat and healthy.

Mike Lamb and his family came out in the evening bringing food and beer, and a friendly Christian family from down the road bought more. For one last night we had our dinner to the accompaniment of Mike's gentle sentimental songs and his sweet sounding guitar. It was day 120 of our adventure.

I'd agreed with Finisia to travel with her into New Mexico and maybe even as far as the coast. I was flexible. The wagon made life much easier for me and for Smokey. No more worries about feed, water, or a place to stay. Smokey was free from the burden of the packs and enjoying Shortcake's bad tempered company. It was all very cushy. With everything taken care of there wasn't really anything I had to worry about but I was conscious of a nagging, guilty feeling. This was supposed to be a solo unsupported ride across the country on a single horse and there was no achievement in knocking off twenty miles each day in the wagon airstream. There was some pretty tough country coming up, though, so I settled with things as they were, for now at least.

Finisia's traveling technique was very different from mine. Smokey and I had become used to taking all day to cover the ideal of twenty miles, what with all the walking I did and the long noon-time break, but Fin went at it full pelt, slamming on the brakes, no rest stops, and the day's travel finished in four or five hours. It took Smokey and me over eight in the saddle. We managed to keep up perfectly well though. I was still stiff but adjusting to and enjoying the new pace, and Smokey didn't seem to mind at all. It was great to be on the road again after all that inactivity at Ropesville and Lubbock. The temperatures were beginning to ease down into the early nineties which was comforting, the nights were cooling down too and each day I looked for a change in the color of the roadside trees.

Day 121 saw us knocking off the twenty miles and a little bit more. Somehow Finisia had arranged to wangle some welding work to the trailer the colt traveled in from a company west of Levelland and we needed to make it there by the evening of Day 121 as the work was to be done first thing in the morning.

The trailer was a makeshift outfit built by Finisia in Florida to house the unexpected baby horse. Not until the creature was born did Finisia suspect her mare was pregnant. A country friend of hers eleven months previously had, for a joke, put the mare in with his stud horse and in Florida Finisia's team had grown by one. The whole gang had had to take two months off to give the colt time enough to grow stronger and to rest the mother. From my position on Smokey behind the trailer I could see there were some major design errors. With each movement of the growing young horse, the trailer swayed and lurched, swinging on its hitch behind the wagon. Some welding on the underside was needed to give it stability.

The people from the factory at Levelland made arrangements with Finisia before they left for the day about fixing the thing in the morning and we set up on good grass alongside the buildings. After the hot ride the horses were all hosed off (though Smokey hated it) fed, watered, and let out to roll and relax in the evening sun, a good day's work behind them. We had the patriotic Texas lady, Betty, with us that night in all her stars and stripes gear and she'd added a dinky little pistol to her get up, no doubt impressed by the one hanging off Finisia's hip. The weapon, small enough to be concealed, looked silly when worn openly. Finisia wanted me to sleep with her rifle in my tent but I laughed and refused.

Betty, the lady in the red, white and blue rattled on with Finisia all evening about the evils of government and the evils of just about everyone, rather boring unless you're both politically minded and paranoid. I chose to stay out of it and was very glad when an old friend from many miles back turned up in his beaten old truck. He was Rual Moody, a cousin of Buster Moody of *Six Flags* fame. I'd met him at the lake party Buster had held, and though Rual had given me his address in Levelland I hadn't thought to call him. His gift of a huge juicy watermelon and beer eased up the two politicals and for the time he was there at least the conversation was a little more varied.

Good humored Rual stayed until dark, leaving as the three women made ready for bed; Fin in the wagon, the tent for me, and Betty on a rather elaborate bed roll in the open made up of tarpaulins from Fin and horse blankets from me. The nights were beginning to cool off slightly but she looked cosy in everybody's spares.

I don't know how Finisia did it but she could get almost anyone to do almost anything, free of charge, however long the job took and often with a donation in her deerskin pockets at the end of it. I would cringe at the amount of nerve she had sometimes. The guys at the factory on the western limit of Levelland did an excellent job of fixing the trailer, also mending the steps which kept falling, and the towing bracket in the bargain. Finisia thanked them kindly enough, several problems fixed in one day, and both she and Betty climbed up and led off.

We were heading directly west along Route 114, with Betty leaving pretty early on for other engagements. Fin and I headed on alone towards Whiteface, the road long, straight, flat and quiet.

"Hey! Come and ride in the wagon a ways!" Finisia shouted back to me as I rode Smokey along the grass verge.

"Okay," I said and pulled up. I unsaddled Smokey and tied her to the corner of the wagon before taking a seat next to Finisia at the reins.

"Click!" she shouted and the wagon lurched forward. There was a sudden jerk of the whole outfit to the right and Smokey trotted past us on the inside, her broken head collar dangling. I quickly jumped down and we put her in one of Finisia's spare halters.

"She'll get used to being led," Fin assured me and off we went again. I sat next to Fin, white-knuckled and anxious, the wagon swaying in response to Smokey's fight to get away from the wagon's side.

"She'll get used to it," Fin repeated. For a short distance Smokey would trot alongside, the rope attached from the head collar to the wagon fully extended, Smokey's body as far away as possible. For a while she'd tolerate the rattling and banging, then in a frenzy of fear and panic, she'd rear and twist in a desperate effort to free herself. With a grim face and sweating hands I witnessed Smokey's struggle with the wagon all day.

"She'll get used to it," Fin said again and again.

By late afternoon we'd only covered twelve miles and with a thunderous build up of heavy dark cloud threatening to release its heavy burden any minute, Fin selected a piece of wide grassy verge and we pulled over. I went to release Smokey from the wagon.

My poor, old, little white mare stood quiet, exhausted and beaten. Her head hung in ugly dejection, the skin under and around the head collar raw and bleeding. All the hair from back hock to heel was gone, blood seeping from ugly scrapes where before her coat had shone with health.

The fence was set up and the horses released as Smokey stood stiff and swollen. I had to lift her feeding bucket off the ground so she could eat, her neck muscles too strained to allow her to lower her head. Her usually glistening black eyes stared ahead in unfocusing sadness.

"Never again," I said over the top of her raw head as she half-heartedly ate.

The rain began to fall. Big heavy drops, starting slowly then increasing until a continuous cooling downpour began to fill the roadside ditch, massaging the torn muscles and aching sores of my battered little pony. She stood there as if the rain washed her clean, soothing the swellings, erasing the day.

As the sky cleared, a police car pulled up.

"There's someone name of Palmer looking for you." the officer shouted at Finisia.

"Who? Never heard of her!" she shouted back. We all wondered who it could be.

By the time a battered old camper van pulled up, horse trailer in tow, I had realized the only possible person it could be was Jeannie Palmer from Chico, Texas. Against all the odds, in little over two weeks, she had sold the property, bought two horses, and made it out to west Texas, finding Smokey and me when I hadn't even told her where we'd be.

As the engine died. I went over, arms outstretched, to meet my old friends, Jeannie and Tom.

"We've been looking for you for two days!" Jeannie barked, excited, pleased and a little bit cross.

"Oops!" I laughed, casting an anxious glance back to Finisia leaning against the wagon.

"Here. Better come meet the Bag Lady."

There were three of us now, waving Texas good-bye.

For Jeannie it had taken one and a half days in the saddle and a lifetime of dreaming. For Finisia and me, it had taken what seemed to be a lot longer.

From the idyllic green eastern counties to the majestic dramatic sweep of the West Texas plains; eight weeks of summer heat covering 600 miles: from the shady pines to the thorny mesquite, from the solitude to the crowded city. Texas was all. It was more, much more than just another

State, the sixth to cross before the long imagined Pacific. Texas had given more and taken more than any other. And so each of us, especially Finisia and me, looked back from the New Mexico-Texas line with a mixture of gladness and regret at leaving the Lone Star State behind.

Texas is a country. It's own place; it's own people. A warm feeling inside and a country where a dreamer on a horse can look back on as home.

Chapter 8

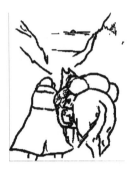

NEW MEXICO
We regret we break from the wagon on the
timeless banks of the Rio Grande. Let's race now,
Smokey, against the ice and snow of a Rocky Mountain winter.

We rode through a landscape as wild, as windswept and as unchanged as
the American West before the white man. Unchanged, that is, if one could
ignore the defacements of the power lines and the arrow-straight sticky
black tarmac. A wide open sky above, a blue barren of birds. So much like
Texas, but somehow different. Everything was different now anyway.
Traveling with the wagon and now with Jeannie too, the atmosphere was
completely changed. No longer did I spend hours planning out water stops
or checking out likely looking properties in which this little English bird
could roost for the night. I didn't need to look to Smokey as my only partner,
her responsibilities having relaxed to being just a horse again. Gone was the
euphoria of dozing under a tree for the hazy heated hours and gone was
the unity. Gone was Texas, too, and it was a little like leaving home.

New Mexico, Land of Enchantment, was foreign and unexplored.

Despite the empty loss of Texas left behind, the new life was full of ease
and laughs. Traveling with Finisia and her wagon afforded me the luxury
of Smokey free of the packs. Finisia kindly stowed them in the heavy

racks hanging beneath the wagon, including all my winter gear, my sleeping bag, everything. The traveling pace was much much faster and freedom from the packs left both Smokey and me unhindered to enjoy it. This new fast twenty mile jog daily was taking ifs toll on Jeannie, though, with her two unconditioned animals. She tried to keep up with the fast moving pace despite Finisia's and my advice to take it gently for a week or two. But poor Jeannie was paranoid about slowing up the team, being last in camp and having to force her sore horse and exhausted mule on.

The first night in this big flat land, we set up camp next to a cattle watering spot and swam in the shallow refreshing pond. What a golden reward after a long hot day! Hay was thrown to all the horses housed behind two sets of electrified ribbon, creating two long big fields alongside the quiet road. The evening settled down to one of talk and coffee, suggestions and memories, plans, religion, and always back to horse talk.

Finisia and I both felt that there was now no need to make the very early starts of the middle Texas days. The temperature was now easing off slightly, even the ninety plus degrees had become welcome after the days in the hundreds. We were half way through September and 7:30 or 8:00 seemed a lot more reasonable than 5 or 5:30 in the morning. We even had time for coffee! However slowly we packed up the night's camp, Jeannie was always way behind. She quickly earned the nickname Two Summers for her lengthy starts, and though when Smokey was saddled up and ready and I'd move on to help Jeannie with her two, she'd snap annoyance at my interference. The dog, Spirit Wolf, was also proving to be less than perfect as a heeler and would wander all over the road, causing me to shut my eyes every time a vehicle passed by. Nor did the dog respond too well to commands!

Poor Jeannie. Early on the realisms of her long dreamt-for trip came crashing in. It would have been much easier for her if just she and I were traveling together, as I would have adjusted my pace, but the wagon would leave regardless of Jeannie and her team. Where she should have bent, she didn't, and her strong nature and stubborn will were spoiling her animals and her trip. Her horse was quickly sore along the back from the saddle, the heat, the pace, and the miles. Her mule, seventeen years old, was completely incapable of work. We decided to take a day off in Tatum and trim down Jeannie's packs.

Tatum was a not much of anything town. Quiet, peaceful, a few shops, a couple of motels. We rode through and Fin picked a spot on the west side, a scrap of land among abandoned buildings. First responsibilities were to the horses, and working as a team, the electrified fence was set up, Finisia banging in the poles with me following threading the narrow ribbon through the insulated loops and their tops. The final piece was tied to the solar powered battery on the wagon and the current switched on. Two fields. Fin's animals in one, Jeannie's and mine in the other. Worked pretty well. Next came water. Two big barrels, one for each field, filled by hose from other big barrels carried at the back of the wagon. Much easier all around than trying to find a place to camp, fenced, with water, or staking Smokey out all night. The wagon carried hay, too, five bales usually, strapped to the sides of the wagon, increasing the overall width to pretty illegal dimensions.

With the fields ready, the horses were freed, the colt unloaded from the trailer at the back and the pressure off for the day. Later, they'd all be fed big buckets of corn, or sweet feed, or oats or whatever was on board, often feed donated by friendly visitors. All the animals were well fed and fat apart from Jeannie's mule. He was going down hill fast. At the end of twenty miles he'd be too exhausted to eat and would lie down as soon as he was let into the makeshift field. Jeannie was hoping he'd shape up as the miles passed by, but he was totally unconditioned and needing a rest.

I put my tent up in the shadow of the wagon, a little step away from the spot selected for the night's campfire. Jeannie did the same. Already visitors had arrived to talk to Finisia, attracted by the dramatic red writing on the canvas sided wagon: "Pulling for Christ, Coast to Coast." I began the rather cruel task of going through Jeannie's equipment, hoping to ease the pressure on the mule.

"You won't need that...You won't need that.... or that." I began, glancing up at Jeannie's depressed expression.

"You won't need that, but that'll be handy," I went on.

"That's essential, but you could get by without that," I continued.

"No! I want that!" she'd object to an occasional lost item. We went through the whole bundle, cutting out the luxuries. A pile of necessities, a pile of maybes. It wasn't easy for a woman so used to being in charge to now be the child of the group. She was fifty, I was nearly half her age. She ground her teeth and went to find a box for the rejects. Finisia, in a break from talking to the locals, went through the pile again, and poor Jeannie lost a bit more. However, at the end of it she had a reasonable amount of equipment and felt encouraged that maybe now her mule would be more able to cope.

To repair her battered ego, she took a room in a motel and we all shared in the luxury of her hot shower.

Rual Moody turned up that day; the guy I'd met at the lakeside party back in Texas, the one from Levelland. Everyone enjoyed his company and had begun to recognize the sound of his noisy old truck as it approached. With his good nature and big round belly, gifts of water melon and feed, he was always a popular visitor. Especially to me, as I knew him first. We became friends.

By the time we pulled out of Tatum on September 18th, Monday morning, we'd had a whole bunch of people over to visit. Two young men with unusual names, Jeno and Istuan from Los Angeles, old friends of Fin's dropped by, and invited both me and Fin on a four year round the world horseback ride. They were both pretty impressed with my little mare and adjusted their plans of using Arabs to considering using the Spanish Mustangs. The ride would have covered many places I cared to go but Fin later told me they'd been talking about this for years and so far had only progressed to having the tee-shirts made up! They planned to leave three months after I predicted completing my own ride. It kept me thinking.

On leaving Tatum, we also had another passenger for the wagon; a young, quiet mannered American boy, named Edward. He was running away from something but it wasn't clear what it might be.

We traveled directly west for three miles before the road swung to the north west; a long straight, direct route to Caprock. Not even a bump in the road for twenty miles. We set up camp in the middle of the Bagley North Oil Field, a few miles before the town, enjoying the afternoon after banging out the twenty miles by two o'clock. Fin, the Bag Lady as she liked to be called, had allowed Jeannie to stash her honed down pile of equipment in the wagon that day to give the mule an extra easy day, and he seemed much recovered by the time they pulled in. She was still trying to keep up with the rapid fire pace so I'd hang back a little to slow Jeannie up.

We stuck with the 380 the next day, too; four miles into Caprock.(a junction in the road) three miles to the edge of the escarpment. Since climbing up the steep mile-long bank back at Post, Texas, to the edge of this drop on Day 127, we'd been traveling over a portion of the Great Plains. By mid-morning we were dropping down the steep westward side with a scream and a holler from the wagon up ahead. I looked up from watching the roadside for glass, and faraway to the west stood out first evidence of the Rocky Mountains — a ghostly specter maybe thirty miles away, but the exhilaration was real and the day was made special. I added my own shouts to Finisia's for it felt like a prize to be closing in on the west. The mountains we'd waited and watched for so many days started that day with the sighting of Sardine Mountain, at 3973 feet, a third of the height of what was to come.

Jeannie was silent. She hadn't earned the right to know what it was to be freed from the central plains, but she smiled at her own pleasure at our excitement. With high spirits and a lively step we took the drop down the Cap Rock and onto Mescalero Sands.

The mile markers passed quickly by. The twentieth became our home for the night.

It was up and at 'em early the next morning with Jeannie and me having our first falling out when I began to offer her advice on folding her saddle blanket to ease pressure on her mare's back. I'd tried every combination there is with a five by four piece of blanket by the time Smokey and I had reached New Mexico, and so I felt qualified to comment. Jeannie felt not. I left ahead and the day was filled with a bad tension. Finisia made it harder for poor Jeannie with her continuous complaints about her slowness breaking camp and Jeannie had become very sensitive to criticism. She took it out on her animals by keeping up with the wagon all day.

We camped again that night after another dead straight twenty miles on Highway 280, ten miles or so from the major town of Roswell.

Day 129 saw us through the pretty tree-lined town with it's old central streets and new out of town shopping malls. We attracted a lot of attention from midday shoppers, people hanging out of office windows and cars pulling up to wave or stare. The racket from the horses and wagon was amplified against the buildings on each side of the narrow streets. We picked up the corn for the horses at a feed store and Jeannie used the machine at the bank to stock up on her cash supplies. The relationship between us was still a little fragile and we were trying to be polite.

At the end of the day's twenty miles, six miles further west of Roswell, her mule was again worn out. She began talking of changing him for another horse and both Finisia and I thought it wise. Her good natured dun colored mare was enduring well, though saddle sores were still a little tender. For some reason Finisia was usually unwilling to allow Jeannie to stack her bags in the wagon, and the mule paid. For a lady professing Christian values, sometimes her nature was hard and unbending. She was continually mentally aggressive to Edward who was planning to ride with us as far as Riodoso, a week away. And she mercilessly picked on

Jeannie. Despite this part of her character we all had a huge respect for her, admired her power, her wonderful stories and history and physical strength rare in a thirty seven year old woman. She was not fussy about the way she looked; she lived well on a little; she was basically happy though I also found her sometimes lonely and very homesick for her Idaho green. She'd been married; she'd been beautiful; she'd been wild. She was still many things, but now was lined by weather and her physically demanding lifestyle. However, she surprised me continually with her criticism of the many well intentioned people that came to speak with her. If they bought food or horse feed and money, she'd be polite, though often glad to see them go, but if they came empty handed, her tongue was bitter when their backs were turned.

"Well, how do you expect me to feed my horses with your 'God Bless You!'" she'd mutter under her breath. It was humorous at the time, and I'd laugh, but it was also sourly meant. She was mean to Jeannie and mean to Edward. She left me alone. She knew I didn't need her to make the west coast, and we liked each other anyway.

"I had prayed for you to come to me," she said. I was fine.

Day 130 took us nineteen miles along more of the arrow straight 30, with the unbroken scenery of shrub and dust and the occasional squeaking windmill. The land was so desolate only very rarely did we see the cattle, it was supposed to support. We were in Lincoln County and heading to the foothills of the white mountains.

Shortly after the morning start on Day 131, we were climbing. Finisia kept her speed up, then rested, ran again, then rested. The wagon with its load of hay and water was very heavy, over 7,000 lbs., and the horses were earning their corn that day. I trotted merrily behind on my Smokey, and Jeannie fortunately kept her pace slow and steady. The hill was steep. It was exciting for me. I had no worries and my spirits were lifted by being in hilly country after so long. What a pleasure if was not to be able to see fifty miles in each direction. It made every bend in the road like a treasure, every new scene an opening gift.

We were aiming for a promise of sweet grass in an apple orchard near Hondo, an offer from the owner and very welcome. It meant twenty-two miles and each one hard on Jeannie, but the prize, after the dusty flat lands, was well worth it.

We made it by late afternoon, dropping away from the road with ifs broken line of motorbikes heading to a meet at Ruidoso and into the quiet of trees. Real trees! And Grass! And Water! The grass was thick and deep and good on the eyes, both for dusty people and hay fed horses. We planned on a couple of days off, and like children on Christmas morning we excitedly set up the fencing and the tents. We all watched with satisfaction as the horses were released, their own pleasure obvious to those who knew them well. Rual was expected to join us that day, too, so there was an extra luxury to look forward to. He was always thoughtful as to food, and horse feed and often cold beer!

Later that evening, Finisia and I stood waiting for him at the junction of the orchard road and the highway; Fin waving her religious banners at passers by. It was quite dark by the time we were able to pick up the sound of Rual's noisy truck, but eventually he was there and we excitedly led him down the maze of bumpy lanes and orchard tracks. There was a party that night, with a bonfire and Rual cooking, cold beer and a day off to look forward to.

I lay in bed the next morning watching the patterns dancing on the tent walls from the sun shining through the apple trees. The early mornings were cooler now, especially since we'd started to climb, and I enjoyed the luxury of my sleeping bag until the sun warmed the tent too much and it was time to be up. A trip to an obscure bush for the loo, then back to my normal morning chore of feeding horses, a toothbrush in the corner of my mouth.

We fed the horses twice a day, two coffee containers of feed each, half a bucket almost. Every horse had his own bucket which was fixed to them by a ribbon behind the ears. That way no horse could steal anothers feed. It worked well, though the first time Smokey was fitted with hers, it was very frightening for her. She quickly learned the bucket was a good thing though, and was soon as good at the technique as the others.

When the chores were over, (which Jeannie and I usually split) Rual took Edward, Jeannie and me into Ruidoso, the next major town along the highway. How exciting it was to be traveling at fifty miles an hour, instead of five! However, both Jeannie and I watched the road carefully, despite our excitement, to learn what to expect in the following twenty six miles.

Ruidoso is a popular place to escape to in the summer to avoid desert temperatures and also to enjoy skiing in the winter. The town nestles along both banks of the Ruidoso River and is surrounded by the steep mountains of the Sierra Blanca. Pine trees provide shade throughout the town, which is situated within the Lincoln National Forest. Bears have been seen wandering the streets at night and their eery calls awake strangers to the sound. The town is designed to attract tourists, with it's lovely main street of wood fronted shops and galleries. There's a race track too, which boasts the running of the world's richest quarter-horse race; a purse of 2.5 million dollars! And that week in September saw a massive meeting of motorbike enthusiasts, an annual event.

Edward was there to pick up a cheap sleeping bag and warm jacket from a charity shop. Also to find a job. Both Jeannie and I were happily enjoying a day away from the horses and the wagon. It felt good. We walked up and down the main street, fingered a few things, looked mainly, ate an ice-cream, watched out for a likely place to camp in a couple of days. Rual did a few things with Jeannie for a while and I sat and watched the leather clad bikers with fascination as they slowly passed up and down the road. Took advantage of a real loo in the gas station too!

We were back at the wagon mid-afternoon to find Finisia in a foul mood. Smokey had run the fence to be back with her friend Shortcake, and Jeannie's two were wandering around loose. Jeannie and I collected the strays with ease, wondering at Fin's bad temper and determination to be difficult; decided it was obvious she'd be happier traveling alone. We talked about leaving her to the solitude she craved.

By the early afternoon of Day 135, we found ourselves camped on the selected spot on the western edge of Ruidoso, New Mexico. Tall grass on an empty plot of land designated for use as a supermarket. Already the orange ended stakes marked out the area from the surveyors work.

It was Finisia's turn for a few hours to escape. I went along too. We found a vet to renew health certificate papers for Fins' now five horses, including a new palomino filly, an addition from Day 134. The results would take a couple of days to arrive so again we were to take some time off.

The day passed by easily, with visitors, newspaper interviews, writing and talking. I made good progress on a pair of deerskin trousers I was making. Rual joined us again, probably for the last time. He was already many long miles from home and his work on the oil fields afforded no more holiday. We all, with much regret, watched his noisy old truck drive back down the eastbound highway, heading to Texas.

Jeannie with her more secure financial position, rented a motel room for the night, and we all took showers. However, she wasn't quite brave enough to admit that she craved a night in a real bed, so without prompting, Finisia took the opportunity and took the clean sheets herself. It meant Jeannie and I had a quiet easy evening, just we two and the horses and dogs and the empty wagon. It was a bit dull. But it was peaceful.

All this hanging around was a bit frustrating, so as soon as the health papers came in, we said good-bye to our strange friend, Edward, and we were off. Both Finisia and Jeannie wanted to stay on the Mescalero Indian Reservation the following night; both felt strongly about their native roots.

The day was an idyllic one of pretty climbs and descents; the road threading it's way through valleys and around peaks, into the Apache Reservation. We followed Cherokee Canyon, onto Dark Canyon. Past Carrizo Mountain and over six thousand feet to our right and Apache Summit to our left. Onto Tularosa Canyon and North Fork Road. Green pastures, tree covered slopes, warm weather, perfect riding. Jeannie and her mule were keeping up well and it felt good to be moving again.

At the end of the seventeen mile pleasure ride nestled the small town of Mescalero, the administration center for the Mescalero Apache Indian Reservation. I was looking forward to picking up mail there, and Jeannie and Fin were excited about being hosted by the Native Americans for this, the first day of October.

The night was not a good one. It was to leave a bitter taste in the mouths of all three of us, each disappointed for different and every reason. The first blow came my way when all my expected mail had been returned to sender several days before my arrival.

"We only hold mail for fourteen days. It's policy." the unsympathetic counter staff said. I had one letter. From Pat. The cruelty seemed personal and I was very low with it.

We filled the water tanks at the gas station while Fin went over to the small city building to ask permission to camp on the reservation that night. Expecting a friendly welcome and a warm heart from a fellow American with Indian heritage, the reception was cold and suspicious and unyielding. Fin, with her strong manner pointed out we hadn't enough daylight to make it on to Federal land again, forced the official into conceding us the use of a piece of land next to the school. Jeannie with her very strong views about white man bad, red man good, felt the insult most strongly.

The scrap of land we'd been allotted was a piece full of wire and glass and broken cement. Nothing could be salvaged to make it safe enough, and with bitterness turned outward we tied all the horses around the fence line and to the wagon. Water was there at least, though from a river under the road and difficult to access. We had hay, and we had visitors, though not all pleasant.

By very first light we were saddled and packed, loaded and ready. With the familiar 'Click' from Finisia to her team, the wagon rolled away from the scrap and wire, torn pieces of cars and used condoms, onto the highway. Away from the suspicious, unwelcoming Apache. The sunny morning felt cloudy to all three.

We gladly dropped away from Mescalero, down the western slopes of the White mountains towards the Tularosa valley and The Malpais (Bad Country). We were on 70 and heading towards the north-south road, Highway 54. As we completed the final descents, the valley bottom lay complete before us; a barren, arid, sand pit of a scene, a hundred miles wide, the San Andreas mountains in the distance. In between that range and this lay the snow white shock of White Sands National Monument - mile after mile of the whitest, cleanest and completely dry shifting sand dunes. We stopped in silence to look, then with eyes downwards and with minds avoiding confronting the thought of crossing the sand, we turned south into Tularosa. For several days we'd be town hopping, carrying hay and stocking up on water whenever it was to be found. Tularosa was green but the country around was not.

Alamogordo came next. One friendly vendor threw me a brightly colored tee-shirt.

"The traffic'll sure notice ya' now!" he shouted, as I pulled it on. We camped in the industrial area, west of town on Highway 70. The ground was hard and stony, and though October, the day hot and dusty.

Smokey's shoes were worn out and one was off. I rang for a horse shoer, found one free and had a handsome new set fitted by a local man and his helper daughter. Felt like putting fuel in the tank!

We left Almogordo behind us on October 4th. Day 141. Over 1800 miles behind us. For Finisia over 5000. We were aiming for the dunes.

The road was long, straight, flat. Both sides harsh looking desert of sharp cactus and cracked earth. Ahead, the white.

I hung back with Jeannie and we did a little tourist shopping outside town before enjoying our own easy pace together, the wagon a dot in the distance.

The wagon grew in size as we approached it later in the day. There was Finisia, hands on hips, fire in her eyes, watching us ride up. She had pulled over at the border of White Sands National Monument and her horses were still in the traces, dozing in the sun. She looked mad and Jeannie and I unintentionally sank in our saddles. "They're letting off some dammed missile," she barked, "and they won't let us go on!" At least it wasn't our fault, both Jeannie and I thought.

"But we're gonna!" she went on.

"Oh, good move," I thought. "Let's get ourselves in trouble with the

United States Army."

"Whatever you say, Fin," I answered, tipping my hat back, shifting in the saddle "We're ready!"

An army guy came over, talked to Fin, warned her about the gun she carried and basically bashed her ego for a bit.

"We'll pay for that later," I thought, as I watched her stride back, her jaw set.

"Set camp!" she barked.

We had to spend the night opposite the gates to the park. Our two long fields strung out along the hard shoulder. Hay for horses. Jeannie and I bought ice-cream from the tourist shop, two each, and enjoyed the splendor of the glistening sands as the sun faded. The white had it's own light, making the dunes eerie and magical, ghostlike and alive. Fascinating, but ominous.

We were in a bit of a fix, geographically. The army was exploding bombs sometime the following morning, and again thirty six hours later. We had to make it across the desert and out of range of the missiles before the second round was set off, otherwise the army was going to force us off and back the way we'd come. It was obvious we couldn't leave until the first explosions were over, there would be a road block out, but we'd have to be ready to make it as far as possible over the desert floor before night. We'd better be first in line at that road block in the morning.

We were up and ready with brakes set behind the road block early the next morning. We passed the time taking photos of the outrider horses riding up and down the dunes that had drifted over the park boundary. We weren't allowed in the park proper.

Before long, the noise from jet engines filled the sky and we heard distant erratic booms from whatever it was these people were doing. With a crackle of conversations on the sentry's radio, the barrier was up and we were waved through, on our way. Finisia immediately set a blasting trot, which she kept up almost continuously, until by the eighteenth mile marker, the light being lost and camp had to be set. We'd lost several hours of light due to the late start.

The night passed without incident, though we were all three restless to be gone from the missile range. The traffic was fast and irregular during the night-time hours. It was the very early truckers who witnessed the wagon making it's rattling, banging, noisy way back onto the highway the morning of Day 142.

"Hey, Lonely Buddy, get a handle on this," we'd hear via Fin's C.B. radio she carried aboard.

"There's some crazy guy in a wagon up here blocking up the dammed highway. Ain't never seen nothin' like it!"

"Some ugly bitch comin' up behind, too, with a cute arsed gal," another trucker would throw in.

"Shouldna' be allowed. Damned hippies!" another would say.

"Hey, that's kinda' neat," a more generous minded one might fill in. "Might do that myself one day."

The comments were all different and kept the three of us amused on the many long lovely stretches. Fin would relate the best at the end of the day if we'd been too far back to hear. It was always amusing to be talked about when the talkers thought we were deaf to their comments.

By early afternoon we were passing White Sands Missile Range Post Area to our left, Rattlesnake Ridge to our right. We began the steep ascent of the Organ Mountains.

We climbed and climbed, watering the horses halfway up the incline, through the San Agustin Pass at 5719 feet. Jeannie was far back again, easing her tired mule along. Fin and I waited for her at the summit, the dramatic desert basin stretched out behind us. It had been a long hard day.

At the first sign of an empty plot, making a twenty one mile day, we pitched camp a little past the small town of Organ. Safe, and two miles off the range. It was dark before chores were finished.

Unfortunately, sometimes, even though the day may have been hard work, it was rarely over when the horses were unhitched. As soon as we stopped, people would be curious to find out our story, especially Finisia's, so it was normal to have visitors until quite late. Fin would mainly talk to the ones who were interested in the religious reasons for such a journey, and I would talk to the horse lovers. My visitor that night in Organ was Bob Rodgers, an owner of two horses, one of them a big mustang gelding. He arrived with a present of a couple of bales of hay. I immediately liked him. He looked like my Canadian. Jeannie usually sat in Fin's shadow and rather uncomfortably made comments on religion she knew nothing about. She admired Fin's belief though, and with that admiration tried to emulate the admired. Religion to me is a much more private affair and I laid off the subject completely.

I was quite happy to talk about horses though, especially my specialist subject, Spanish Mustangs, in particular, my little Smokey. She was faultless and flawless in my eyes. We had grown a little less dependent on each other the last few weeks. She had her new friend 'the spare mare,' the new palomino of Fin's, and I had my two companions. She was still just as special though, despite the new drawing of lines.

Bob finally left and quiet descended on the dozing animals as three tired women their rolled gladly into their beds.

It was time for another rest. After the strenuous crossing of the Tularosa Basin and the stony desert, Jeannie's mule was exhausted. She had to find a home for him and a replacement horse. We all agreed to spend the weekend down by the Rio Grande at Las Cruces.

Las Cruces began as a graveyard. When New Mexico was being settled by the Spanish, they were frequently set upon by the unfriendly Apache Indians and slaughtered. In the 1700's several oxcart drivers were found murdered here, and the crosses erected to mark their graves were joined forty-three years later by a party of thirty travelers from Taos who met the same fate. The place began to be known as *La Placita de las Cruces,* the Place of the Crosses. Las Cruces today is the second largest city in New Mexico. And, luckily for travelers, the Indians are more friendly.

The wagon and outriders pulled through the pretty town with its colorful buildings and historic center on Day 144. We took the most direct route, Fin's impeccable sense of direction faultless in a city with many twists, turns, junctions, lights and distractions. Just before the wide flowing waters of the Rio Grande, we took a drop, and she pulled her team to a stop on the lush green grassy eastern bank. Another heavenly prospect of grazing horses, fresh flowing water, and a bit of rest.

Camp was quickly set. All the insulated poles were used to make the biggest areas possible for grazing in the long grass. West of Las Cruces lay nothing but desert stretching forever it seemed, so we planned to take full advantage of this lull before the storm.

Not long after the wagon had pulled to a stop, visitors began to arrive, curious at the old-style scene. Most waited until the horses were released and fed and watered before joining us. One of them was Bob Rodger, from the night before, with another present of more hay. Though the horses didn't need it, I split one bale between the two fields. The wagon was holding it's maximum capacity.

With Fin talking to a large family with Mexican heritage and strong religious beliefs, I was free to hang back and talk to Bob. The night before I'd mentioned my preference in equestrian events was the cross-country part, and with two horses of his own and a cross country clinic to go to the following day, he invited me to ride with him. I gently refused, not wanting to break my neck so far into my trip but said I'd be glad to go along and watch, and to ride his second horse in the arena for a bit, later.

Bob picked me up the next morning, took me back to his empty house. His wife and daughter were away in Las Vegas for a couple of days. We loaded the horse he was to ride in the trailer, arriving in good time for the start of the clinic. About twelve or fourteen riders and their horses were already there, and were going through the ritual of grooming, saddling, warming up their horses over small jumps, cantering and trotting. The cross- country course itself was off to the left, maybe two miles and twelve jumps through the mesquite and cactus, with a good, soft, dusty red dirt surface.

With the sun beginning to climb, the lady instructor strode out of the house, all jodhpurs and a big voice. Each rider was paying forty dollars for the mornings tuition.

One at a time, the jumps were taken; the lady teacher picking up good points and trying to correct bad points. When all the jumps were completed each horse and rider took the cross country course complete in a race against the clock. Bob and his big thoroughbred gelding seemed to do well. His riding was certainly much better than mine and I was glad I'd refused his offer of the other horse. Some of the jumps were quite daunting.

Flushed and excited, he unsaddled, loaded up and we drove back to his house close to Hacienda Acres on Highway 70. I rode the big mustang in his arena for a short while, stopping finally for lunch. By this time, Bob was flirting like mad, trying to convince me that a quickie affair with him while his wife was away was an okay thing.

"If she doesn't know, she doesn't mind," he told me.

"Yeah, right," I thought.

"Look Bob," I said, " I think you're very nice but I'm not in the habit of bonking married men." I must have said it a dozen times.

He tried and tried, but eventually dropped me back at the wagon to Jeannie, busy with arrangements for the mule and Fin in a simmering mood. There was a horse trailer parked on the grass , "Kiss My Ass, Mules," was painted on the side. Jeannie had found a wonderful home for her old mule. It was a specialist ranch that just dealt with donkeys and mules for enthusiastic lovers of the sad looking creatures. They were glad to give Jeannie's a good home. For a minimum sale price, they loaded and drove him away. Another trailer arrived later in the afternoon with a possible horse to replace the mule. Both Jeannie and Fin gave it a good looking over. Seemed okay. Sold. Looked like it was going to be Jeannie's lucky day. I hung back by my tent -- it seemed for some reason as if I was in trouble.

There were no shoes on the new horse so Jeannie was busy phoning farriers to come out as soon as possible. Her new purchase settled down quickly with the other animals. Fin was quiet, hidden in the wagon.

By the end of the afternoon, Jeannie was back. A horse shoer had been arranged for two days time. She disappeared into the wagon with Fin.

By night fall, something was definitely brewing.

The middle of Day 146, the following day, Fin came out of the wagon and threw a bale of hay only to her horses and stomped back inside. My temper blew. For the whole time we'd been together, Jeannie and I had fed all the horses, including hers, twice a day, with water, too. Fin, by feeding just hers was trying to make a statement, trying to pick a fight. We snapped at each other briefly. Shortly after, she emptied all my equipment out of the wagon. I let her simmer and simmered some myself until the visitors had gone and it was night time again.

"What's going on, Fin?" I asked, standing on the wagon steps.

"Nothin'" she answered

"Why's all my stuff outside then, and why are you in such a stinky mood? Doesn't look much like nothing."

"I don't much care for your attitude towards these good Christian people that are only trying to be nice, and I don't much care for your carrying on with a married man," she finally hurled at me.

"What!" was my astonished reply

"You're so bitchy about all these people behind their backs and it's poisoning me!" she spat.

I was amazed. For the four weeks we'd been together I'd witnessed her constant criticism of almost all empty-handed people. And Jeannie. And Edward. She'd never picked on me.

"And the way you're so mean to Jeannie," she went on.

"Oh right!" I shouted back.

"You're poisoning me!" she continued.

We talked some more, got nowhere. I said I'd leave.

Early next morning, after arranging with Jeannie to meet her in a couple of days - she'd also had enough of the Bag lady's tongue «-1 saddled up Smokey, packs and all, mounted up and turned to go.

"Wait! Wait!" Fin shouted, waving and running towards me.

I turned Smokey's head. Fin caught up, panting a little, put her hand on Smokey's neck. Looked at me. Stopped.

"Thank you," she said quietly, tears running down her cheeks.

"Thank you," I replied, sad-eyed too.

For maybe a minute we both stood, looking at each other. Finally, I turned Smokey's head and rode away. It took me a long time to work out why my friend Finisia had wanted me to leave, though the answer was a simple one. Underneath all the hard surface she was quite a good woman, or she tried to be. Her temper took over often, and her bad moods became directed at others. Now and again she'd realize she was far from her ideal of a loving Jesus. She'd try to get back. The whole time Jeannie had been with us, Finisia had been mean. Like a bully in a school playground, picking on the new boy. Her criticism of people was in the way she saw them: as wanting something from her and giving nothing in return. It would last a while, then something would happen and she'd look at herself and not like the way she'd become. That happened in Las Cruces and she had to make it up. Jeannie had planned to leave, driven away by Fin's cutting remarks. She'd be heading off on her own, but Fin saw her as incapable of surviving alone though Jeannie couldn't see it that way. If I hadn't been pushed out, I'd have left with Fin in one direction, Jeannie another. Guilt came flooding in to Finisia's basically good heart, and Emma, the already proven distance rider-survivor, had to go. Fin had to make it up to Jeannie. Make it up to her Jesus.

"Thank you," she'd said as I'd left. I didn't understand it then, but I do now.

"Thank you," I'd replied to the sad faced woman looking up at me.

"For it all." I said to myself.

"Just you and me now, Smokey."

Loneliness. Anger. Sadness. Regret. And Fear. After having it all on a plate, was I capable of it anymore? Where was I going to find water? What about feed and hay? Where would I stay? What about those deserts? And goodness knows about those mountains! There's a thousand miles yet!

A dread filled my early morning hours.

"At least Jeannie will be along in a couple of days," I'd comfort myself. We'd have a short day and call it quits. At least there was grass along the Rio Grande and I'd stick with that for a way at least. Fin was going west. We'd head north.

A sandy path ran along the bank of the Rio Grande that day, sometimes on both sides and with the mild temperatures and calming river, my battered spirit was slowly soothed. I'd done this before. I'd found water before. And places to stay. And feed and hay. I knew what to expect from the deserts and the mountains are no big deal. I can do this. I must.

"Just you and me now, Smokey."

Someone was ahead and my natural suspicions and new insecurity caused me to unsnap the safety strap across the long blade knife I wore at my waist. For added effect I slipped the buckle of the leather pouch and played the 'I have a serious weapon in here' routine. Sonny Melendrez wasn't fussed. He came striding up, all smiles and good nature and offered a place for the night's stop.

"That'd be great," I told him. A friend when I needed one. I should have known better than to doubt the American people. Of course I would get to the coast, because America would take me there. Wonderful, wonderful, interested people!

"This night at least will work out okay," I thought in my pessimism,

Before too long, Smokey was in Sonny's neighbor's corral chowing down on good local alfalfa hay. Sonny and I went back to Las Cruces to eat.

The food was good, the beer was great. Sonny was a pleasure to be with ~ a great humor bubbling continuously — exactly what I needed for my bruised self. We enjoyed each other enormously, but I benefited the most. Back at his house, he offered a home for whenever I needed it, and frightened me a bit with his honest fear of the mountains ahead. He wanted me to rest up for a few days while he finished business to do with chili farming or film directing (he did both) a few days away. He wanted to find a horse trailer and take me through. Snow was predicted by the weekend. However, I decided to move on. I had to keep visible for Jeannie, leaving messages so she'd find me.

With a sore head from the night before, but my spirit much recovered, Day 148 began. It was out of the small dirt road leading to Sonny's place and onto 185 following the river. 1897 long miles were behind us and the toughest yet to come. Many miles to my left I could see the Black Range. Long slung, threatening dark clouds hid the peaks.

With only a mile gone, a trailer pulled up, one I recognized, and Bob was it's driver.

"Thought you might want some company," he said.

"Okay, Bob".

The path of yesterday that had followed the river had ended at Radwin Springs, near Sonny's place, but it did begin again a few miles up the road, at Hatch. Bob and I decided to load Smokey up and drive the two horses the ten or twelve miles to the more pleasurable riding country.

For several hours we rode along the graveled, quiet, path, the river, fascinating, to our left. There was a break for lunch, the two horses staked out to graze, Bob and I, sitting, toes in the river. He tried for the last time to seduce me, gave up, and left me with his address.

"Oh, by the way, Jeannie and the wagon have gone."

Lonely again.

Smokey and I had crossed the Rio Grande between Deny and Arrey on Route 187. I said good-bye to the last of the alfalfa fields that lined its fertile banks. The road could take us all the way to Truth or Consequences, a town named after a radio and television game show, but we were to leave it at Caballo and head west on 152.

At the junction between these two roads was a campground. Pretty large but not suitable for Smokey and me even if we had been allowed, the ground was barren of grass. At the gas station I asked around for a night's stop.

"Sure! You can stay with my Dad and me," piped up Hoss Bates, a local from Caballo. 'Caballo' appropriately meaning 'horse'.

"Great!" I said, and took directions.

It meant a mile out of our way, but the area we were in was desolate shrub land, scarcely populated, and dry. Despite a twenty mile day, we took the offer.

A couple of hundred yards from Hoss's front gate, he met me on a bicycle.

"My Dad says you can't stay. Your horse will frighten the cattle." he said.

"Oh it's alright. She's really used to cows," I replied.

"I think he doesn't want you there," was his answer.

I looked up to see an overweight man in work pants standing at the gates.

"Clear off!" I heard him shout.

"It's getting dark, you know," I said to Hoss,, "and we've come out of our way." Panic was creeping into my voice.

"What about you selling me some hay at least," I added.

"He says he doesn't want you there," Hoss guiltily replied and turned away.

"Piss off!" I heard from up the road.

"Very friendly!" I screamed back. I turned Smokey back down the road and away. My guts were twisted in anger, disappointment and worry about the night's stop.

There were houses all around this dusty area, spread out on large lots. Mostly quiet and unlived in looking. Broken bottles spoiled back yards and out front I could see wilted, frost damaged plants. I left the Highway and went among them.

One house I tried, empty, had a horse behind it in a small corral. A big stack of hay stood to one side.

"If the worst comes to the worst," I thought, "I'll steal some of that."

I asked at the house opposite when the owners might be back.

"Might be back later," answered Craig Swainston. "Can't really tell."

I asked about buying some of the hay, and a place to stay, water for the horse.

"You could stay in the Community center," Craig suggested, indicating an area alongside his property. "It's fenced and I could find you hay."

I shook his hand in gratitude. I'd found a good man.

Craig and his lovely wife, Laurie, were more than true to their word. They saw Smokey fed and watered and free to roam the abandoned looking community center next to their house. They took me for a drive to see the dramatic Caballo Dam and to pick up fresh hay. They fed me good country cooking and we talked and laughed until late. They marveled at my trip and admired my courage. (Though I hadn't felt very courageous recently.) By the time I was curled up in my sleeping bag on the cement steps of the empty building, I was once again feeling halfway content.

All night, the lightening flashed silently to the south.

With a cheery start and exchange of addresses, I said goodbye to my two new friends in Caballo in the early morning of Day 149. Smokey had half a bale of hay strapped over the saddle, enough for two days, and I was walking.

It wasn't too long before we were back at the junction with 152 at the gas station. I stocked up on chocolate and strawberry-kiwi Snapple, a drink much to be preferred over the moldy water in my canteen.

The road was quiet, and long; a gradual climb, a bend, a drop and more long steady climbs. Dried river beds passed underneath. Ahead rose the Black Range, the Mimbres Mountains, the Elk Mountains, the Mogollon Mountains. Each range higher than the last. We had a long day ahead, climbing, seventeen miles and me walking beside my horse. The whole area was open grazing though the feed was poor. Cattle grids crossed the road in places and we'd have to find a lose wire and a way around.

As well as the hard climbs, the temperature was dropping. The day turned to grey. We needed to make it to Hillsboro before dark.

A small pickup with a cover on the back pulled over ahead of me and stopped. An intelligent looking, forty or so year old man made his way back down the road to talk to me.

"Hello. How are you? My name is John Flannery. I wondered if you could do with a drink?"

"That'd be lovely," I smiled in response. For half an hour or so I sat on the tail gate of John's truck drinking a couple of cans he'd bought from his house and enjoying the sandwiches specially made.

He'd even thought to bring water out for Smokey. We liked each other and he offered a place to stay for the night.

"That'd be great," I replied, and we arranged to meet further up the road. As a bonus, John took my hay with him, so I was now able to climb into the saddle.

The road became steeper, more bending, with dramatic views of the foothills behind us and the cloud-covered black mountains ahead. John met us one more time on the road to make sure we were okay. I was confident we had a good caring host for the night.

Arriving at Hillsboro, we passed from summer to autumn. Dancing orange leaves fell from mature trees lining the pretty woods faced town. Old time America. Pretty. Unpretentious. Chilly. John met me at the junction of his dirt lane road with the main street. My spirits soared from the new air we found ourselves surrounded by. Trees and grass and friendly people. An autumn oasis.

John had a pretty one story house in a small orchard a little way back from the dirt road. He'd cleared a space for Smokey to stay and a comfortable camper van for me. The clouds were building, thick and heavy rain was inevitable. But Smokey had a well roofed garage for shelter and I had the camper van. It could rain a plenty for all of me..

The hour or so before dark, John took me for some more hay. After Smokey was settled, it was a hot bath up at the house for me, the smell of good cooking drifting under the door from the kitchen. John had to leave in the morning for Texas, but kindly offered me the use of his home for as long as I liked. I gratefully accepted another day.

Day 151. The rain beat down almost without a break. It had awakened me during the night, the drumming sound on the camper roof alien to me for it had been weeks since I'd last heard it. From my view back up at the house I could see Smokey dozing in the garage, out of the wet, which she hated.

John was gone, so the day was one of peace, quiet, laundry, TV, food, watching Smokey. How lucky to be in a house and not in the tent! It was pretty amazing, I thought, the trust that a stranger could grant a stranger. I was in John's house and though he hardly knew me, he gave me a free rein to stay there without him. My trust was equal to his with acceptance of his offer of a place to stay. Thank goodness people are still able to give like that.

By the morning of Day 152, the rain had stopped, thought the dark clouds still blocked the sun and threatened more heavy falls later. Snow had been predicted for the day we planned to cross the big mountain pass. We could be snowed in. I went down to saddle Smokey.

Halfway through the loading of the packs, I looked down to see the smooth glossy line of a rattlesnake. With a quick flick, I unhooked Smokey's lead rope and swung the big heavy brass clip round and round over my head. When the speed was fast, I dropped the arc to bring the brass catch closer to the poisonous angry snake. A change of angle, a hit and the snake was dead. To be sure, I chopped off his head. Usually, my admiration for these fascinating creatures would have sent me backing away, but this time, the coiling body and rattling tail were too close to my beloved horse and I couldn't risk a strike. I picked up the remaining inert piece and packed it in a plastic bag for the night's meal.

Guiltily leaving a horse-poop strewn mess in the garage, I hung the horse feed and hay for the next three days over the saddle, and pulled on the waterproofs John had given me. We headed back onto 152. We were racing against the weather.

We made it as far as Kingston. A nine mile walk and difficult. There was some rain which kept me dressed up in John's waterproofs all day - they were, however, very difficult to walk in. I had, under the yellow plastic, a pair of thermal leggings and the deerskin trousers I'd made in the wagon days. The climb was steep and twisted but it was a day of freedom from everything, apart from thoughts of the mountain ahead. Emory Pass. 8,228 feet. Occasionally the sun would break through but not warm enough to dry the tarmacked road. There was very little traffic. I began to sing again.

Kingston was a tiny little village along a single lane running parallel to the 152. We went in, found nowhere to stay, and turned around. Just outside the small hamlet was a tiny little campground belonging to the Gila National Forest. They didn't allow horses but I had to risk it. There was nowhere else. After tying Smokey to a tree her head was quickly in the long grass. I asked the two other groups camped there if they'd mind a horse as a neighbor for the night.

"Hell no! Help ya' self, friend!" was their joyful answer.

With relief I unsaddled, set up the tent, fed extra hay to Smokey, gave her water, lit a small fire in the blackened circle from an earlier camper. It was going to be a cold night. One group of youngsters on a day trip from the deserts offered me hamburgers, chicken and milk which I gladly accepted. Then the larger group invited me to a bonfire party complete with beer and food later that night. How could I have ever felt lonely after the split with Jeannie and Finisia — this was America! Before I left for the second meal, I found a

Volvo hubcap on the side of the road, and in a little water from the river, cooked the rattlesnake from the morning. Hamburgers were to be had that night, so I shoved the snake back in the bag for the next day. It smelled pretty awful!

Even close to the big blazing fire that night, the cold, crept in. I wore all the clothes I owned.

Very early the next morning I was up, dressing reluctantly, losing the warmth from my sleeping bag as I moved around. Outside my packs were white with their frosted coating. Smokey nickered her morning greeting, the air swirling white around her nose.

She was fed, loaded, watered, hay stashed, bridle hung over the saddle horn, before our hosts of the night before were truly awake. I said good bye and gave my thanks again for their kindness. Smokey and I set off for the cloud-covered Emery Peak.

The rain began early. A light drizzle. Enough to cool a horse and walker from the exertions of the steep, then steeper, ascents. The road turned and backed, climbed then switched, forever up towards the black mountain ahead. The peak lost in mist, the valleys lost in mist. Eight miles of tough trekking and we were at the pass. No snow fortunately but the temperature would have been bitter if the wind hadn't been still. Both Smokey and I were wet; me with unevaporated sweat from the work of walking uphill, and Smokey from the constant drizzly rain. I was glad I couldn't see how high we were.

Without time to read the plaque that marks the pass, we moved on. Down mainly, hoping for San Lorenzo before nightfall. I didn't rest Smokey all day, and kept the hay slung over the saddle 185 - My Kingdom is a Horse

in case we were snowed in and needed to hole up in the woods somewhere. I kept my compass out, keeping track of our position throughout the day, just in case.

After twenty five miles of hard slog, and in the dark, we pulled into San Lorenzo. It was pointless trying to find a place to stay by knocking on doors - due to the wet, ugly, dejected picture we made. I was red faced, hobbling on blistered swollen feet, soaked. Smokey's mane hung down her metal grey neck, water dripping from it's wiry ends; the packs, like a shopping cart, loaded untidily.

I pulled Smokey into an empty corral behind an abandoned house, released her of her burden. After feeding and watering my good natured, hard-working mare, I sat on the steps of the empty house, chewing on the unsavory snake. I won't say it wasn't good, but I'd probably never serve it to guests.

By the end of the following day, we were down the mountain, past the 2000 mile point and back into civilization.

We'd been through the small towns of Hanover and Turnerville, and the ugly city of Central. Even though we were tired, and I could hardly walk with my swollen feet, I pushed Smokey and myself on as far as nineteen miles, finding a friendly farmer with a good corral, horse feed and a quiet spot to camp. I'd managed to get some riding in that day after sticking my thumb out up in the hills. A curious passer by had stopped and I'd cadged a ride for the bulky hay and horse feed, arranging to pick it up at a designated mile marker further down the road. Though it was an embarrassing procedure, I was excited about the technique.

I took advantage of a convenient Wal-Mart the next morning, buying a wonderful big polystyrene cup of coffee, and replacing the Sony Walkman I'd left in the beaten-down grass beside the Rio Grande. E.T.Collingsworth stopped me in the parking lot, and kindly moved my hay up the road ten miles. I was able to ride and rest my beaten up muscles and ugly feet, victims of the Black Mountain.

Shortly after leaving Silver City, Smokey and I were crossing over the Continental Divide. From now on all rivers would be draining west rather than to the east. We were closing in on the Pacific. Maggie O'Brien hauled the hay further that day. She also arranged for us to stop at Jerry's place; a sort of friend of hers. We pulled in by mid-afternoon after a sixteen mile day.

Jerry was a packer. He took groups of city people, hunters, bird watchers, tourists, romantics, into the tough mountainous country surrounding his ranch, using horses and mules. He had a heap of Indian heritage. Very good looking, very charming. He showed me where to put Smokey and opened up the unused house as a place for me. He offered me tea up at his house when I'd finished cleaning up.

Jerry lived in a fascinating house built underground. The front door was in the side of the hill, almost unnoticeable. Terra cotta tile floor and natural colorings. An open side at the back lead out into an overgrown jungle-like garden full of late flowers and weeds, cacti and vegetables. A sauna area stood to one side, half hidden in the brush and with spectacular views surrounding this unusual and sympathetic home.

Jerry showed me around, proud to exhibit his dream house. With deep set, black twinkling eyes, he watched for my reaction at each new scene. I admired it fully, but watched him slyly.

He was very charming. Very 'attentive'. A spiritual type person. I'm not all that comfortable with those types, maybe I'm too shallow, but thought he'd be great for my academic vegetarian younger sister. A man, maybe forty, but long dark hair unstreaked with grey and his merry dancing eyes made him difficult to truly age. He was a hawk, and a cat; a snake and a wolf.

When he offered to share my shower, I knew I'd have to keep sharp.

Maybe two hours we sat at the table. Jerry quietly, and he thought successfully, trying to win me into his bed. I was sober and therefore impossible to fool.

"What the hell are you doing here!" I turned around quickly from the table to see a wild-eyed, curly-haired woman staring at me. She hurled her spite at the man opposite.

"How could you! How COULD you!" she screamed. I sat in silence, a little bit shocked to be at the center of a scene.

"You promised, you bastard! After the last time, you PROMISED!" It seemed like a good time to slip away.

From behind the locked door of the bunk house, I could hear the screaming tires and scattering gravel as Jerry's berserk girlfriend drove around the property. She continued her drunken minute, then burned rubber along the highway and away.

"Phew!" I thought, and went to check up on Smokey.

Maybe ten minutes later as the night was falling over the ranch, Maggie turned up.

"Oh God! I'm so sorry!" she exclaimed after I'd told her the evening events. "I didn't know she was still around. She's a nutcase."

"Oh, it was pretty entertaining really," I replied. We talked a while, Maggie bringing out her presents of food and beer. A squeal on the highway made us both look north. 'She' was coming back.

"Hell! Ya'd better hide!" Maggie shouted.

"What on Earth for? I haven't done anything," I said. Within a minute, the poor distraught woman had pulled her car to a stop next to Maggie's.

"What d'ya have to come here for!" she yelled at me. "He's nothin' to you! He promised me it wouldn't happen again! He said that was the last time! And now, YOU! How could you - he's mine, ya hear me - He's MINE!..." she shouted.

"Whoa! Hold on a minute," I said, putting down my beer and walking up to the car.

"First of all, let's get it straight, friend," I said to her. "Jerry's nothing to me — I'm just passing through. I'm riding a horse cross country and needed a place to stop for the night. I've never met the guy before." She cast a red-eyed glance over to the ghost like horse grazing contentedly in the corral.

"He ain't got no right," she began again, "he said he wouldn't never do nothin' like last time!"

"Look - if there's a last time, there'll be a next time, but it isn't going to be with me! Quit the guy if he's that much of a sod!"

Maggie agreed, and she calmed down a little.

"He said he wanted to sleep with you and be with you," she sadly added.

"Well, he's a complete loser than, get ya'self a new one for sure. This one ain't doing ya' no good!" offered Maggie.

Both Maggie and I and the sad eyed lady talked on . She began to believe my story.

It was truly dark by the time I was free to return to the bunk house. I slept one ear open for Smokey, the other for a car with a woman nursing a dangerous broken heart.

With a guilty look, Jerry said goodbye to me in the morning. He wanted me to stay; or to come back, and to write anyway. I said 'Sure,' but I didn't ask for an address.

I stayed at the fairgrounds at Cliff the next day after some of the most spectacular scenery in the country. Grand rolling hills surrounded by majestic mountains; clouds scurrying across a Mediterranean blue sky - birds flying south in V formation. Fresh, fresh, fresh air! Wonderful! Both Smokey and I felt great!

My visitor for the night at the fairgrounds was quiet, intelligent, kindly Janet. She brought out her little stove and made me corn tortillas with a sweet potato and Worcestershire sauce topping. Heavenly! Still one of my favorites today! She also told me she'd seen Finisia. Jeannie was with her. They'd gone west together.

I was to leave New Mexico, my Land of Enchantment and of many things on Day 159. We were on Highway 78 out of Mule Creek, an almost deserted stretch of spectacular road; more magical countryside with each turn in the highway; cool days and frosty nights. I had an aim. The coast by December 18th, Rual had said. My dear devoted friend Rual Moody had driven all the way from Lubbock, Texas, to see me. See if I was okay, offer me and my Smokey a ride home.

"Be there by December 18th and I'll be there, too, with a horse trailer and a tank load of Texas gas!" It was a remarkable offer. If Rual could get us as far back as Levelland, I could ride Smokey back across Texas to her home farm in

Marshall in time for my March 28th return flight to England. I was ecstatic!

"Oh Rual. You are so WONDERFUL!!" I screamed wrapping my skinny arms around him. "What can I say? Thank you! Thank you! Thank you!"

It was October 22nd. Day 159. Mile 2071. A simple green sign on a quiet mountainous road.

Welcome to Arizona, it said. Grand Canyon State.

Westbound.

Chapter 9

ARIZONA
When I have a bad dream, it's Arizona on my mind.
Hunger, thirst, exhaustion, pain. Barbarous mountains
and tortuous deserts haunt me still.

"Easy does it, Smokey. Gently now." We were edging our way down the dramatic steep sided western drops of the Big Lue Mountains, taking it slowly but hoping to cover the twenty seven miles to Three Ways before dark. I was walking. It was too steep to ride. My two hosts, Mr. and Mrs. Ford from the night before had the hay and it was thanks to them that Smokey and I had a place to aim for that night. We were to be made welcome at the Forest Service Headquarters at the junction of 78, 191 and 75. Three Ways. In Arizona.

We could see the junction from high up on Mule Creek Road, but it was Black Jack Canyon and a drop of 5000 feet to be covered in the dark before we'd pass onto Forest Service Land, praying all the way that the Fords would be lighting the way with their car headlights. We waved good-bye at the fence line and the good natured uniformed man in charge led me to the corrals in back.

Hay was thrown out to Smokey, and horse feed, too. Water was freshened up in the big trough and with a hearty handshake and wishes of good luck, the officer left me to the horses and the stars. I set up the tent, sat in it's door, and rubbed my swollen feet with horse liniment. I did Smokey's knee next; it was also a bit enlarged from the down hill work. And we'd only just started.

"Arizona, my dear horsey friend," I said to Smokey as I massaged her stiffening joints, "Arizona, I'm afraid, is going to be a bit of a bitch."

The morning sun rises late on the valley floor, hidden behind the mountains to the east, keeping this stiff traveler and her woolly coated horse cold until work warms muscles and bones.

With a screaming left hip, a tortured knee and swollen feet, I led my loaded pony out in the early light of Day 160. It would be another long hard slog ahead. We took the 191 away from Three Ways climbing steeply into the Peloncillo Mountains and into Tollhouse Canyon. Within a few miles I was very uncomfortable. I struck out my thumb to passing traffic.

"Hey! Hey! Hey! What the hell ya doin' stickin' out ya thumb? Don't ya know ya got a horse behind ya?" A small red pickup had pulled over ahead and two well oiled cowboys hung out the cab windows laughing merrily. They told me they'd been gambling all night at the casino on the Indian Reservation. We joked around a bit, me feigning surprise at finding a horse walking alongside. After a few minutes, I persuaded them to carry the hay to a mile marker fifteen miles further on, which they found a difficult request to understand in their condition, with a confused look, they loaded up the two flakes in the truck. I wasn't sure whether I'd see it again.

I now had the option of riding. With a sigh, Smokey accepted the extra weight and we moved on.

For the next fifteen miles, I rode to ease my bad hip, knee and feet, then walked to ease Smokey's now swollen knee. She was always glad when I climbed down; I was always glad to climb up.

We were on a stretch of nothing. Of course, when you're inside a speeding car, the air conditioner on, an icy drink in your hand, it is beautiful. Very Spectacular. A mountain range to the west, one behind you to the east. One climbed the other yet to climb. But for me and Smokey, what we saw was no sign of water; rocky cactus desert to each side; no feed or food or place to stay. The first town, a small hamlet west of Safford, would be too far at thirty-five miles to make in our condition. Nothing to be done. We plodded wearily on.

The hay was there at the fifteenth mile marker. I was surprised. At least Smokey had food. I kept looking back up the highway, hoping for a horse trailer, or at least a visitor.

Nobody stopped that day. No visitors with a cold Coke or a bucket of water for Smokey, like we'd been spoilt with the day before by the Fords. No sandwiches or offers of places to stay. With the light being lost behind Pinaleno mountains to the west, I pulled Smokey off the road and into the sand and stones along Highway 70. There was nowhere more comfortable to go. We had had no water in twenty five miles and none here for sure. I emptied out the half a cup from the canteen into Smokey's feed bucket, the water lightly flavored with powered GatorAde still moldy smelling and warm. She sucked it gratefully down. Though I gave her hay, without water, she didn't eat. With a guilty feeling I opened up a can of Beenie-Weenies, ate it with the spoon, sucked on a beaver tail cactus for the water, and watched Smokey's dissatisfaction.

"Sorry, Smokey...." It was all I could do for her. There was not a sound that night. No coyote. No insects. No call from the wild burros. Not a stir. Not a whisper. Only Smokey grinding her teeth, craving a drink.

By nine o'clock the following morning, Smokey was swallowing her fill from a hosepipe from a small house on the outside of Solomon. She drank and drank and drank. Her eyes half closed, her ears twitching back and forth with every swallow. Eventually she lifted her head and with slurpy satisfaction allowed the water to wash around her mouth and down her black nose. Finally, she turned, head down to the home owners' lawn.

I took her as far as a grassy bank on the way to Safford, could go no further, sank gratefully down in the soft green. Water ran behind my back in a little irrigation ditch on its way to fields of late crops and alfalfa grass. The Gila River was somewhere to the north; we were in its valley. I was very tired; very sore. Each yank on the lead rope from Smokey sent cruel jabs of pain up from my right knee and left hip. I looked at the Arizona pages of what was to come. My spirit sank. We weren't even in the tough stuff yet. Smokey had a couple of hours grazing on the deep Bermuda grass before I loaded her up for the second time that day. With huge reluctance we set off once again along the highway. We needed to find a good night.

Within five more miles we were in the tree lined cool suburbs of the town of Safford. Smokey and I angled off into the back streets and at the first opportunity, asked about a place to stay.

"Hello, my name is Emma Crosby, I'm from England and doing a bit of traveling with my horse in this area and wondered if you'd be kind enough to let me borrow your pasture for the night. We'd be no bother I promise, and I'd be glad to pay you..." They must have seen the need in my face, the desperation in the appeal because Carl and Dorrill Johnson couldn't have been kinder. With pleasure they helped me to see Smokey housed in their waist high pasture behind the house; water clean and deep in the trough. Despite my objections to handing over my disgraceful pile of worn out, dusty, smelly clothes, Carl wouldn't take a no, demanding that they should be cleaned and made liveable again. Their own camper van next to the paddock became my home for my stay; the bed, a double, royally covered with the deep inviting luxury of a feather mattress. With the strain of the last few days and the night before, we were both in heaven; on hold were the barbarous mountains and treacherous deserts.

Smokey and I stayed with the Johnson's another day. Both our knees were rested; my hip was given a chance to recover. There was excellent food, the intoxicating luxury of drinking cocktails, watching my horse happily grazing in the long, protein rich grass. The local reporter came out and seemed to enjoy the interview as I took a trip to the supermarket. A 'trip' it was, too! So much food! So many choices! I stocked up on cans of Beanie-Weenies and for a special treat in the future, when I needed a lift, I invested in a tin of fruit cocktail. Dorrill also drove me to the offices of the Bureau of Land Management and the Forest Service to find out what was to come; enlist their help.

On the morning of Day 163, the 26th of October, Smokey and I set out smartly from Safford.. No packs, no hay, no feed to carry. The Johnson's were kindly going to drop them off at around four in the afternoon. Once again, we were free to just ride; to enjoy the day. And what a beautiful day it was too!

We made it to Fort Thomas, six miles short of the San Carlos Indian Reservation, twenty two miles gone. An old widowed gentleman agreed to us using his paddock for the night, then shyly and graciously made me hamburgers for an evening meal, despite his difficulty in moving after a recent stroke. He apologized for not thinking it wise to have me stay in his house, but he felt it best not to give the neighbors food for gossip. He must have been at least seventy.

With a full belly of bacon and eggs in the morning and three days supply of hay over the saddle, I sadly said good-bye to my king host of Day 163, Mr. McEwen. I didn't know what to expect for the next two nights — we'd be on the reservation — so my comfortable night with him was doubly welcome.

After my experience of the Apache at Mescalero, I was, putting it mildly, concerned about being forced to spend two nights in their company again. We were heading away from the fertile Gila Valley and away from water. The 70 would take us Northwest slightly, skirting around the San Carlos Lake towards Globe over three days away. However I paced the next two days, it meant staying in the reservation at night.

Very quickly the land became more desolate. Alfalfa gave way to mesquite and cacti, pretty little town birds gave way to birds of prey.

I stopped at Bylas, highway 70 dividing the town through it's center. A wild horse roamed down the rocky verge. It was hot. Dogs barked.

I watered Smokey then went into the icy air-conditioned coolness of the gas station to ask about a place to stay and buy a drink. We'd only done eleven miles but there was nothing to the west. A customer buying gas said she'd be glad to put us up. With thanks, I took the lady's directions and led Smokey that way. We were to leave 70, dropping into the bottle and litter strewn series of buildings to the northern side. Small streets lined with barking dogs, laughing children, people shouting, calm eyed grandparents, led me to the address I'd been given. It was early yet. Darlene, my host, and her husband met us, leading the way past the barking dogs, a calm and dignified smile on her handsome Apache face.

We were to spend the night in a small enclosure. The house stood to one side, along the others, buildings, small horse corrals, a fence, a gate. There was an awful lot of trash around, a smoldering fire. I secretly cleared Smokey's pen of wire and glass, fed her a flake of hay and some grain; worried whether the weak-looking fence would hold her.

With the extra hours of daylight I caught up on some letter writing and watched Smokey. I was treated kindly by Darlene and her family. With quiet respect, she'd bring me a bit of soup, or some coffee, a small stove, and a blanket. She wouldn't stay but quietly came and went. A small office-like building forty feet away from the house had been cleared for my home for the night. A good roof, running water, a loo. Very welcome. Two pretty teenage girls came by for half an hour on their way out to a house party. It was a good place to stop. I could sleep well.

With it being so dark so early in the evenings now, bedtime was not long after everyone came home from work. Usually by 6 p.m. I was wrapped up in my sleeping bag, and that's if I could make it that long! Sometimes exhaustion would make the end of my day even sooner. I could sleep quite happily for twelve or thirteen hours!

Day 165 saw us up early and on the road shivering gladly with the cool temperatures. Before very long the sun would have climbed over the mountains and warmed the morning air. I was in the saddle for a ten mile stretch - my hosts were on their way to San Carlos and were carrying the hay for me -- so, well rested and pretty fit, we headed west, the sun warming rapidly on our backs.

With the strain of these early Arizona miles, I was comforting myself with the thought of Rual's offer of a ride back to Texas. At least I wouldn't have all these miles to ride over again on the west-east trip. And we weren't even in the difficult bit yet! West of Phoenix was where it counted. Gila Bend to California. If I was struggling with East Arizona, just you wait Emma, you ain't seen nothin' yet...

The hay wasn't at the designated mile marker. I walked anxiously on, more and more panicked by the idea of no food for Smokey that night. It was painful for me the thought of letting her down after her day after day of heroic efforts. She was still fat, but I wanted her to stay fat. I had an orange string vest that I'd been given by someone to make me more visible which I usually gave to my hay carriers to tie to the mile marker the hay was hidden close to. The designated one for Darlene and her husband, was bare. They must have forgotten and driven on by.

Td almost given up hope before seeing the orange vest flapping in the breeze almost half a mile further on. The orange vest meant hay back on the saddle and being closer to self sufficient. With huge kindness and thoughtfulness they'd also left Smokey a big bucket of cooling water.

Our second night on the reservation was in a sea of glass. From my first view on top of the rolling hill, I thought a lake lay before us in the afternoon sun. A shimmering, glittering coolness lay ahead and my heart leapt for the thought of a night by the cool water. There was no lake on my very detailed map. The closer we approached the desert land mirage, the more the sadness of broken beer bottles and cans imitating silvery water became obvious, and I wondered at the myth of the Native American respect for the land.

We stayed our second night on the reservation, just short of San Carlos with it's very popular Casino. A small tree shaded the tent from the evening sun in the large yard of a large Apache family. The house was simple, quite big and plain. The children lively, fun loving, very curious and lots of them. Smokey was again in a corral subtlety cleared of wire and trash. Dogs and youngsters came in and out of my tent, exploring my bags and my way of life. We'd covered twenty-three miles.

It was dark before I could free myself from the smiling, runny-nosed children. They were called to eat and bed. I sat in the tent door and had a tin of Beanie-Weenies, tired out but feeling pretty well. Good job, too. The next day, we'd be starting to climb again.

It was a long walk. I'd wanted to stop at Cutter but there was nothing there. We dragged along to near Globe. An eighteen mile slog; my knee again a tortuous hotspot. We were off the reservation by half a mile.

On the northern side of the same Highway 70, a green garden and a well kept house after the last few dusty miles tipped Smokey off for a likely nights stay. She stopped in her tracks and waited while we went through the normal ritual of me trying to make her move on, then giving up. When I'd finished my usual struggles, Smokey calmly turned her head to the right.

"What about there?" she seemed to say.

"Hmmm...." I answered her, scratching my head "Looks a bit posh for us."

Not long after, I was sitting on the steps to my very own recreational vehicle, calmly eating a chunky home-made sandwich, Smokey tied to the wheel contentedly grazing on the kind owners well kept lawn.

"You're getting pretty good at this, Smokey." I offered.

"Hmmm," she said, looking at me through half closed eyes.

Nothing sets you up like a good plate of home-cooked breakfast, and even as importantly, a big steaming cup of good fresh coffee on a cool morning. How I appreciated that welcome brew after having to give up the stove in Texas. I missed my morning coffee the most.

Day 167 saw me back on the road, well spoiled in both departments: good coffee and a big plate of bacon and eggs. Our hosts, Mr and Mrs. Frank Stephenson just outside of Globe had treated us royally, with their kind loan of the big RV and two good, much needed meals. Smokey enjoyed the luxury of a choice between grass and hay, and there was the possibility of mail at Globe. We left in very good spirits.

The town of Globe is the first in a series of towns almost continuously lining this stretch of Highway 70 climbing up into the Pinal Mountains. A big mining area with names like Quartzite Peak, Granite Point, Inspiration and Chrome Butte. Steep cliffs crowd in on the road, squeezing out horse and rider. Big trucks rule. We were headed for a few tricky miles.

What was to come didn't spoil our enjoyment of those early morning moments; the cool temperatures, the sunny day. We came into Globe at a good paced walk after little more than an hour since leaving the last night's stop. The town was still half asleep. One of the early risers, a man in a pickup truck, pulled over ahead of us, waited for us to ride up. "Hi! How ya doin'?" he called out when we were close enough to hear.

"Good. How 'bout you?" I replied. The tall, good looking man introduced himself as Howard Horinek; he was a horse shoer.

"Don't fancy a job do you?" I asked hopefully, pointing at Smokey's paper thin shoes.

"Sure," he said.

While Howard replaced the worn out set of steel shoes with new, we traded stories of how we came to be where we were. My new friend was a hard working cowboy living a few miles away at the Sheppard Ranch, shoeing horses now and again and a talented saddle maker also. He showed me his latest piece; a lovely leather lightweight saddle, very comfortable. The design was his own and I admired it immensely.

"One day," I promised him, "I'll have a saddle like that." How I wished I could have had Howard build me one of those right then ~ they weren't expensive, but EVERYTHING was out of my price range! I sighed and saved the image as something to dream about.

Howard also had a load of contacts in the area who'd be possible for places to stay. With Smokey newly shod all round, he drove off to find out.

We met up a little later in the morning. Two addresses he had for the next two nights. I was very grateful as the map described rather a lonely stretch coming up. Howard also very kindly bought out a bag of alfalfa nuts to refill Smokey's feed sacks hanging down empty from the saddle horn.

As we said good-bye, I hoped my warm handshake conveyed to Howard my gratitude for his going out of his way to help me on that morning at the end of October. Probably didn't realize how glad I was to meet him: Smokey's shoes had broken in two when he'd pulled them off they'd been so worn out, and with no feed on board, I worried about her being disappointed at the end of the day. An extra bonus, very welcome, was the two nights of no worries. Thanks Howard..

It was only ten miles to the first address I'd been given that morning, but by the time we'd made the dangerous climb to the ranch gates, it was already late afternoon. The sun was casting it's last amber hues on the high peaks overhead, while Smokey and I were fading into the blues of the steep-sided canyon walls.

We'd just passed the 2200 mile mark.

Opening the gate was a struggle with wire wrapped very tightly around the post and very unyielding. Ranch traffic used the cattle grid entrance to the left. My fingers were sore and my temper red by the time I had Smokey off the highway and onto the property.

Looking around, I could see small well kept houses, pretty and neatly edged with green lawn and flower beds. Maybe two hundred yards of dirt lane led up to the main house giving me a few minutes to cool off my mood, fortunately. To the right fat cattle with calves grazed the short grass around a pond. A horse called from a corral I couldn't see.

We followed the little dirt road up to the main buildings, tying Smokey to the high chain link fence. Big and little dogs threw themselves against the wire barking furiously but wagging their tails. Johnny and Helen Shultze came out to welcome us.

"Oh, don't worry about them!" Johnny shouted over his noisy pets, "they're very friendly really."

Johnny and Helen proved very friendly, too. Glamorous Helen cooked up a splendid fish dinner seemingly without effort, while Johnny saw Smokey turned out on the grass, extra feed and hay in the trough. One of the buildings lay empty and I was offered it's use for the night which I was glad to accept. It was fully furnished.

Back at the house, the evening passed quickly with lively conversation and good humor. Both Johnny and Helen were real characters; fiin loving and popular. Bill Scott, a neighbor and local reporter came over with his wife and took a casual interview in a party atmosphere for the local paper and radio station. I think I may have had a beer or two.

Much of the conversation covered the country Smokey and I had already been over, but it often turned back to what to expect ahead.

"It's pretty bad down there," said Johnny, "don't know if it's even possible to get through. You see, there's all them trucks tearing by — they don't take no notice of nothin' on the side of the road. Hell, they don't even slow down round them bends and there's some pretty bad ones, I can tell ya. The road, ifs pretty steep and narrow in places and then of course, you know about the tunnel..." "The tunnel???" I said.

"Yeah. That great long tunnel through the mountain up by Devil's Canyon. It's pretty bad ~ don't know if it's even possible. Ain't no hard shoulder I should think."

"Oh.... a tunnel," I repeated, sinking in my chair. There was no tunnel on my map. Tunnels are very sobering.

"Tell ya what though," Johnny went on, "I've got a truck I can get and take you across myself in the morning." I argued just long enough about the use of a horse trailer to convince my hosts I wasn't a coward, then reluctantly folded to their offer.

"Well, if you really think it's impassable for a horse -1 guess that'll be great if you'd take us through, Johnny. That's really kind," I said, an argued down sort of smile on my face.

"Thank God!" I thought to myself.

The road was indeed very dangerous. Steep, sharp bends, huge trucks, blinding sun sometimes dropping into dusk like darkness. Smokey had surprised me by very happily jumping up into the back of a five ton truck. It wasn't exactly designed to transport a horse. Johnny had her tied to the wooden frame, and I rode a bit anxiously in the cab.

She traveled well, the wind in her face, her long mane flying out behind.

From the cab window I could see her black nose poked over the top of the truck side, her nostrils flared, her eyes alert, enjoying the ride. Even with the noisy granite-laden eighteen wheelers whizzing by, she wasn't fussed. I turned to Johnny.

"Pretty good horse, eh?" I said tossing my head towards Smokey.

"Oh yeah. She's a good 'un," he replied, smiling.

We were in and out of the tunnel very quickly; an orange tinted darkness then blinding sun.

"She did alright," I said to Johnny.

"Oh yeah, she did alright," he agreed. We were to stay at Dan's that night; only a four mile ride after being dropped off by Johnny in Superior. He'd had to back the truck up to a soft bank for Smokey to be able to jump down without hurting herself. With such a short distance to cover, I treated myself to an ice-cream at the Dairy Queen; went to the Post office, too, and ate some of the candy Bill the reporter had kindly given me. It was a warm day, promising a cold night.

Dan was glad to be able to help. We camped early behind his house in a small collection of corrals. Howard, the horse shoer, had dropped off a new set of feed bags he'd especially made for me, and the remainder of the horse feed I hadn't been able to carry before. The bags were beautiful and very tough wearing. I gladly threw away the worn out old burlap sacks I'd been using. They'd lasted since Post, Texas. The remainder of the day I spent in letter writing and while the light lasted, I watched my precious Smokey and mused on her character. She was chewing contentedly on her evening hay. I remembered her joyous face of that morning, when the wind had whipped through her mane and her black eyes had shone with the coldness of the wind chill and with excitement. I looked at her now, grazing in the fading light; quiet. Is she real, I thought.

It was the first of November. Day 169. 2212 miles behind us and plenty yet to go. We took our last big climb early in the afternoon, followed by Gonzales Pass and down. The Rocky Mountains, with it's many ranges, were just about behind us.

Good. And bad. Good as no more pressure on Smokey's knees from those steep downhill grades. And bad -- now, just deserts; finding water.

We pulled in to a wholesale jewelry store at the junction of Highway 60 and Route 79. There were some deserted buildings behind the store that had attracted my attention and I asked about their possible use for the night. A rather tall, domineering woman listened grim faced to my request.

"Oo, my dear, 'course you can." she returned in a slight German accent, a charming smile breaking out on her well cared for face.

"Tell me vat you're doin'." I went briefly over my journey so far, which she seemed to enjoy.

"Veil! I do admire you!" she said and shoveled a whole collection of tinned goodies into a bag for my use.

The building I'd selected was an empty house; it's grounds completely fenced. There was a little bit of grass surviving from what once had been a lawn. Though my friendly host opened the house, I chose to camp outside in the tent. The house was a little musty. I saw Smokey unsaddled and settled, then returned to the jewelry store for coffee and chat with the tall boss lady and her couple of staff.

I drank the coffee pot dry. Also irresistible was a small black stone frog with turquoise eyes crafted by a Navajo Indian that, with a generous discount, was almost given to me. Added to this box were small pieces of turquoise in various stages of polishing, for good luck, she said. In my turn, I was able to hand over an eagle feather I wore in my black hat. The lady had admired it as a present for her husband (the real eagle feathers were very rare). It made a good change for me to actually have something to give as a gift. There wasn't much I owned that people would want.

When the shop was closed up for the night and everyone had gone home, I sat in the tent door, watching Smokey eating from one of the new cans I'd been given. For the first and only time on the whole trip, I ate asparagus tips! The caffeine in my system kept me awake most of the night.

We had two nights with Bob and Rae Phillips at their lovely home in Florence. A real bed; excellent food; a trip to town to buy some replacement jeans (my other ones were pretty indecent). Generally, a welcome break. We were saddled up and ready to go the morning after the first night but heavy rain set in and it was easy to take advantage of their kind offer of an extra night.

It was great to be able to walk around the pretty little town of Florence, alone, without the worry of Smokey hurrying me on. I visited several shops to luxuriously waste time and a restaurant tempted me in for a bowl of wonderful clam chowder. I could easily imagine what it must be like to have the responsibility of children twenty-four hours a day, and then, briefly to be free of them for awhile. Real freedom! Wonderful!

One of my slowly selected purchases was a decent tube of glue, which, back at the house, I used to repair the worn out soles of my boots. For several days I'd been carrying around torn up pieces of truck tires I'd picked up from the side of the road and the glue bonded them beautifully to the holey soles. It was lovely to walk on half inch bouncy rubber! Made for interesting footprints, too!

Day 172 was an easy ten miles along the back roads away from Florence. A cool, sunny morning followed by a comfortable warm afternoon. Puddles made finding a drink for Smokey easy, and with no hay over the saddle, I was able to ride again. We were in farming country so finding a meal for Smokey shouldn't be a problem. We were following the fertile Gila River Valley, with Phoenix to the north-west out of a view but a huge orange block on my map. The next Indian Reservation lay to the west. I stopped Smokey just short of it's western boundary.

We camped in a barn belonging to a friendly farmer, surrounded by the last of the flat green and brown fields. The owner very generously brought out a fresh bale of sweet alfalfa hay which he refused payment for.

"Make yaself at home," he said "You're sure welcome here."

The night was peaceful and quiet.

The Gila River Indian Reservation stretched over thirty miles of our east-west route, so one night around it's main town of Sacaton should be all we'd need before being out the other side. Sacaton marked the halfway point across Arizona and pretty much the end of the 'easy' stuff.

The cultivated fields stayed with us a little way into the reservation, but as the morning wore on, they faded into land of bush and rock. The low lying hills of the Sacaton mountains to the north and south wedged against the narrowing band of flat country we traveled through . This was the land of the Pima Indian.

Many of the buildings on the outside of town seemed almost new, but empty; others seemed broken up and lived in. There were a few horses around, usually colorful black and white ponies, and scrawny suspicious-eyed dogs. Rubbish collection was either very sporadic or didn't exist. As in most of the reservation land I'd been through, glass and cans lay like an outside carpet in most people's back yards. We were along Route 1 and passing an area of new development and grander housing. Not many homes had gone by before a bunch of men and women sitting under a tree called to us as we plodded along the road.

"Hey! Where yagoin'?!" one shouted.

"Oh...Sacaton!" I called back.

"Come on over and have a beer!" one round faced woman yelled out, "It's my birthday." An easy offer, not to be refused. I tied Smokey under another tree and joined the Indian group in the shade. Friends and family gathered around the already red-eyed Melinda Whitson, most enjoying the cold Budweiser beers from the outside fridge. Pretty faced, brown-eyed children played with the toys around the adult's feet; broken glass and Superman figures sharing the same spot.

After the second beer, I accepted their welcome offer of a stop for the night. We'd covered thirteen miles.

Smokey was unsaddled and tied on her long rope to a fence at the neighbor's house. Thick green grass around her feet soon had her undivided attention. I ferried the packs over to Melinda's spare room, at least, it was made into a spare room for me.

The inside of the house was dark, sparsely furnished and, like my little cottage back in England, home to spiders and dust. The sitting room held only a long green sofa and a chair beside the big screen television. A young, quiet couple held each other on the sofa. I could hear a baby chatting to a young girl. The kitchen was very dark, the stove black with greasy spatterings of old fat. A table covered in a plastic cloth had a hasty washing. There was a cheap print on a wall and a pile of clean laundry in a basket. The kitchen led to the back yard where another young child played on a mattress. Old cars stood rusting against the property edge; glass and trash were everywhere. A much lived in place.

The beer was almost gone, so the party broke up to restock. Three full blooded Pima Indian men, Melinda and I, all, apart from the driver in various stages of inebriation, piled into a beaten up old wide bodied car and headed up the highway. We were drinking the last of the'Bud'.

Maybe six miles on, we pulled into the parking area outside an out-of-town combination grocery store and gas station. Iron bars covered every window. "Pay before you pump" was printed boldly on the door. We were off the reservation.

"No alcohol sold on the Rez," Melinda's friend said. I thought from all the evidence of cans and bottles inside the reservation, this halfhearted control to keep the inhabitants alcohol free was something less than totally successful. It actually seemed to cause car-loads of alcohol-saturated drivers to race up and down the highway on their way to the nearest liquor store. Curious.

We picked up a couple of six packs and headed back, taking a detour to visit some of the sacred spots inside the reservation. Various rocks and marks on the mountain sides were pointed out to me by the driver; a tall thirty-something handsome man with a deep knowledge of his home and history. As he described each new place we visited, the stones and the land took on more depth. The other passengers in the car quieted down their loud jokes and infectious laughter and listened to the often told stories, their thoughts reflecting back to their ancestors and their proud heritage. Why, then, with their love for this rocky country around them, did they care so little for keeping it clean? I didn't understand the contradiction.

Before the tour was over, Linda had passed out in the front seat; her snores accompanied us back to the house.

The party broke up. I checked up on Smokey, found her happy and went to my own bed. With a quick sweep of my hand, I brushed away the cockroaches from my mattress in the spare room and laid out my sleeping bag. Despite the baby crying down the corridor, sleep came easily.

Melinda made a wonderful breakfast of potatoes and eggs and bacon. Coffee followed. Her gang were taking her on a trip to town that day as a birthday treat, then another party to follow. She pleaded with me to come along. I didn't think my stamina could hold up against these party loving people for a whole day, so as politely as possible refused the kind invitation.

"Sorry Linda. Got to catch a ride in San Diego on the 18th and I'm pushed for time. I'd really love to normally..."

The neighbors and friends and family watched quietly as I loaded Smokey up and moved back out on to the highway. "Bye; Linda. I had a great time last night and thanks for the tour and I wish I could stay. Have a lovely time today and thanks again..."

We exchanged addresses and a hug and I led Smokey on, waving back to my new friends; the fun loving and very friendly Pima people.

Route 1, a little traveled highway, took us as far west as Sacaton where we left if for Seed Farm Road. We were aiming for Maricopa, a small town just west of the reservation boundary. I was walking. The day was sunny and clear, a comfortable seventy-five or eighty degrees by noon. Out quiet little lane was a pleasure to travel along, the tarmac soon giving way to soft dirt. Scavenger birds accompanied us overhead. A canal still held water to the south of us and there was another to the north. I watered Smokey midday at an irrigation channel next to an orange grove. Gently turning windmills worked silently amongst the trees. There was no one around.

By early afternoon we'd left the cool orange groves behind us and set out over a stretch of desert-barren land around Camp Rivers, a site of ruins on the top of Sacaton Butte, a hill of 1570 feet. A car sat at the bottom of the hill, it's passengers a few colorful splashes against the sandy colored rock following the footpath to the peak. The soft road we now followed was straining the tendon in my right heel, and the further we traveled, the more painful it became. Smokey was fine. I pushed on, wanting to make it to Maricopa and water before dark.

We left the ruins behind us; traveled directly west along Smith-Enke Road. In the desert shrub, the bleached bones of dozens of cattle lined our path, like something out of an old John Wayne film.

Nineteen miles went by before I felt I couldn't go on. My heel had become so sore the first sign of a hidden away camping site drew my last resources and I led Smokey off the road. We were in a pecan orchard, and though there was only a shallow puddle for water, it was quiet and private. I couldn't make the extra four miles to Maricopa.

Favoring my right leg, I set up the tent; led Smokey to the puddle for her last chance of water that day; fed her; fed myself, then sank to the ground at the tent door. I couldn't remove my boot, the heel was so swollen and painful. Unpacking the horse liniment I'd been given way back in Texas, I dribbled some of the potent smelling liquid into my sock and let it soak on down inside the boot. 'For veterinary use only' it said on the label. DMSO - it had been banned for human use after causing often weird side effects, but I needed it then. The throbbing would keep me awake only briefly; exhausted after walking nineteen miles, I slept well.

Smokey drank deeply from the puddle early the next morning, our 175th on the road. Picking up the tent and our shared belongings had taken me twice as long as usual with my sore foot and stiff muscles. Finally I swung carefully into the saddle and picked up the reins. Smokey set off automatically. A flake of hay lay unused back at the campsite.

We came into Maricopa just over an hour and a half later. The gate to the feed store was open and I steered Smokey in. Dall Dankworth, the owner, was working the till.

"Howdy! How ya doin'?" he said.

Before too long he'd found out my name; where I was from; what I was doing; where I was going; what I needed at the feed store. The only question I couldn't answer clearly was what the hell was I doing it for. Just couldn't think of a reasonable reply.

"Oh.... for fun, mainly," I finally said, resting my swollen foot over my dust-covered and torn left knee.

I spent the night at Dall's house. His Dad, Ralph, came by and cooked up a giant plate of home-made French fries to go along with barbecued chicken and steak. I ate as much as I possibly could, which was a pitifully small amount with my shrunken stomach, while my clothes span rhythmically around in the clothes washer.

Clean hair, clean clothes, good food, good people. Somewhere dry and warm for the night; somewhere safe for Smokey ~ all the ingredients to a perfect night's stay. Dall and Ralph Dankworth kindly gave me all of these things for our one night in Maricopa and all they asked in return was a postcard from the West Coast. That's a very good trade.

"That'll be the least I can do," I said as I thanked them the next morning, waving good-bye. In the hours I'd sat around the feed store, I'd met quite a few people as they'd come in to pick up a few things or chat to Dall, and one young woman, Sue Handka, had become my friend. She had eagerly agreed to my request of ferrying the hay along Route 238, leaving me free to ride and rest that bad heel, and she promised to bring out water for Smokey, too, before the day was through. With the worry of feed and water over, I set out on Day 176, the 8th of November, aiming to spend the night at Mobile on the eastern edge of the South Maricopa Mountains Wilderness, a sixteen mile trek.

The road was a simple, flat, two lane highway passing through Heaton, Enid and on the Mobile. These small dots on the map rather grandly described a settlement of maybe two or three houses. I watered Smokey at Enid and rode on. Running parallel to the road were the shining steel tracks of the Southern Pacific Railroad. They'd be accompanying us for many miles yet.

The dusty dry river beds from Waterman Wash passed under the road. Cactus, prickly bushes, spine covered plants, coyote footprints and snake tracks, birds of prey circling way up in the dense blue overhead. All these kept us company as we progressed slowly along.

Sue caught up with us just before Mobile, and as promised filled the bucket with good clear water for Smokey. When she'd had her fill, once again, I hooked the three days worth of hay over the saddle horn and across the saddle back. The new feed bags from Howard were swelled to maximum with fresh, high quality, sweet feed, and I added these last to Smokey's load. I thanked my kind new friend for making such a difference to our day and we left with my regrets at seeing her drive away.

Just outside of town which lay a little north of the highway, stood a handsome, well tended school. A cattle grid barred our entrance to the grounds proper, but the bus driver parked across the entrance, waiting for a late class to finish, gave us permission to use the empty rough land on ifs eastern boundary. I led Smokey through the downed wire fence and we dropped out of sight behind several trees and some broken building foundations. I unloaded Smokey and fed her on a short lead. Not until darkness gave us full cover did I pitch the tent and free Smokey to the full length of her rope. When all was quiet, I climbed, with some difficulty, the chain link fence surrounding the school buildings, and with one of their landscaping hoses, I filled Smokey's flexible blue bucket.

The squeals and high pitched yelps of the coyotes in the rough country all around accompanied my dreams through the star-rich night.

Before the sun was truly complete in the morning sky, Smokey and I were on the road and heading west. A cool start soon gave itself up to a warm day, as the tarmacked road soon conceded to the rusty colored dirt. Within a mile or so of walking on the soft path, my rested but not mended heel began it's objectionable nagging pain. We had two days of hay over the saddle so I had no option but to walk. We were crossing Forty Mile Desert.

As the sun climbed, the temperature escalated. Fortunately it was well into November and we were well seasoned to the heat with our August crossing of Texas. However, Smokey had quickly grown a thick woolly winter coat through the frosty nights in the Rockies and she found that being back in summer again, she was a tad overdressed. I tied her mane up to let her sweat more freely.

I was hoping to maybe stop at Estrella that day, half way across the desert, splitting the crossing into two packages, but when we plodded into the spot where Estrella should have been, there was... nothing. And lots of it. Just the dust and the tall Seguaro cactus and the thorny mesquite. Hugely disappointed, we moved on. By this time, I was holding on to Smokey's tail and she was pulling me along.

The next chance of water wouldn't be until Shawmut, over six miles further.

There was nothing at Shawmut. And the same thing happened at Bosque. No water there, either. These small settlements had once been watering holes in the times of the steam train. In my time, there was nothing. Just to dust to quench our thirst; just the stunted thorny bushes to give us shade. Without a break we moved on. I couldn't stop. If I sat down, my swollen feet would seize up and we'd be stuck overnight without water. We had to cover the thirty-four miles to Gila Bend. The dirt road we left our footprints along was a lonely untraveled route; just Smokey and me, and a one time westbound freight train.

I just couldn't do it. Those extra miles on that bad foot took the last of my strength. After a twenty-eight mile day. I had to stop. We followed a little track off to the right which looked promising as a camp site. There were picnic tables and rubbish bins, and a sign saying Such-and-Such Gun Club. There were shelters and parking spots, barbecue pits and paths leading off into the desert. But there was no water. I tied Smokey to one of the shelters and fed her a flake of hay. She ignored it. I gave her the little water I had in the canteen which was a thousandth of what she should have had after the long hot day she'd just been through. Too tired to eat, I unfolded my sleeping bag and collapsed on top of a picnic table.

It was the only time I wished someone would turn up at night.

I slept in snatches. Smokey was pacing, grinding her teeth, seriously in need of a drink. I felt terrible for making her suffer. In the pitch black of three in the morning, I put away the sleeping bag and loaded her up. By ten past three we were back on the dusty road, me in the saddle. I'd left the remaining hay at the shooting range.

Riding in the dark was a very strange disorientating experience. I had the flashlight positioned so I could see if any snakes lay across out path sucking up the warmth from yesterday's sun. The beam passed over Smokey's right shoulder and fell ten or so feet ahead. Smokey didn't like the black hole in the light's center, and couldn't understand why she never caught up with it. Apart from the stars and the faint orange glow from Gila Bend ahead, there were no other lights. It was like swimming in the dark - hard to pinpoint which way was up and which down. I found myself slipping off the saddle several times and I could only be sure we were moving by the rippling muscles of Smokey's shoulder seen in the peripheral of the torch beam. I couldn't even work out east and west and many times looked for the change in the sky in the wrong place.

Finally, the black universe became stretched with an aquiline blue then lighter, off-pink. Early clouds caught the rosy glow and the invisible road became clearer and real. In the very first hour of true morning, Smokey was drinking deeply from a water faucet in Gila Bend.

We made quite a sight. As I pushed open the door to the popular little cafe on the main street, the diners there fell silent.

"Mornin'," I said to several of them as I passed between the tables. I wasn't sure I was going to be allowed to stay. From the once black hat with it's friendly rattle from two long dead snakes, to the four leaf clover on my worn out spurs; to the once blue checkered lumber man's jacket, to the self-taylored deerskin trousers with the bobcat toe-bone buttons, to the wiry plait of uncared for hair, to the broken chipped nails on my hands, I was one color - the color of the pinkish-brown dust of the Maricopa Desert. I wasn't exactly the picture of sartorial elegance. The only contrasting color to my drab ensemble were my blue eyes shining out of a dusty pink-brown face.

"Coffee, please." I whispered to the dark haired waitress. Conversation started back up. I took a seat against a window, next to Smokey. She was outside, contentedly munching down on a big bucket of feed. One friendly guy turned around from his table opposite.

"You're not from round here," he said, smiling.

"No, you're right, I'm not." I smiled back.

There was a letter from home waiting for us at the Post Office. It felt like Christmas Day! Food and coffee, a letter; civilization. Very welcome. We had some tough country ahead. 120 miles from Gila Bend to Yuma and no clear way to travel. The most direct route was Interstate 8 which could take us all the way. Trouble was, no horses were allowed on the freeway. The longer route meant a whole package of countryside like the Maricopa Mountain Wilderness: deserts, low barren mountains, no water. Not much of a decision really. I'd rather be in trouble with the Highway Patrol than follow Day 177 with another miserable one like it. For one day at least, we'd be okay. The Gila Bend Canal, still deep with dark, slow moving water, would accompany us as far as Piedra.

I stocked up on three day's worth of hay and topped up the feed sacks from a huge feed lot at Theba. Though I tried for half an hour to find a worker in the huge complex of grain bins, tanks, cattle holding units and horse sheds, there was no one about. Rather anxiously, I slipped into the feed shed and took what I needed. I left three dollars on the bin lid with a note explaining why I'd taken it and where I could be found if I hadn't left enough. The note was a slight exaggeration. I only *had* three dollars. I loaded Smokey up and we turned westwards.

Where we stayed the night wasn't so much of a worry with the water from the canal to our left and the hay and feed slung over the saddle. Privacy was the only missing ingredient. In the elbow of the canal, as it swung away to the north and under the freeway a dip in the sand became our home for Day 178. I tied Smokey to a big piece of concrete piping and freed her of the heavy load. With a groan of pleasure, she dropped to her knees. Over on her back she turned, rolling and twisting in the soft luxury of the desert sand, scratching herself, having a horse bath. She polished off the sweat with her luxurious rolling — last night we'd been on gravel. Her big woolly head; her broad muscled back; her strong legs and wide neck, she cleaned them all of our long day before. With a hearty shake she shook off the loose sand, then a buck and a jump and she stood king of the castle on a sandy hill. For a few seconds she watched the Interstate traffic passing a few hundred feet to our north, and the lonely howl of the freight trains alongside made her pick up her ears to listen, then with a snort, she'd race down the bank of her small mountain of sand, through my dip and up the other side, a little buck for good measure as she reached its summit. She felt fabulous! And what a pleasure it was for me to see her so happy after the awful night before. We had all the water we needed, good hay and fresh feed. I felt rich that night!

From my map I could work out that the next town of Sentinel at twenty-three miles was our best, and pretty much, our *only* chance of water on this next desolate stretch. If I could sneak Smokey through as far as Exit 78 on the freeway, eight miles past Sentinel, we could pick up the Old Highway that ran alongside from there. We should be able to find water at Dateland, twenty miles on from Sentinel, and from there I could take Smokey cross-country to the back end of the Mohawk Valley. It meant a day and a half of illegal travel. It was worth the risk.

For two miles west of our night's campsite we enjoyed the luxury of a tarmacked farm road running our way. As it ended we were stopped by a friendly farmer. Luck was on our side. This tall, good natured visitor was on his way to Sentinel and could carry the hay for us. He even offered to stock it up with enough to take us as far as the fertile Mohawk Valley. I hadn't been looking forward to twenty-three miles on my bad heel, so was visibly relieved when he made his offer.

"Oh! That would be brilliant," I exclaimed, shaking his hand enthusiastically.

"No problem," he kindly replied.

The tarmacked road ended against a small copse of willowy trees. A wired fence and an ominous sign declared the property ahead private, belonging to the Southern Pacific Railroad. NO Trespassing. A cattle grid barred our entrance to the Interstate to the right, but I didn't look to cross that, because through the trees, on the other side of the wired up gate and the faded sign, I could see a path. A sandy lane ran parallel to the steel tracks. Westbound. Our way on.

With nervous hands, I unbound the constraining wire and led Smokey on through. With it safely closed again we began our long day to Sentinel.

Slowly, very slowly it seemed, the miles drifted by. Sometimes I rode, sometimes I walked; resting my foot, then resting my horse. The land was flat, the path soft and sandy. To the right I could see the Painted Rock Mountains, and to the left was the Barry Goldwater Air Force Range. The steady hum from the freeway traffic accompanied us for a while then faded away as the train tracks came nearer or further away from the road. The sandy path was for Smokey and me only - no one else was seen all day. Sometimes the company of a mile long freight train would invade the quiet, break the monotony. With it's loud warning call and it's violent clackety-clack over the tracks, it would hurl it's cargo by. I'd wave enthusiastically. Southern Pacific Railroad. We were nearly there.

It was late evening by the time we left the railroad path for the small town of Sentinel. Dark threatening clouds were bringing the night on early and we had to think quickly about a place to stay. The hay was there, as promised, behind the gas station on the edge of town, a good healthy half bale of alfalfa. I asked inside about staying at the deserted RV park behind the buildings.

"Don't belong to me," the man at the till said. "I go home in ten minutes."

That meant a yes to my mind and I bought the biggest cup of coffee he had.

I tied Smokey to a tree on the grassy patch, out of the light but not completely out of view. The wind was picking up, and before the tent was fixed and the coffee finished, it was a dark, rain heavy night.

Smokey was enjoying the novelty of short green grass at our camp spot, and round and round the tree she walked, her head down, chewing away. Within half an hour, I looked up from my meal of cold Beanie-Weenies to see her lying on her back, her legs in the air, the long lead rope tight around her feet.

"Oh Smokey, you silly fool!" I said sternly, leaping up from the tent door to help her out. She'd been around the tree so many times the rope had become too short, had caught her feet and pulled her over. Without panic, she lay on her back while I unwound the rope. She watched me with those big, calm, black eyes; complete trust we had.

I rigged up another rope to another tree to stop the same thing happening again, then with a prayer that the tent would hold off the rain, I went to bed.

There wasn't any shortage of water the next day; each rut along our sandy track held enough for ten horses. The heavy cloud of the night before had fed the desert with it's welcome rain, washing the dust from the thirsty, stunted trees, freshening up the colors and making the air rich with the smell of sage and mesquite.

The tent had kept me warm and dry and Smokey's tree had kept her mainly sheltered, so we had splashed our way out of the sodden RV park and back onto the sandy path paralleling the steel tracks in good temper and refreshed. I was back to walking beside my big white friend, still having to favor the sore right heel. The horse liniment seemed to give some relief but the first mile or so was a tortuous painful stretch as I worked out the stiff muscles. I hadn't been able to remove my boot for three days.

The long hard slog of Day 179 was repeated almost unchanged on Day 180. Slowly, mile by mile dropped behind us, as without a break, we covered the twenty miles on to Dateland.We lucked out again that night, with a sheltered, half-hidden spot behind a cafe. The owner's daughter, Rachelle Dale, kept us company while I settled Smokey and put up the tent. She kept her eyes on the horse, admiring her; a pretty young teenager lonely for a pony of her own. I knew what it felt like.

I slept deeply after the twenty mile walk, helped by the fried chicken-steak dinner I'd eaten at the cafe. Also soothing was the news I'd had from Rual, over the phone, that he was still happy to pick us up from San Diego around the 18th December. That was only just over a month away. Rual also told me he'd spoken to Jeannie — she'd headed home with her two horses after the cold weather in the Rockies had made traveling too uncomfortable for her. The dog, Spirit Wolf, had finally been killed by a car.

The Southern Pacific Railroad track had saved us many miles of difficult desert crossing to the north, but with our safe arrival in Dateland, we'd be able to leave it behind. The shiny metal rails disappeared off to the southwest, the most northern end of the Mohawk mountains, directly west of Dateland. If my map was to be believed, we'd be in green fields again before the end of the day.

Much of the country west of Dateland was owned by the state of Arizona (mauve blocks on my map) and The Bureau of Land Management (light brown blocks). The public was allowed access to this unfenced land. Smokey and I took advantage of this freedom and gladly struck out across the sandy mesquite-studded stretch taking a direct line toward the mountains to the west.

The surface we traveled began as mainly flat, but frequent dry washes soon began to cross our path. The dry sand had been sculptured from heavy rain and must have often been swept through with raging flood water; the sand was moved this way and that; broken trees lay banked up against each other, trapped in a narrow gully.

Undeterred by the unsafe environment they made their home, the furry faced groundhogs developed huge underground complexes of tunnel workings. One time as we went over, rather than around one of these mounds, the whole groundhog housing development collapsed and Smokey and I were suddenly plunging through sand up to her belly. It shook me up from my step-by-automatic-step progress.

A lone house in the middle of this hot scene drew us as to a mirage. It seemed incredible that anyone would care to live out here. Ray and Michael Graber did though. As their primary home in Maine began to freeze up in the late Autumn, they'd pack up and move down to the desert for the winter. Many people from the north lived this way and had earned themselves the nickname of snowbirds. All over the western deserts I was to meet up with these warm weather seekers.

Ray and Michael kindly allowed me to water Smokey, and to take a drink myself, before we set off again westward.

Not ten minutes after leaving the cactus landscaped home of the Grabers, Smokey was struck at by a lethally poisonous Sidewinder Rattlesnake. We'd been plodding merrily along, up and down the gently undulating sandy hills, seeking our own route through the stunted bush. I was walking, with my space on the saddle bag taken up by a load of hay, and to distract myself from my painful heel, I was listening to the Los Angeles radio. In the middle of a favorite country song, the lead rope jerked out of my hand, twisting my shoulder painfully backwards.

"What the...." I began turning angrily at Smokey. She was standing to one side, a writhing, twisting, angry sand colored snake spitting at her, a rattling tail held over the coils shaking in warning. Of all the rattlers, the sidewinder was said to be the most vicious, with it's long striking distance ability and an aggression that when upset would drive the snake to pursue, rather than remain in one place. My footprints behind me in the sand showed a path right over it's head. Smokey took a wide circuit around the beautiful though very frightening creature, and with shaking hands I checked her over for the tell tale puncture wounds. She was okay. The radio was off for the rest of that desert day.

As soon as we hit the green irrigated land of the eastern Mohawk Valley, I unloaded Smokey for a much deserved feast on the fresh alfalfa grass. It was worth the risk of an angry faced farmer just to see the ecstatic pleasure in her kind dark eyes. She'd bought us across some pretty difficult country and I was going to let her eat until she'd had enough. Fortunately, no one stopped us.

With Smokey well full, I took the suggestion of an irrigation employee to spend the night in an abandoned house next to the farm land he worked. The grass was deep and long in the back yard, and water supplied to the fields through a concrete channel, supplied us, too. My Spanish speaking farm worker, Javier Jimenez Ramos, joined us later that evening, bringing out burritos and a whole six pack of Cokes. As if that wasn't enough, he kindly pushed a ten dollar bill in my hand before he left me that night. I wished my Spanish had been good enough to thank him fully.

Day 182 saw us in perfect riding country. A smooth raised dirt road ran along the bank of the wide Mohawk Canal. Once again, I was able to climb into the saddle - feed shouldn't be a problem to find in this green country. The canal skirted around the edge of the Mohawk Mountains, twisting south-west back toward Interstate 8. Though the mountainous scene to our left was rocky and dry, to our right lay a patchwork valley of all sorts of colorful foods: lettuce; cauliflower; carrots and onions, all meticulously laid out by alien looking machines, harvested by gangs of mainly dark-skinned Mexican laborers; colorful hats and head scarfs shading the women from the warm sun.

Smokey and I ambled comfortably along all day, finally quitting after fourteen miles. I set up the tent on a piece of rough land east of a town.

Long Bermuda grass, Smokey's meal for the night. Water had to be ferried from the canal a hundred feet away, using my blue waterproof sleeping bag holder. To make the container work I'd tie a rope to the straps, place a rock inside, and throw it into the canal. The concrete sides were too steep for me to risk climbing down but this technique meant I could collect water from however low the level might be, even from a bridge. When the bag had sunk, I'd haul it out, seal the neck and carry it back to camp. Worked very well.

As a special reward for finally pulling the boot over my swollen heel, I allowed myself the luxury of an inspection of my face in the two by three inch mirror. It's funny how absorbing that can be! (I supposed I looked pretty rough). Follow that with the tons of things you can do with a Swiss Army knife, and you've had a pretty entertaining evening! That was mine, on Day 182.

We carried on our westerly path through the orange groves and irrigated green of the valley as far as Wellton, thirteen miles on. On recommendation from one of the town's people there, I took Smokey over the Interstate and onto the property of Joe and Linda Daily. They adopted us unconditionally.

That night I slept between clean cotton sheets, well fed, washed, and thankful that we'd been directed to such a lovely couple's home. Linda absolutely refused to hear of me starting out the next day, insisting on a day of relaxation and recuperation from the strenuous last two-hundred miles. Also, they both thought it might be helpful if they drove me over to west of Yuma so I could see the challenging country early on in our final state of California.

Having a day off was exactly what my battered body and tired out spirit needed. It had been nearly two weeks since the last one in Florence, 185 miles back. Smokey, though fit and well, always felt full of energy after having a rest day. The Daily's kind offer of an extra night with them in Wellton couldn't have been more welcome.

I spent most of the day with Linda. We did a little shopping, then met her cousin, Dale Ronnie, for lunch at a local restaurant. The food and conversation went down well, until not realizing what I'd said, the table went quiet. I looked up.

"What was that?" Linda asked

"Um...Well... I was just saying my permission to enter stamp on my passport expired ages ago ~ I'm just not able to take a trip up to Phoenix or somewhere, when I have Smokey, to get a renewal. It's okay....It doesn't matter...I've done it before."

"Well Emma, I think it might matter," Linda continued, "Ask Dale. He's the Head of Immigration at Andrade."

The color drained quickly from my face, and the food lodged uncomfortably in my throat. "Oh," I said, "Oops."

Not one to make a drama out of a crisis, Linda's kind-hearted cousin ushered me through the immigration system on the Mexican border at Andrade, stamping my passport with a further six months visa. It was a huge relief to be legal again. That could have been the end of my trip right there, and for the most frustrating of reasons.

Sleep was impossible that night. Every thought I had led back to the monstrous country I'd been shown west of Yuma. Images of soft sided mountains of sand, stretching for miles, shifting in the evening wind, unstable, unavoidable, tortured my confidence. It was the only time in the whole of our long journey that I'd been truly frightened, truly worried about being able to make it. I worried about the wisdom of going on. Maybe the ride should be finished 160 miles short of the coast, for, blocking our way westward, lay this eternally long barrier of sand: The Algododnes Dunes.

Joe had set us up with places to stay all the way into Yuma; three nights worth. It felt like money in the bank! What a great way to finish our time in Arizona where almost every mile had been a search for hay and water. Now for our final three days at least, I could simply relax in the saddle and enjoy the last of this austere state; the pressure off.

Day 185 was a totally idyllic fifteen miles of quiet dirt roads between fertile fields, water plentiful in the concrete irrigation channels cris-crossing the countryside. We were to spend the night at a feed lot on Avenue 19, east, the Gila Mountains to our left, the Muggins Mountains to the right.

Our host for the night was Tod Kammann, a young fun-loving man, badly disabled in a motorbike accident when he was a boy. He kindly invited me into his trailer where we sloppily cooked up a feast of hamburgers; Tod's difficulty in moving about didn't affect his astounding sense of humor. We shared the evening together, laughing heartily at our comical lives.

I slept soundly after the poor night I'd had before, the trailer next to Tod's quiet and warm. My worries about the sand dunes no longer tortured my sleep ~ one step at a time, I'd told myself.

The Wellton-Mohawk canal took us away from Tod's, following a circuitous route around the low peaked mountain. From our high vantage point on the canal bank, we made our slow-paced way past Kinter and south towards Blaisdell. As the canal squeezed between two mountain peaks, the green fields ended, only to be displayed in all their glorious greens as the land opened up again further to the south.

We left the dark water of the canal at the bridge with Highway 95. Our second address was a couple of short miles along the road. Bill Daily, Joe's brother, and family, were expecting us.

For our forth night in a row, I enjoyed cotton sheets, good food, hot shower and clean clothes. Good company, too, with Bill and Vickie and all their extensive family making me feel very welcome and at home. A good night's stop again, thanks to Joe.

Our final twelve miles to Yuma passed peacefully and luxuriously by, the canal bank was again our road westwards. A cool wind blew down over the fields from the north, while the autumn sunshine warmed my back through the morning and my face in the afternoon. It was nearly the 19th of November, our 187th day of the journey. Nearly four hundred miles of the spectacular state of Arizona lay behind us; nearly four hundred miles of the most grandeur and the most grueling country. With a night already promised at Scott and Charlotte, Jo and Jennifer Pray's house in Yuma, our last few hours of travel in our eighth American State were free for looking back, for briefly touching on the bad bits — for Arizona had showed us plenty of those. And we were free to be amazed, as a third person would surely be, to look back and be astounded by the stamina of my little, fat, healthy mustang mare over so many hard miles. Amazed, too, at the unconditional generosity and friendly nature of people all over; from the Fords on our first day to the family we'd yet to meet that night. With honesty, I could say I was very glad Arizona was almost over, every miles was deeply etched in my memory with sweat and frozen toes, with swollen joints and stiff muscles. But that state which cost me so much in effort, had given me a personally rewarding challenge, rewarded me so well on these last very western miles. All I had to do to forgive Arizona for being Arizona, was run my hand down the thick healthy coat of the pony beneath me. She'd come across. I'd made it too.

Two nights we stopped at the home of the Pray family. They spoiled me extensively - wonderful bed, delicious food, a day of rest and Christmas shopping. The meat loaf Charlotte made, I think I'll never forget, it was so heavenly! But everyone was a treasure - we were tired and Scott and his family allowed us the comforts to restock our energies and rebuild our strength. I made up a package to send to England, caught up on some letters long overdue and scanned the new maps for our best route west. Once again, I decided, it'd be a canal that takes us on. The All

American. Put away those worn out Arizona pages. Rest well. Tomorrow is not just another day.

As the song says, California, Here I Come.

Chapter 10

CALIFORNIA

Our wonderful adventure finally ends in the golden light of a West Coast sunset, but another adventure begins.

We left late from Scotfs that morning, day 189, after posting off the parcel to England. It was five weeks to Christmas, and the trip was nearly over. I was eager to see it finished but I also longed for it to never end, so it was with a mixture of excitement and dread that I led Smokey over the complex of bridges spanning the Colorado River and into our ninth and final state, California.

We had a short day ahead of us, planning to stop for the night at the Esso gas station and RV park close to the Algodones Dunes on Interstate 8. We were asked over for breakfast by a tall, good-looking local farmer, Dan Sugden, so although still within sight of Arizona, I was glad to accept. It was encouraging to be made so welcome in a state that has often been painted as unfriendly and dangerous. As I spent the next forty minutes talking with Dan about local history and adventures, I felt reassured that California would be no less welcoming than the eight states behind us.

That morning we paralleled the interstate for several miles, through the small town of Winterhaven, swollen with the winter visitors from the north, and the Fort Yuma Indian Reservation, stopping briefly to see the abandoned adobe buildings on the old wooden road, once the only road westward. Only the width of an old Ford car, most of the railroad ties that made the crossing of this sandy area possible had been stolen or lost in the drifting sand, but it was still possible to get an idea of what an uncomfortable and risky drive it would have been.

We left the hard black top road ourselves shortly after, to follow the Southern Pacific railroad, to pass by the agricultural inspection station unnoticed. All Smokey's papers were up to date, and I was almost sure they were complete, but with the different regulations for each state, it was never with total confidence that things would go smoothly if I met the State's attention.

By early afternoon I was tying up to the 'Welcome' sign at the Esso station praying that Jo Daily had left the hay as promised, and the manager wouldn't object to an overnight stay. The familiar line of "You must be the girl going cross country" came from a well built man striding towards me, carrying a child — always a good sign. We talked a little, patted the pony, before I asked about staying. He reluctantly agreed after ascertaining it would be for just one night. But a 'yes' was all I needed tonight, however unwilling, after the strengthening two nights I'd spent with the wonderful Pray family. The hay was waiting for us, so we were in great shape.

I tied Smokey to the fence running behind the gas station, fed her a third of the fresh green hay, ferried water in the blue sack from the faucet up by the buildings, and gave her some of the mixed oats and sweet feed. I asked the owners of the RV closest to us if they'd object to us camping next to them, before setting up the tent in the early evening sun. We'd traveled ten miles that day, an easy ride, and with the rest day we'd had in Yuma, I felt we were both ready to cross the ominous looking sand dunes stretching away into the distant setting sun.

I packed up camp in the early light of dawn. Smokey was carrying two day's worth of hay, and from the pictures the maps detailed there would be little chance of more before the irrigated land around El Centro, on the other side of the dunes, over forty miles away. As Smokey finished her last mouthful of grain from the folding bucket, I hooked the hay over the saddle horn, tied it across the jack, picked up the lead rope and we set off down the stony dirt road that wound it's way between the sleeping campers. Sidewinder Road took us as far as the All American Canal which runs along the border with Mexico. This deep, wide, fast flowing canal was our lifesaver. The water made the crossing of southern California and these dunes possible. Without it, we'd have had to detour hundreds of miles to the north. Without it, an unsupported crossing would be impossible.

The day became overcast as we clambered down the steep bank onto the irrigation company's road running along the north side of the canal. There'd been some windy weather recently, and the sand had drifted across the track making progress tiring. The toes of my boots were soon full of sand that found the holes in the sides and soles. This forced my feet to bunch up, and before long the effort of walking on the soft ground made me strip to my long Johns and socks.

After five or six miles, the canal veered northwest, away from the border and through the biggest of the dunes. They were mostly hidden by the steep banks of the canal, but I still felt like an unwelcome intruder in a land of shifting sand. I kept my eyes on the increasingly difficult path, moving as fast as I could. Within two hours we were passing under the interstate, only a few feet above Smokey's head. She had been quite spirited all morning and I was relieved to reach the other side without event. The canal turned sharply south-west and before too long the path was finally lost to the drifting sand. With the lead rope in one hand and Smokey's tail in the other, we plunged up the soft sided dune to stand panting at its top, witnesses to the desolate, wind-swept scene stretching in each direction. Smokey snatched a mouthful of hay from the nets across her shoulders, and we plunged down the other side. Without a break we were up the next, and then the next. The mosquito whine of the many all-terrain vehicles racing around on the dunes that day, kept Smokey spooky and eager to reach the top each time, despite the sweat that covered her body. I was relieved it was a Tuesday, rather than a weekend, and we were passing through before the Thanksgiving holiday. The whole area would have been alive with the irritating high-pitched noise, and Smokey would have been difficult to hold. I threw the drivers angry glances when they came closer to get a better look at the single, dust-covered traveler being hauled up the dunes in her long Johns by the tail of a sweat-covered grey pony. Nobody said hello.

We left them behind as the dunes leveled out, leaving the canal for the old road west, the Evan Hewes Highway. An old black top road, cracked and little used was very welcome after the energy draining sand. We were hoping to cover at least twenty miles that day, but when an oasis-like RV park appeared like a mirage at sixteen miles, exhaustion and the promise of a warm shower drew us like a magnet through the entrance of beaver tail cactus. We were immediately made welcome by the friendly owners, Elmer and Ana Maria Brill. I erected the tent in one of the prettiest spots since east Texas, with flowering bushes and domesticated cacti sheltering us from the late afternoon wind. I fed Smokey, then spent the next forty minutes sitting of the floor of the shower while the hot stinging water brought relief to my aching muscles.

I felt very content that evening, sitting on the remaining hay, eating sweet corn out of a can and watching Smokey, knowing the big dunes were behind us. I had expected to be camped somewhere in the sand dunes that night, anxious to a avoid a meeting with a desperate Mexican illegally entering the States, hoping for a better life. So I sincerely thanked God for bringing us safely through another day and to the security of the beautiful spot we found ourselves in. As the shadows lengthened, and the evening sky became increasingly dark, I set my watch back one hour, to Pacific time. By four-thirty, I was asleep.

Day 191 started well, with hot coffee and fresh banana bread from Ana Maria, her dark eyes reflecting the morning sun. By six-thirty camp was packed, Smokey was loaded, and the area was cleaned of all evidence of our night's stay. We followed the road for several hours before taking the overpass across the interstate, to rejoin the irrigation road running along the canal bank. The weather was warm and sunny, and the way straight and flat. Before many minutes had passed, an irrigation worker caught up with us in his white pick-up truck, and I steeled myself for a bad scene, as, legally, we were trespassing. But he couldn't have been more kind. His name was Jesse Agguilar, an American with Mexican roots. Thick dark hair, black eyes shining in a sun-bronzed face. He visited us several times throughout the fifteen mile day, bringing sodas, sandwiches and detailed maps of the irrigation system in the El Centro area. The land to each side of us was desolate and uninhabited, with the water from the All American canal destined for use further west.

Jesse was the only person we met that day, until turning into a compound of company worker's houses to look for the night's stop we were met by Chris and Missy Schrum, brother and cousin. They suggested we stop on an empty property on the outer side of this group of houses, but before long their hospitable parents, Don and Rosemary, had installed Smokey in their well kept and fenced yard, and I had the luxury of their recreational vehicle next to her. Chris, a quiet, easy going teenager immediately took over the care of Smokey, seeing her fed and watered. Hay was fetched from a neighbor, the plants were covered to try to protect them from Smoke/s curious taste buds, and I had the complete menu that goes to make up a perfect day: hot food, shower, laundry, no tent, and Smokey off the long rope for the night. As I sat on the steps of the RV that night, watching Smokey chew contentedly under a blanket of stars, I felt completely happy. Tomorrow we were taking the day off. It was Thanksgiving and I'd been invited to stay. The chance of a hot turkey dinner was something I wouldn't dream of turning down. California was off to a good start.

Usually up at the first light of dawn, I had the luxury of a lie-in the next morning, knowing that Chris was outside feeding and watering Smokey. What a pleasure it was to stay curled up in the warm blankets on a comfortable bed, until the sun was more than just a hint in the early morning sky.

There was a full day ahead of us. I'd promised Missy and Chris they could ride, and before long the relatives would all be arriving for this traditional American holiday. History says it had started with the Pilgrims giving a feast with the Indians, and the meal of turkey, ham and pumpkin pie was probably little changed, apart from the alcohol. I also needed to talk with a neighbor who might be able to offer advice on the best route up the final range of mountains, eighty miles away.

After a breakfast of pecan pie, Chris had his first ride on a horse, taking to it naturally. Within a few minutes he was riding without me leading, even having a short trot. He had gentle hands, and he and Smokey seemed to understand each other early on, so it was with almost complete confidence that later that night, I let him ride alone, bareback.

That morning, Don and Rosemary took me on a tour of the hydro-electric station on the canal where Don was a manager. It was fascinating to see the huge turbines at work, and hear the stories about the unfortunate Mexicans who had lost their lives in the strong current of the canal while trying to cross to a better life in the States, only to be found in the water filters by the power station workers. Nine people were found dead the previous year. Moor hens swam dangerously close to the swirling green water being channeled into the pitiless turbines forty feet below the surface. Sometimes they'd swim too close, and unable to resist the currents would be sucked through the generator to be spat out the other side, fifty feet lower, occasionally alive, but always ugly!

It was November 24, but the meal I shared with the fifteen or twenty relatives of the Shrum family later that day was laid out like a picnic in the warm sun. We sat in little groups around the well-laden tables, balancing paper plates of turkey, potatoes, salads and biscuits on our best-dressed knees. Children ran under table legs and hung over the fence trying to stroke the white horse. Old people sat comfortably in their chairs, chatting to relatives not often seen, their plates refilled by sons and daughters. I never knew where my next hot meal would be, so savored each mouthful of the delicious food. Only the pumpkin pie with ifs bland flavor didn't appeal to me. With one eye on the children trying to pet Smokey, I told the story of the trip to anyone who wanted to know, and it was here that I met Jack Fortenberry who would later be a big help to me.

It was a lovely afternoon. A perfect place to spend our day off, knowing the worst of California was already behind us. We were way ahead of the date set to meet Rual in San Diego, and with 2504 miles behind us and maybe 140 to go, there was no pressure to push forward.

As the sun sank lower and everyone returned home, I relaxed in front of a good film, while Chris and Missy took turns riding Smokey around the compound. What a great feeling to know that I had a bed again that night. I'm sure if I'd have been a cat, I would have purred! Tomorrow Smokey would have no hay to carry, so I could ride. What a luxury. Purrrr! It was back to the canal road early next morning, but before long, the desert to each side gave way to the shocking green of alfalfa fields, and the geometric rigidity of lettuce, onions, carrots and greens. Huge stacks of fresh hay lined the roads, but no horses. Every couple of hours we'd stop, and I'd let Smokey graze on the green grass, the first she'd seen in quite a while. It was worth risking trouble from a farmer to see the look on her face as she grabbed mouthful after mouthful.

We spent all day on the minor roads running between the fields, always looking for a bit of pasture where Smokey could graze for a night, but it wasn't until quite late that we turned into property of the Miranda family, attracted by the fat cattle and goats they kept as pets behind the house. The son, Frank, took time off from his chores to help me with Smokey, and make me welcome. We hung over the fence. Me, dusty from the day's ride. Frank, clean and fresh in shorts and shirt, watching Smokey discouraging too close a scrutiny from the young cows. He told me of the time he'd been bitten by a rattlesnake on the back porch, and had been flown for emergency treatment in a helicopter to San Diego. He was lucky not to have lost his leg, which had swollen to a frightening size. With the horse settled, he showed me cracks in the stucco sided house caused by the minor earthquakes common in the area. They were living three miles from the San Andreas fault, and at continuous risk from a major quake.

When Frank's parents returned home later that night, they were equally hospitable. The wind was becoming stronger and they were eager for me to stay in the house, normally an unrefusable offer, but as the tent was already set up I didn't want to risk it blowing away in the night. Also, everyone was so well dressed and healthy looking. I couldn't help but cringe at my tatty sleeve on the polished table, and my leather trousers with the hanging fringe looked so mountain-man against Emily's smart pantsuit bottoms. I felt like a gun-dog in a city flat; out of place and clumsy. I belonged outside in the swirling dust, with the cows and the white horse. I said goodnight to my friendly hosts and with the promise of a good breakfast in the morning, I curled up in my down sleeping bag, all my equipment inside the tent holding down the corners. Despite the strong winds, I slept soundly, as usual.

I woke up the next morning to the sound of a full blown gale, and the flying sand stung my eyes when I went to check on Smokey first thing. She was backed to the wind, her head low, but still nickered her approval on seeing her early morning feed passed through the fence. I went up to the house for a luxurious, lengthy breakfast, one of the best I'd had, with an extended Miranda family. We had been seen a few days ago on the television news and were made to feel very special by their obvious interest in our trip, and their words of encouragement. By the time the meal was over, the wind was severe, but with an address to aim to for the night, and a bandana over my nose and mouth, I climbed into the saddle, and we left.

Horses don't usually like the wind; they often become spooky and irrational. But Smokey, with her calm and sensible nature lowered her head, and pushed on into the dust-filled head wind. When I tried to rest her back a couple of hours later by walking alongside, I was unable to walk, the wind was so strong, and I had to climb back in the saddle, my head bent low over Smokey's neck to reduce the work she was having to do. We were stopped several times that day, by people offering help or accommodation, but with only a thirteen mile ride to the address we'd been given, we pushed on.

By early evening, I was watching television and eating Caesar salad with the son of the owner of the horse boarding farm we found ourselves at. Father and son weren't the best of friends. While the elder lived in the house, the younger lived in a converted shed, six feet by seven feet, in the stable yard. I had heard him banging nails into wooden boards, final fixing-ups to his tiny shack, from where I sat on the saddlebags in Smokey's pen. The slightly scruffy young man called me over from my little perch to show off his craftsmanship. It was pretty cosy! A single bed, a TV, a clock. We spent the evening swapping jokes and stories and watching the big screen television that took up half of one wall, eating the salad with plastic forks. However, I did sympathize with the father whom I felt was irritated by his son's lack of ambition, and also with the son, for his father's lack of flexibility. It was a fun evening.

By the next morning, the wind had died down. We rode on, following the dirt roads into the suburbs of El Centro, the major city in the area. People were just starting to come out of their warm and comfortable houses for the real life pastimes of Saturday shopping, or to wash the car or mow the lawn. As the traffic increased, we were back on the old Evan Hewes Highway heading away from the city. In the distance were the Jacumba Mountains, the first in a series of ranges that would take us all the way to the coast. First, we had to cross the Yuha Desert that stretched from the end of the irrigated farmlands, to the foot of the big climb at Ocotillo. I wanted to camp that night as close to the desert as possible, without losing access to water and hay. I knew that day, our 195th on the road, would probably be the last without the inconvenience of having to carry hay. Tomorrow I'd be on foot again, with the three days supply of feed hooked over the saddle horn.

By late afternoon, I'd found what I thought would be a perfect spot for the night. A cattle feed lot called Kuhn Farms, which had long grass for Smokey and was also on the very edge of the cultivated area. But here we had our first and only rejection for a place to stay in the whole of California. It was always a shock to be refused, even though I expected to hear it each time I asked at a stranger's door. We left immediately, apologizing for taking up the farmer's time. Not wanting to leave the hay country, we headed north hoping for better luck at some farms I could see in the distance. We tried a couple but no one was home, so I loaded Smokey with hay from a broken bale that had fallen from a big stack at the side of a field, and looked for a campsite next to the canal for the night. Nowhere seemed safe enough, it was such exposed, flat land. Finally I gave up, watered Smokey from the canal, and turned her head westwards. On the edge of the desert, the very last building was *The Wind and Sand Cafe.*

It was getting dark, so with nothing to lose, I asked at the bar about stopping behind the fence, in the broken glass, cans and empty beer bottles. Though the place looked less than the ideal, there was water. And we had hay and feed, a good tree to tie up to and the tent was out of view of the road. After an okay from the pretty Mexican woman serving behind the counter I cleared a space in the rubbish, setting up the tent in the dusky light. The sun had set behind the range of mountains to the west. The coyotes began their hungry yapping in the desert country we edged. A pitbull dog barked from behind broken wooden boards at the back of the cafe, a long chain straining from the heavy collar around its neck. Cars came and went from the parking lot alongside the peeling painted buildings, picking up an easy meal. The sign swung on its rusty hinge, squeaking in the wind.

After the usual chores were over, I reversed my sweatshirt to make me feel I was dressing to go out, washed my hands and face under the broken faucet, and sitting at the counter in the cafe, enjoyed the best breakfast burritos ever, along with a good cold beer. With my heavily restrictive budget, to eat out at this small Mexican cafe and bar, was as exciting as dining in a Parisian restaurant! With a full stomach, and sleepy from the single beer, I returned in the dark to the tent, satisfied and happy.

I slept well, until I woke with a start around three in the morning. Scanning the area with my flashlight, I could see no sign of Smokey, and feeling sick to the stomach, leapt out of the tent. She was lying in a hollow behind an old bonfire, and when she heard me racing around, lifted up her big white head, looked at me as if to say, "Well, what now?" and with a big sigh went back to sleep. I sat in the tent door with my heart racing. The thought of losing Smokey so close to the end of the ride was disturbing. Ever since Mississippi I had been paranoid about her disappearing during the night, not because it would be an awful inconvenience, but because she was my friend and partner, and I loved the silly old mare. With her common sense, strength and peaceful nature, I wouldn't be able to replace her, nor would I want to.

Finally, I slept. I woke to the peaceful sound of Smokey chewing on hay, and to the nicker she greeted me with each morning.

The road was straight and little traveled, most traffic using the interstate running parallel to us a couple of miles to the south. The land to each side was sand and scrub, dry and uninhabited. As the morning sun climbed higher, the plasterboard factory that had started off as a little dot in the distance, grew and grew, until we were crossing the tracks that led into the warehouses, dwarfed by the noisy chimneys and buildings towering above us. Huge trucks loaded with fresh white plasterboard passed us continually that morning, most driving with kind consideration to the horse on the side of the road.

With each step, we were coming closer to the Jacumba Mountains. The only way up the eleven mile gradient, that began at Ocotillo and took us to the small town of Jacumba, was Interstate 8, which was illegal for us to use, and I still didn't have a plan to get around this problem. It looked like the sensible thing to do would be to take a trailer ride to the top of the mountain, where the old road, Highway 94, began. Jack Fortenberry, whom I'd met at the Thanksgiving party, had been kind enough to make such an offer. I gave him a call at Coyote Wells, an abandoned gas station with a working telephone. We made an arrangement to meet in the morning, and Smokey and I carried on to Ocotillo, leaving the Yuhu Desert behind us.

The word, 'desert' brings to mind sand and dust and unbearable heat, but crossing these barren stretches in the winter, the weather couldn't have been more ideal. Still warm, short sleeved shirt weather, but not so hot that water for Smokey was a continuous worry. The nights were cold, which made the luxury of my down sleeping bag always a thrill, each time I crawled inside. Every night, I thanked my parents for giving me the gift of comfort that this bag gave me. Even though it was now six years old, and I'd slept in it around the world, I never got used to it.

At Ocotillo, I watered Smokey at a gas station, and enjoyed the luxury of a wooden bench and a frozen yoghurt. The owners were rather unfriendly, but answered civilly enough my questions on a place to stay. Several people voiced their congratulations and admiration after seeing us on the local news, and in the paper, which compensated for the cold reception from the gas station. With directions for a possible corral and campsite, we headed for the outskirts of this tiny settlement. This was always my most stressful time of day. We were both tired, the light was fading, and I never knew the reception we'd receive when I knocked at a door. This was not a horsey town which increased the pressure to be lucky early on.

I read the directions wrong, taking south's instead of north's, ending up at a pretty RV park on the edge of town. I interrupted Lloyd Pierce, a retiree from Oregon, who was working on the engine of his old red truck. He treated me like a friend he hadn't seen for a long time, excited by my story and the courage he felt I must have. He'd also read the article in the paper, and I was surprised to hear that I'd been quoted as saying Smokey was to be given to a nine year old girl when the trip was over. It was rare that I read the results of the many interviews I gave without finding some sort of exaggeration or fabrication, but it always irritated me. Especially this time, as this untruth made me out to be more heroic than I actually was. I didn't have the courage to correct this false impression, not because I wanted to deceive, but because I hated to disappoint.

Lloyd took us up to the office, where I was introduced to John and Harlene Jackson, and their son, Bill. Between them they lovingly ran the RV park, home to many escapees from the northern winter. Palm trees, potted plants, tidy yards. All were carefully attended by the friendly owners, giving off an atmosphere of lazy retirement. That night I asked for nothing, but received everything. Smokey was led to a corral close by, fed and watered, immediately dominating the quarter-horse mare that shared the pen with her. Though there were plenty of places I could have put my tent, and the weather was warm and clear, I was given the use of a luxurious RV by these kind people. John lent me his own television, and Harlene sent over the most wonderful home-made turkey soup, sandwiches and refreshing cranberry juice, complete with napkins and chocolate. But the thing that I appreciated most from them, though they probably didn't realize it, was being left alone to enjoy all this luxury. Usually I had to trade a hot meal or a relaxing bath, for my tales of what it was like to ride coast to coast alone. Just to watch a film on the television and write a few letters on a table by electric light, without having to be witty and entertaining, was the grail I was always hoping for. I was often asked whether I found it lonely traveling on my own, but the real problem was not loneliness, but finding time for myself at the end of the day.

That evening I sat outside in a comfortable armchair, looking back on the 196 days and 2548 miles behind us, thinking how incredibly lucky we'd been, and the wonderfully helpful people we'd met. How quickly you forget the bad ones and the bad days, and how easy it is to remember the friends and thrill of daily achievement.

We left the next morning, leaving behind our new old friends. Jack Fortenberry was meeting us at ten o'clock at the ramp leading onto the interstate, and we were also to be interviewed by an El Centro reporter. Both groups arrived at the same time. I was in a good mood after the night we'd had at the RV park, and looking forward with pleasure to the trailer ride up the mountain so I think I gave a good story while the photographer took two or three rolls of photos.

The climb up the mountain was spectacular. Huge boulders in total disarray, free of vegetation and order. Jack's truck labored up the steep gradient, through Devil's Canyon, to the peak at 4000 feet. The mountain seemed to be made of piles and piles of the apricot colored boulders, with nothing solid or flat. Within twenty minutes, we were off the interstate, and onto the windy, tree lined Old Highway 80. It would have taken us over half the day without Jack's help, and as each stolen mile flew past, I became more and more reluctant to call a stop.

"Far enough Jack," I finally said, and we pulled over in the small village of Boulevard. The leafy road and small houses reminded me of the mountain towns of New Mexico and Arizona. It was wonderful to see trees again, and best of all, grass.

It was much cooler at this altitude. I needed both my thick lumberjack's shirt and fluffy Helly Hansen sailing jacket to keep warm while I loaded Smokey up with the packs for the second time that day. Jack waited until I was ready before tucking a twenty dollar bill into my gloved hand, stammering a hurried good-bye. Sometimes it was hard to put across to the people that helped us how much I appreciated them. Jack was one of those. He'd driven from El Centro, forty miles away, after borrowing a horse trailer from a friend, changing long standing appointments to be there when I needed him. The only thing he needed in return, was to know he'd made a difference.

We left Old Highway 80, at the fork at Manzanita, joining up with the picturesque 94. For six miles we climbed rocky peaks, dropping into tree lined valleys. We were on the last leg to the coast. With all the deserts and big climbs behind us, the next seventy miles would be just pleasure riding, and I sang lively country songs to Smokey as we plodded along. It was the 29th of November. We had nineteen days until the planned date to meet with Rual, so I wanted to take as long as possible to cover the short distance to San Diego.

The first likely looking place to stay was at the junction with Oak Springs Road, a white fenced cattle ranch, with a pretty, old house and well maintained out buildings. A big bull was dozing in the sun, while a couple of well fed yearlings watched our progress up the driveway. Huge American oak trees, their branches swaying in the heavy wind, cast dancing shadows over the green pasture and wintry looking garden. It was quite a way until the next town, so I pulled Smokey in and tied her to the gate. Before I'd had time to finish the quick release knot, Jan Haselton was holding out her hands in welcome.

Jan, her husband Scott, and their two daughters, a close, Christian family, believed every stranger they met may be a visiting angel. It showed in the way they did everything they could to make my stay more comfortable and enjoyable. With their good humor and relaxed and loving nature, I was made to feel at home. I learned they had been managing the ranch for many years, and because of their good work, the absentee landowners had given them the house and the surrounding twelve acres.

The kitchen was furnished with Judy Garland's old cabinets and the dozens of chickens Jan collected, and every room contained hand made cushions, curtains and crafted pieces. That night I enjoyed the novelty of singing a song in Judy Garland's old bath, followed by steaming bowls of chilli with the family. Scott and his eldest daughter left shortly after the meal to clean the border patrol station, fourteen miles away. They also forwarded three days supply of hay, so the following day I'd be able to ride.

For the second night in a row, I enjoyed clean sheets and a comfortable bed. I could hear my clothes going round and around in the dryer in the next room, and Charity, the youngest daughter, who suffered from water-on-the-brain, studying for a test at school the next day. It was the end to another great day. What a charmed life we led!

The morning started off sunny, but cool and windy. After not seeing any real trees since the mountain passes of New Mexico and Arizona, I couldn't help but be fascinated by the branches dancing in the breeze. The fallen leaves, with their rich reds and browns, softened the sound of Smokey's steel shoes on the hard narrow road. When we climbed, we left behind the big trees and grassy verges, for the rocky, scrub covered peaks, only to drop again a few miles further, into the shade and the pastures. What a wonderful day we had. Only fourteen miles to Campo, where I planned we'd spend the night, a lazy, easy day. We stopped several times for Smokey to graze on the roadside grass, while I enjoyed the muffins, made fresh for me that morning by Jan. The only concern that day was the traffic tearing around the corners on this narrow winding road. Most places had a hard shoulder where I could ride Smokey in safety, but on a few bends, I had to listen carefully and move quickly.

We picked up the hay at the border patrol station in the middle of the afternoon, and walked through the small village of Camapo. There was an atmosphere of a once prosperous little town, that had now been almost emptied. Many of the buildings were deserted, with broken windows and overgrown gardens. There was a big railway museum, which was closed, but the oldest building of all, belonging to the historical society, attracted my attention as a possible night's stop, with its grassy land and pretty stream. As I stood on the corner, thinking about crossing the little bridge to the beautiful stone museum, a car pulled over, and an excited Beverley Rathman jumped out. She wanted to know everything about our trip, but after finding out she would be owning her own horse soon, I pushed Smokey's lead rope in her hand, and skipped over the bridge to get Smokey that grassy night's rest.

I interrupted Ruth, an older volunteer helper at the museum, who took me to see Roger, the director and old style American. He had grown a wonderful pair of handlebar moustaches, and with his unusual hat and dated clothes, he could have stepped out of the last century. He made a phone call just to be sure, and we had our place to stay.

It was hard to interrupt their questions, but I finally managed to race back across the bridge to relieve Beverley of Smokey. She expressed her concern about the road we were about to follow the next day, saying it was narrow, with a steep descent, and impossible for a horse to safely walk the four miles to the bottom. This sort of comment, the one that said "impossible"or "you can't do that" always irritated me, and always bought the same response: "Never say Never!" I was glad of any information on the route ahead, but many times on the ride my blood had been made to boil by this negative attitude. Anything is possible if you're determined enough, or you have no choice. I don't care for the word 'impossible'. I took her address, promising to write WHEN we safely reached the coast, and led Smokey to where Roger and the museum staff were all waiting for us.

I tied Smokey on her long rope to a tree growing on the grassy bank of the clear, fast flowing stream behind the museum. After coffee with Ruth and her husband, Scott, I put up the tent in a little picnic area, with big boulders towering behind us, and the old stagecoach route to San Diego at the door.

I'd been invited to eat with Ruth and Scottie in the trailer they shared with their nineteen cats. So when camp was ready, I reversed my sweatshirt, washed my face and hands in the stream, and went to join them. After the thick and nourishing stew, Scott began pouring what was to the first of many vodkas and 7-Ups. With each refill, his American accent slipped more and more into a strong Scottish brogue, as he told me of his disturbing and exciting life as a professional soldier, and despite his mature years, the dreams he still had for his future with Ruth in the States. Ruth, in her uniform of a volunteer at the museum, nodded and smiled at the often told stories, a small grin on her good natured lined face. As the evening wore on, both Scottie and I slipped lower and lower into the soft mobile home seats, eyes glazing over with a vodka induced mist. Tall Scottie talked of England, the States, war and the place of his birth with an increasingly slurred Highland accent until he was unrecognizable from the upright American of a few hours ago. I'm sure my speech suffered the same treatment!

I often had the feeling with many people I met on this journey, that they still thought of themselves as settlers in this country. Many times, conversation would turn to where they came from, even though it may have been generations back. Grandparents from Germany, or ancestors from Italy. If they were proud to be Americans, I felt that part of them would always want to boast of their 'old country' roots.

I staggered back to the tent late that night, after an intoxicating evening with Scott, Ruth and the nineteen cats. With sore eyes from cigarette smoke, and a runny nose from my allergy to cats, I crawled into my luxurious sleeping bag, anaesthetized to the frosty night by the vodka. I watched Smokey for a few minutes, as I usually did, but was unable to stop her image dancing in the moonlight. I closed one eye and went to sleep.

It had been arranged that I would give a talk the next morning to a group of young adults on a volunteer program, based in San Diego, in the exhibition room above the museum. So a little later than usual, and with an aching head, I loaded Smokey, on our 199th day, tying her to the steps to eat her morning feed. Roger arrived, kindly bringing hay and corn to top up the supply Smokey was carrying, his pet goat being the donor. Shortly after, the students arrived, and I juggled talking about the trip with eating the excellent home-made chocolate chip cookies Roger's wife, Betty, had sent.

I don't take naturally to talking in front of a group of people, but it is something that I'd like to be better at doing, and the only way to become more able, is to practice. It helped me if I adopted a 'giving-a-talk' character. I mixed information, with funny and serious stories, observations and reflections, questions and answers. They were mostly curious about what it was like to be a woman traveling alone. Whether I was scared. Whether the single six inch knife I carried on my hip was enough protection. Whether my bum became sore from so many hours in the saddle. Did I get lonely. What was the funniest thing, and the most scary. Did I fry in the desert, or freeze in the mountains. What I ate, and what I thought of the States and the people here. When I talked to young people I met on the way, I tried to leave them wanting to stick their necks out a little, to go after that dream they kept hidden but were maybe a little scared to chase. I tried to put across my belief that it is better to regret the things you have done, than the things you haven't.

The talk went well that morning. The newspaper reporter was there, and thanked me for a captivating two hours. And many of the young people came to see me after, wanting to know more and to shake my hand. It amazed and flattered me, as it always did, that so much interest was shown, in what, to me, was just a big long pony ride, my holiday. They kindly gave me a little pin from the organization they all belonged to, and we went downstairs to meet the real star of the show, the little Spanish Mustang who once ran wild in the mountains of Nevada, "Who's never ridden a pony before?" I shouted, and a couple of the braver ones went home that night with the boast of riding a coast to coast horse.

I could easily have spent the whole day there, talking and listening to the students and museum staff, but we had nine miles to Potrero, the next town along, and already the morning was half gone. Finally, I hooked the hay over the saddle horn, said our last goodbye, promising a postcard from the coast, only fifty miles away. Roger opened the gate, and once again, we were on the road, heading west.

I had twenty dollars in my pocket, donated by a kind Mexican lady after the talk, and my head had cleared of the after effects of last night's drinking. It was cool, but sunny, with enough breeze to move the trees, and the whispering in the branches accompanied the country and western songs I sang to Smokey as we walked along. The brim of my hat caught the falling leaves.

Towards the middle of the afternoon, after several hours of steep climbs and heady descents, a car pulled over in front of us, parking dangerously close to a blind bend. The driver, an older, attractive woman, introduced herself as Heidi Fokker.

She had a small ranch in Potrero where we were aiming to spend the night, and she had the courage to agree to us staying with her, despite being a widow, and living on her own. I wrote down the directions she gave me on a scrap of paper I found in my wallet, waving good-bye as she drove on, down the hill.

I could see Potrero below us, nestled in the valley bottom, surrounded by boulder covered mountains. It took us two hours to make the four mile descent, but finally the road leveled, and I was leading Smokey through the first buildings of a quiet little town. The directions were good, and within a few minutes, Heidi was opening the gates that led into her immaculate yard.

I spent that evening quietly watching television, and enjoying the wood fire, though it wasn't really cold enough to need one. Heidi dozed in her reclining chair, after a tuna casserole dinner in front of the early news. By nine o'clock, I was showered and asleep, dreaming of the Pacific Ocean, only a couple of days away.

The farrier came the next morning to replace Smokey's front shoes, which were wearing out quickly on the steep gradients. So it was another late start by the time I climbed into the saddle and said good-bye.

Beverly Rathman, from Campo, had been right about the road being dangerous for a horse. After a steep climb from Potrero, we began the difficult descent to Barrett Junction. The traffic was heavy with Christmas shoppers on their way to San Diego, and the hard shoulder in many places disappeared. Smokey wasn't carrying hay that day, but the drop was so steep, I dismounted and led her to ease the stress on her knees. We walked on the same side the vehicles traveled. Some drivers, in their impatience to reach the city, drove without consideration for the horse at the side of the narrow road, which made for a stressful few hours. At one point, I looked back up the mountain road to see an eighteen wheeler truck hurtling around the bends, heading towards us. I would see him each time he came around the outside corner, and wondered how long it would be before he saw the white horse on the road ahead of him, and slowed down. Smokey and I had traffic to our left, and a steep cliff dropping away only a few inches to our right. There was nowhere we could go. As the truck came around the last bend, I knew he wasn't going to slow down. He was going to have to pass us in the same lane, which was hardly wide enough for him, let alone with the added width of a well packed pony. As he carried on at his reckless speed I could see the ride was going to end with a tragedy. The only thing I could do was warn Smokey of the speeding truck. I turned her head, and for a few seconds let her watch the trucks approach, then I straightened her and tightened my grip on her lead rope. I was sure the truck was going to hit us — it seemed so unavoidable. I didn't feel alarmed or panicky, just disappointed we were going to fail to cover the last forty miles to the coast, after coming so far. I would have liked to have seen the Pacific. I watched the heavily laden, eighteen wheel truck speed past Smokey's saddlebags with four inches to spare. The wind alone nearly sent me over the cliff edge, my hat flying taut against the leather strings around my neck, grit in my eyes. Smokey hadn't moved a muscle. I felt for the hundredth time on this ride that she was, still is, no ordinary horse.

We arrived in Barrett Junction at one thirty in the afternoon, tired after only eight miles. I tied Smokey outside the sleepy looking cafe and went inside to get something to eat and to ask about a place to stay. All eyes turned my way when I walked in.

"I hope you're not going to leave your horse there long," the woman behind the counter spat out. "As long as it takes you to make my cheeseburger," I replied.

She was one of those Californians I'd been warned about, unfriendly and aggressive. The cafe was large but almost empty. Faded posters from the eighties gathered dust on the grey walls. A cabinet along one end held old-looking chocolate bars and packets of gum. The few customers there were ate hunched over their polystyrene plates, and talked to each other in lowered tones with mouths full of food. But the food did look good.

I gave the surly woman behind the counter my biggest smile as she handed over my meal in a bag, and left with the music of my spurs as they hit the linoleum floor.

I was followed by two women whom I'd noticed watching me inside the cafe. I had mistaken their nervous glances and whispers as suspicion, whereas they had really been trying to find the courage to talk to me. They overcame their shyness (an uncommon trait in an American) as I led Smokey back across the parking lot. They hurriedly asked the usual questions: Where are you going? Where are you coming from? Aren't you scared? They were kind and enthusiastic. And they dispelled the bad mood I was in after the unfriendly treatment from the woman behind the counter. They pointed out the Taylor Ranch, a thoroughbred farm on the other side of the road as a likely place to stay the night, knowing the owners to be friendly towards unusual equestrians. Earlier in the year they had played hosts to a high dollar coast to coast wagon ride, finding room for the eight massive Belgian horses that pulled the beautifully restored rig. They bet five dollars that the Taylors would help

I left the two woman outside the cafe, leading Smokey with one hand and finishing a cheeseburger in the other. The Taylor Ranch was only a hundred yards or so further along, on Highway 94, at the bottom of a two and a half mile climb to Little Tecate Peak. To our right, White Mountain glowed yellow in the early afternoon sun.

Mike Taylor wasn't expected back until three thirty in the afternoon, an hour before dark. I sat under a shady tree to wait. It was a beautiful property, nestled in the valley bottom. Handsome, well fed thoroughbreds grazed in the green pastures. A well kept dirt road wound it's way between the worker's homes, and across a shallow river to the barn below. One of the Mexican stable hands gave me a huge red apple and a coke. Mike arrived on time, listened to my story, and assented to us stopping there for one night. He led us down to the barn, where the foreman housed Smokey in one of the handsome pens, and I was offered the use of the small quarters inside the barn that were used by the night watchman during foaling time. Mike Taylor became increasingly friendly, taking me through the ranch in his pick-up truck, and up the hill behind, to feed the horses there. It was a lovely evening, and a beautiful spot to spend one of the last nights of the trip.

After a good hot shower, and a short rest, Mike and his bubbly, beautiful wife, took me and another friend out to dinner at the Dulzura Cafe, a few miles away. I could only eat a fraction of the huge plate of Mexican food I'd ordered, but had a really enjoyable evening drinking beer and trading stories with the lively Taylors. Back at the ranch, the party continued in the kitchen, drinking good quality brandy and champagne. Mike spent a few minutes on the phone, arranging places for Smokey and me, for the next two nights it would take us to reach the coast.

We stayed up late that night, drinking too much, laughing at everything, and celebrating the near end of almost eight months on the road. Just in time, Mike drove me back down to the barn, where I collapsed gratefully on the comfortable bed in the night watchman's quarters, with a hand over one eye, to stop the room from spinning around.

We left the Taylor Ranch a little late the next morning, with a sore head, but in good spirits. It was a glorious cool, sunny day. We set off for the last time on dangerous Highway 94, climbing steeply, then narrow difficult descents. After several strenuous hours, we dropped into Dulzura, and I went into the cafe there, tying Smokey under a tree in the parking lot. I could watch her from my table inside, as she dozed in the morning sun, one back foot resting and her eyes half closed. I met again the two women who'd told me about the Taylor Ranch and thanked them. Several people came to me to offer advice on the road ahead, standing open mouthed when they learnt how far the little pony and I had come. One man came up to offer his congratulations and to shake my hand. He gave me five dollars to pay for my breakfast. One couple wanted to trailer Smokey to the bottom of the approaching hill, worried about how dangerous it would be to ride, but I gently refused.

I left amazed, yet again, at the interest shown in what, after all, was just my little holiday. It had been a long ride from Georgia, and at times, pretty hard going, but never THAT hard. Not as hard as looking after children or working with enthusiasm in a repetitive job. Not as hard as living with an unfaithful husband or an infirm parent. I felt this praise wasn't really for completing a coast to coast ride, but admiration at daring to live a dream; jumping off the deep end; having the courage to take that plunge. Many people I met wanted to ride across the country, or thought they did, and the claps on the back, and the handshakes, and the five dollar bills were small tokens of thanks to someone, a ninety-five pound English girl, who made them feel that, yes, anything is possible. Just take a deep breath and jump.

I was stopped on the road later that day by Rual, the Mexican farm worker who'd kindly agreed to putting us up that night. He drove ahead slowly, leading us to his ranch.

I spent a quiet evening watching television with his family, in the tense atmosphere when communication is difficult because of ignorance of each others language. Neither Rual or any of his family spoke much English, and were unable to understand my poor Spanish with an English accent. I excused myself as the sun dropped behind the hills we were to cover the next day, and sat outside in the dusky light, almost able to smell the ocean eighteen miles away. This was our last night on the road.

Smokey was ignoring Rual's handsome stallion racing up and down the fence line trying to get her attention. Instead she grazed contentedly on the fresh alfalfa hay, occasionally taking a mouthful of the high protein sweet feed from her folding bucket. I noted with much satisfaction, that she'd finish her 2640 miles and 202 days in perfect condition. She was fat. Her dark grey mane had grown five inches since the start of the ride — a sign of a healthy happy horse. Her long woolly coat was clean and thick, and her body and her back were free from sores or injuries. In the gentle evening breeze, I could just pick up her sweet horsey smell. Only one more day, her work would be done. We set off in the early light of dawn, the sun still hidden behind the mountains we'd crossed the previous day, and it would be a while before it would climb high enough to warm my frozen toes. I wore all my cold weather clothes that morning. A little of Smokey's warmth came through the treeless saddle, like a luxurious heated car seat, but before long, I was jogging alongside. It was December 3rd, and today we would see the ocean.

We needed to travel quickly to cover the estimated twenty-five miles to the ranch Mike Taylor had arranged for the night's stop. It was two miles from the beach, in the shadow of the Mexican border. To get there meant miles of city roads and Christmas traffic, and we needed to be off the streets before lighting up time, at four thirty.

I pushed Smokey on, alternating between riding and walking. She could sense my anxiety, responding with a good, forward moving fast walk. We made good time, reaching our halfway point, the Otay Lakes Reservoir bridge by midday. We left behind the trees, and wide green sweeps, the cattle and friendly country people when we made a left onto Telegraph Canyon Road. My highly detailed 1993 DeLorme map was already inaccurate, not showing the new growth of the rapidly expanding city. Fluttering real estate company flags competed for attention on both sides of the road, advertising large and luxurious looking new family homes. We rode down the cycle lane on the expanded road, attracting hostile looks from the many cyclists riding in their weekend groups. We passed new shopping malls, many of the stores still waiting for new businesses to give them life. There were huge parking lots, mostly empty, and pockets of newly landscaped green areas planted with labeled trees, and regimented flowers I mostly didn't recognize. It was a good looking and well thought out suburb waiting to be filled by people, like a huge toy town with no children to play with the pieces.

We passed under Interstate 805 and into downtown Chula Vista, part of the conglomerate that goes to make up San Diego. Traffic seemed heavy after being so long away from the big city, but it was a Sunday, so it could have been much worse. Smokey, as always, was faultless. She passed under roads, and over. She crossed major intersections, after standing patiently at red lights. She ignored heavy traffic and the deafening sirens of police cars. We pushed on, through the business area on L Street, climbed a rise, and spread out before us, three or four miles to the west, shimmered the Pacific Ocean. What a thrill. After all those miles and months in the saddle, here we were, safe and well. My heart swelled with gratitude to the long- maned little white horse that had brought me safely all the way from the green Georgia swamps, through tension filled Alabama, hospitable Mississippi, seven weeks of hot, hot Texas, and through the mountains and deserts of the west. The achievement for me, lay in her: Her healthy white coat, big, clear black eyes and round, well-fed belly. Her two black tipped ears listened to the busy rush hour traffic surrounding us, unaware that her long ride was over. I wrapped my arms around Smokey's strong grey neck as we waited for the filter light to change to green. I was very proud of my little wild pony, together we had made it. There wasn't time however to dwell on our first sighting of the sparkling blue water, the sun was already quite low, and we had several more miles of city to cross before dark. We turned south, riding along the stressful busy Third Avenue, with ifs many shops, garages, and restaurants. I hadn't eaten that day, but there was no time to stop. We moved over to a parallel street, and pushed on. People wanted us to stand a while and talk, but guiltily I rode quickly by. There was no time. If we were caught in the city at night, there'd be nowhere to safely camp, and we had no lights for night riding. We crossed our second interstate into a residential area, occasionally glimpsing the ocean to our right. As the sun sank behind the houses, we came into Hollister Street. I saw a man riding a horse in the dusky light, and I knew we were safe.

On each side of the road there were places to board your horse, or to rent one for a ride to the beach. There were breeding farms for arabs and thoroughbreds, all along this one street, on the edge of the big city. We passed several other people out for a late ride, but they weren't very friendly. They went by without a word or a curious glance. At the end of Hollister Street there was a steep sided hill — the border with Mexico - and nestled at the base of this floodlit bank, lay Suncoast Thoroughbred Farm.

It took two days before I finally saddled Smokey for the two mile ride to the beach. She didn't like the soft sand, and with stubborn determination refused to dip her feet in the waves, but it really wasn't important. We took the final photographs in the Californian sunshine and sealed the lid on nearly eight months of wonderful memories.

It was the 4th December. We'd traveled for 202 days, covered 2641 miles, with no scars to show, just a few muscles we might otherwise not have had. Smokey was fat, her character unchanged after her long trip. She was still hard headed, and a bit moody when hungry. She liked Granola Bars over apples, her fascination still lay with cattle and things far away. I've changed At least I hope I have. I hope I've learned patience. And respect. And the things that are really important in this world; clean clothes, hot food, a warm bed, a cold drink, friendly people. And a good horse.

As I looked out over the Pacific Ocean stretching away to the west, the satisfaction was not in completing an old dream or covering the huge, beautiful country of the United States of America, but of arriving at the coast with my little white pony happy, healthy, fat and well. Her thick, shiny, grey speckled coat, and glittering black eyes were my reward; my prize, my West Coast sunset.

Ifs the 4th of March today, three months have gone by since I rode Smokey in through the gates at Suncoast Thoroughbred Farm. I'm still here, though Smokey's gone. Mike Spurling, my very good friend, and owner of the horse ranch here, drove us back to her home farm in the pine covered, rolling green hills of east Texas. It took three days to cover what had taken five months in the saddle, though they were very long days! We pulled into Karma Farms in the dark, so without trumpets or a big fuss, I let Smokey go in the big old pasture where she'd spent so many years. With a determined step and her ears forward, she disappeared into the night. She knew she was home.

After a good nights sleep at Motel 6, Mike and I went back to Karma Farms to say our last good-bye to the little grey Spanish Mustang, and to thank, once again, Vickie Ives Speir and her wonderful family, husband Tom, daughters Tori and Tomi, for all the help, enthusiasm and encouragement they'd freely given.

I took Mike for a walk, through the woods and sunlit pastures, over the stream and up the hill, looking for Smokey. We passed small herds of Spanish Mustangs, the original American Indian Horse, grazing contentedly in the morning sun. And little bunches of white tailed deer skipped into the bushes as we walked by. Smokey was in the furthest corner of the 140 acre property with her old gang of friends. She was watching us approach. I could see her thinking. To her, Emma Crosby meant either food or work. I wasn't carrying her blue folding feed bucket, so it had to be work. She was thinking about running. But she didn't. She let me slowly approach her, as I'd done a thousand times before, to scratch her stocky neck and stroke her silky nose. She blew her sweet breath into my ear, then turned, looked at her herd, and ran, bucking and playing, back to the colorful bunch of mares and geldings, young and old.

We saw her one more time that morning. From the big picture window inside the house, we all watched Smokey and her herd wind their way down the hill, and across the stream to the feed bins and mineral licks in the pasture alongside the house. They were led by Moon, an old retired patriarch, who pushed aside a younger bunch enjoying the salt. Smokey was in high spirits. Her tail in the air, running between the horses, up and down the fence line. She stopped and stared at the horse trailer parked in the yard, wondering. But she was there to stay. The trailer was no longer for her. She's staying at Karma Farms to have babies, and as a coast to coast mustang in the Supreme Horse Hall of Fame, to promote the farm and her historic breed. She may even do a little competitive trail riding. She'll have a good life, nothing less than she deserves.

That was the last time I saw Smoking Spear, my little wild horse. She touched a lot of people's lives, and changed some too. I miss her, so does everyone else that knew her. But when I see her worn saddle and the packs she carried all the way across this beautiful country, empty and unused, I remember the look in her eye as she turned and ran, bucking and showing her spirit, back to her colorful band of Spanish Mustangs in that east Texas sunshine. She's not with me, but she's where she belongs.

I'm back with Mike at the ranch in sunny Southern California, writing at the dining room table. I have a huge pile of letters to send to the many people I met on the way, who are anxious to know that a ninety-eight pound English girl and her fourteen hand pony have made it safely to the west coast. Yes, we have. Thanks to you.

I've put on twenty pounds, and replaced my worn out clothes, since first riding through those iron gates. I think I might have found a home here with Mike, his two children, Matt and Amy, and the dogs, cat and horses. I'm hopeful. Outside, in a pen, far away to the right, dozes a well bred quarter horse mare. She may be in foal. In three or four years, that foal may be ready to ride.

To where...?

EPILOGUE

Sometimes I have a dream. A dream so improbable, so fairy landish and so absorbing, it causes me to stretch with pleasure in my sleep, a smile on my lips, a purr deep in my throat. I dream about a horse. A little white American Indian pony; a white mustang mare, and a small boyish round faced English girl. Both heading west.

The scenes change from the dense greenery of faraway places (for my dreams are always color) to the heated stretches under a glaring sun that seem to last forever. I curl up with cold at some point as mountains appear then drop away, and before I awake I see a glittering ocean ahead. But the tale is not finished by the edge of the rolling surf, but goes on. It passes to see the silky fat horse grazing in the Texan green and on to a party in an historic fifteenth century English hotel. The round faced girl is very changed, wearing a long ivory silk dress with flowers in her hair. Around her stand family and friends and officials, and next to her a tall, shiny-faced, blushing American man, the same that saw the white pony home. He stumbles over words and slides a gold band on a left hand finger and steals her back to the Southern California sunshine.

When I tell this dream to someone who asks to hear it, they laugh and throw their hands in the air, "Oh sure!" they say. "No! No! It's really true," I reply.

"I rode across the United States, 2641 miles, 202 days in the saddle, on my own and unsupported, unarmed and on a budget of twenty dollars a week, right through the gates of Suncoast Thoroughbred Farm and into the arms of Michael Spurling, and there I stayed!"

"Oh right, yeah, really...." A smile on their lips and a teasing unbelieving look on their faces, and they change the subject, mentally logging this English woman as a crank.

But there's a shiny faced, good natured American man an few feet away, a steady grin on his handsome features, a gold band on a left hand finger. A flash of understanding passes between us and a knowing smile, husband to wife. If you could read the message sent between these two happy people, you'd believe too. The message is always the same. Always as strong. And always as simple. And it's for everyone.

Dreams, you know, can come true. *THE END?*

EQUIPMENT
Smokey:
Bob Marshall treeless barrel racing saddle
2 saddle pads
1 saddle blanket
2 feed bags
2 hay nets (winter)
Fly spray
Hoof pick, brush
Veterinary equipment
Vitamins and minerals
Me:
Buck knife
Mini Maglite flashlight
Sony Walkman
Akubra hat
Australian stockman's coat
Swiss Army knife
Behind the saddle:
VanDe two man lightweight tent
Lumberjack shirt
Helly Hansen thermal jacket (winter)
Thick coat (winter)
Marco Polo Down sleeping bag (winter)

The packs:
Small gas stove (summer) and pot (summer)
2 tee-shirts
3 socks, 3 underwear
2 trousers
1 pair thermal Helly Hansen trousers (winter)
1 set silk thermal underwear (winter)
1 sweatshirt
Repair kit (glue, needle and thread, patches)
Lighter and matches
Yashica T3 Super automatic camera and film
Stationery
Toiletries
Maps
Waterproof trousers (winter)
Spoon
Plastic bags for rubbish and manure collecting
Plastic seaside spade (never used but legal requirement)
Outside the packs:
2 x 30ft rope
curly peg
2 pint water canteen
Ortlieb folding bucket

Printed in Great Britain
by Amazon